Creative Music Production

Joe Meek's BOLD Techniques

by Barry Cleveland

mixbarry@yahoo.com

MIX BOOKS

236 Georgia Street, Suite 100
Vallejo, CA 94590

Library of Congress Catalog Card Number: 2001087622

Production Staff: Mike Lawson, Publisher; Patrick Runkle, Editorial Director; Stephen Ramirez, Art Director

MixBooks is an imprint of artistpro.com, LLC
236 Georgia Street, Suite 100
Vallejo, CA 94590
707-554-1935

Also from MixBooks

The AudioPro Home Recording Course, Volumes I, II, and III
I Hate the Man Who Runs This Bar!
Professional Sound Reinforcement Techniques
The Art of Mixing: A Visual Guide to Recording, Engineering, and Production
The Mixing Engineer's Handbook
The Mastering Engineer's Handbook
Music Publishing: The Real Road to Music Business Success, Rev. and Exp. 4th Ed.
How to Run a Recording Session
The Professional Musician's Internet Guide
The Songwriters Guide to Collaboration, Rev. and Exp. 2nd Ed.
Critical Listening and Auditory Perception
Modular Digital Multitracks: The Power User's Guide, Rev. Ed.
The Dictionary of Music Business Terms
Professional Microphone Techniques
Sound for Picture, 2nd Ed.
Music Producers, 2nd Ed.
Live Sound Reinforcement

Also from EMBooks

The Independent Working Musician
Making the Ultimate Demo, 2nd Ed.
Remix: The Electronic Music Explosion
Making Music with Your Computer, 2nd Ed.
Anatomy of a Home Studio
The EM Guide to the Roland VS-880

Printed in Auburn Hills, MI
ISBN 1-931140-08-1

Contents

Sources and Acknowledgements

Information for this book was obtained from the following sources:

INTERVIEWS:

Dave Adams (Fall 2000) *Vocalist, songwriter, and keyboardist who worked with Meek throughout his career, beginning in 1958. Adams played piano and sang on hundreds of demos, recorded as an artist under various names, and was a member of Joy and Dave, Heinz and the Wild Boys, and other Meek-related groups. Adams also constructed Meek's studio at 304 Holloway Road.* (**www.bigglethwaite.com/telstar/artistes/adams/tw-adams-idx.htm**)

Ritchie Blackmore (Summer 2000) *Guitarist who worked with Meek between 1962 and 1965. Blackmore played on many Meek sessions, and was a member of the Outlaws and Heinz and the Wild Boys. He is best known for his work with rock groups Deep Purple and Rainbow.* (**www.ritchieblackmore.com**)

Ted Fletcher (Fall 2000) *Vocalist who worked with Meek between 1963 and 1965 as a session singer and a member of the Cameos. Fletcher later founded Joemeek, Ltd., which manufactures compressors, equalizers, and microphone preamplifiers.* (**www.joemeek.com**)

Ken Harvey (Winter 2001) *Saxophonist and singer who worked with Meek from 1959 to 1962 as a member of the Blue Men and the Stonehenge Men.*

Steve Howe (Summer 2000) *Guitarist who worked with Meek circa 1964 as a member of the Syndicats. Best known for his work with progressive rock groups Yes and Asia.* (**http://yesworld.com/Steve.Howe**)

Adrian Kerridge (Fall 2000) *Recording engineer who worked with Meek at IBC and Lansdowne studios between 1955 and 1959. Kerridge became a prominent producer and a key figure in the British recording industry. He currently heads CTS-Lansdowne studios.* (**www.cts-lansdowne.co.uk/lrs**)

Peter Miller (Spring 2000) *Guitarist, songwriter, producer, recording engineer, and educator. Miller worked with Meek during 1963 and 1964 as guitarist for Peter Jay and the Jaywalkers. He currently heads the Audio Institute of America.* (**www.audioinstitute.com and www.bigboypete.com**)

Les Paul (Spring 2000) *Visionary guitarist, composer, inventor, and recording innovator. Paul had a hit with Meek's "Put A Ring On My Finger." Other accomplishments include inventing the electric guitar and the multitrack tape recorder.*

TAPED INTERVIEWS PROVIDED COURTESY OF JOHN REPSCH:

Interview with **Adrian Kerridge** by John Repsch (1983/84)

Interview with **Denis Preston** and **Adrian Kerridge** by Chris Knight (1976?) *Preston, now deceased, was the first independent producer in England. He worked with Meek at IBC and Lansdowne studios from 1955 to 1959, and specialized in jazz and world-fusion music.*

Interview with **Tony Kent** by Chris Knight and Jim Blake (1972) *Meek's secretary for a few months circa 1961.*

Interview with **Tony Kent** by John Repsch (1983)

Interview with **Harry Moss** (1985) *A disc-cutting engineer at EMI/Abbey Road who cut many of Meek's early records.*

Interview with **Ray Prickett** (1983) *A Senior Engineer who worked alongside Meek at IBC.*

RECORDINGS OF JOE MEEK:

Joe's Story recorded by Joe Meek circa 1957. Originally intended to be edited into a one-hour program. Meek tells his story to that point in great detail.

Studio Tour recorded November 1962 for use by *Audio Record Review* magazine, but never published.

BOOKS:

The Legendary Joe Meek, the Telstar Man, First Edition (1989), John Repsch. Woodford House, London. *An extensively researched general biography of Joe Meek covering his entire life and career. The original edition was published privately in the UK. A revised second edition was published in 2001 by Cherry Red Publishing, UK. (**www.cherryred.co.uk**)*

Halfway To Paradise, Britpop, 1955-1962 (1996) Spencer Leigh, John Firminger. Finbarr, Folkestone.

Play Like Elvis, How British Musicians Bought The American Dream (2000), Mo Foster. Sanctuary Publishing, London.

The Sound Of The City, The Rise Of Rock And Roll Revised & Expanded Edition (1970/1983) Charlie Gillett. Pantheon Books, New York.

All Music Guide To Rock (1997) Various editors. Miller Freeman Books, San Francisco.

Rock Of Ages (1986) Ed Ward, Geoffrey Stokes, and Ken Tucker. Summit Books, New York.

Meeksville: The Recordings of Joe Meek (1960-1965). Pastime Publications, South Yorkshire, 1991.

REISSUE CD LINER NOTES (VARIOUS RECORD LABELS):

R. W Dopson
A. D. Blackburn

RADIO:

Meek & Wild BBC Radio Kent. Produced by Andy Garland.

TELEVISION:

The Very Strange Story of Joe Meek BBC Television Arena

WORLD WIDE WEB:

TelstarWeb—*www.concentric.net/~meekweb/telstar.htm*
Joe Meek Appreciation Society—*www.rgmsound.co.uk*

SPECIAL THANKS TO:

Alex Artaud
Michael Batory
Denis Blackham
John Cavanagh
Dennis Diken
Steve Fay
Brett Lowden
Julie Shorter
Mark Straton
Nigel Woodward

and

Barry Fox at Tannoy
Andy Garland and **Paul James** at BBC Kent
Andy Linehan at the Sound Archive of the British Museum
Mark Newson and **Craig Newton** at the Joe Meek Appreciation Society
Sarita Stewart at AKG Acoustics
Johan von Schoultz at Lyrec
George West for the information on Vortexion
(www.gwest56.freeserve.co.uk/ferrograph/index.html)
Todd W. White at Altec

VERY SPECIAL THANKS TO:

Shaun Brennan for making hundreds of Joe Meek's recordings available, providing information on the artists, reviewing the manuscript, and keeping the jokes coming.
Kim Lowden for her tireless efforts, which included providing audio and video materials, facilitating contacts, answering scores of questions, and reviewing the manuscript.
John O' Kill for providing considerable technical and historical insights, his writings on Meek's equipment and the history of British recording, photographs, and professional encouragement.
John Repsch for generously providing taped interviews, photographs, contact information, and numerous other materials that were invaluable to the creation and presentation of this book.

This book could never have taken its present form without the assistance of these four outstanding individuals.

Introduction

Since the publication of John Repsch's *The Legendary Joe Meek* in 1989, and the broadcast of the BBC *Arena* [1] documentary shortly thereafter, interest in the Telstar Man has gone into orbit. There are at present over fifty CD collections of his productions, and prices for his highly collectable original records continue to rise. There are even several competing fan clubs, each with their own slant, offering more Meek to all comers. Thirty-five years after his death, Joe Meek has truly achieved legendary status.

But as with any legend, it is sometimes difficult to separate who and what Joe Meek actually was from the many stories and myths that have taken on a life of their own since his death in early 1967. People who knew Joe personally and were first-hand witnesses to his life and work are increasingly difficult to find, and in just the last year several of his most significant friends and associates have died. And to be honest, even the accounts of those closest to Joe are often contradictory, sometimes wildly so.

There is an old saw that "a moving target is more difficult to hit," and whether Meek was familiar with it or not, it is an adage that he fully put into practice. Joe Meek was a wild card, and he very rarely tipped his hand. People who knew him generally speak fondly of him, and he obviously earned a special place in their hearts. But the truth is that he was a difficult person to really get to know, and he kept his own heart—a very large one by all accounts [2]—far away from his sleeve. Many of his actions were covert, and he could change quickly and often inexplicably according to mood and circumstance.

It is the combination of all that we know about Joe Meek, and the many things that we do not know, that makes him such a fascinating figure. You might be drawn into the Meek mythos for any one of dozens of reasons, only to find once you're inside that you have entered a vast and largely uncharted realm. For Meek is an extremely enigmatic figure, who presents the subtle smile of the Sphinx—or at least the Cheshire Cat—to those who would attempt to fathom his personal mysteries.

Fortunately, our task is not quite so daunting. This book does tell Joe's story, including a brief account of his highly influential formative years [3], but it does so primarily from the perspective of his work within the recording and music industries. The main focus is on the 12 years of his professional career, from 1955 until 1967, and always with an eye on his production techniques, the equipment he used, and the effects that his work had on the world around him.

But Joe Meek didn't just produce records; he also engineered them, wrote lyrics and music (though he was tone-deaf and had no musical abilities), signed artists (in some cases acting as their personal manager), and negotiated licensing agreements with major record labels. He even briefly operated his own independent record label—one of the first indies in England. Joe was also something of an inventor; he modified, serviced, and in some cases built his own equipment.

Joe Meek in many ways embodied what audio professionals were destined to become. If you record music in a personal recording studio, or would like to; if you work as a professional audio engineer or producer; or if you are involved with an independent record label, you owe something to Joe Meek, probably without realizing it. Meek was a key "prototype," if you will, for modern-day studio denizens, independent record label executives, and others trying to eke out an existence in a musical universe dominated by huge corporations.

But while Joe has been adopted as the patron saint of rebels and progressives, he was not really an "outsider" in the way that he is often portrayed. Meek began his professional career working on commercial sessions for major artists at the major labels, and nearly all of his records were licensed to majors for release. He proudly proclaimed his dedication to producing records "for the commercial market," that is, for teenagers. He repeatedly signed "answer to" artists presumably to capitalize on current trends. He repackaged the same chords, melodies and sounds that had been successful once, obviously hoping the lightening would strike twice. And he usually based his A&R decisions more on looks than on talent or vocal abilities.

At the same time, Joe couldn't abide working under what he considered to be the artistically and personally restrictive conditions present in major British recording studios in the late 1950's, and he opted to establish himself as an independent. His recordings, while intended to sell records, were "commercial" in a sense that was peculiar to him, if not downright peculiar. He ran practically every sound through compressors; routinely ran his input and tape levels into the red; drenched nearly everything in reverb, echo, and delay; recorded bass big enough to cause the stylus to jump the grooves; sometimes added homemade sound effects; and often sped everything up to give it more personality.

Joe Meek was also responsible for many firsts, at least in England. He was one of the first mobile DJs; he was the first engineer to put microphones directly in front of, close to, and sometimes inside sound sources; he was the first to intentionally overload preamplifier inputs and to print "hot" signals to tape; he was the first to use compressors and limiters aggressively in creative rather than corrective applications; he was the first to "flange" sounds using two synchronized recorders (1957!); he was one of the first to experiment professionally with sound-on-sound overdubbing; and he built one of the first spring reverb units (1957).

Of course, in order to understand the significance of Joe Meek's achievements it is necessary to place them in context. Much of what he did that seemed entirely radical at the time has been so thoroughly absorbed by the recording and music industries that it is now commonplace and barely noticeable. Looking back, many of Meek's production and musical ideas seem quaint and even naive and it is difficult to understand how they could have triggered such an intense backlash from nearly every quarter of the British record industry. But then again, as Americans, we generally have little understanding of that industry.

Americans tend to think that British pop music began with the Beatles. But what did John, Paul, George, and Ringo grow up listening to? In the late forties and early fifties much of the music that was recorded in England had its roots in pre-WWII British music hall, which was similar to American vaudeville music from the same period. Crooning, comedy, song 'n' dance sort of stuff went over well in the post-war "feel good" period. The mid-fifties saw the emergence of trad jazz, which was basically a re-working of New Orleans-style dixieland; and skiffle, which was similar, but also incorporated elements of blues, folk, and country music. Almost all of this music was related in some way to American music, but it had a decidedly British twist.

By 1955, when Joe Meek began working professionally, Bill Haley had officially ushered in the Golden Age of rock and roll, and American radio was beginning to resonate to the sounds of Chuck Berry, Little Richard, Fats Domino, and Bo Diddly, with Elvis warming up in the wings. Elvis would soon ride the Mystery Train to the top of the charts, laying the tracks for Gene Vincent, Eddie Cochran, and Buddy Holly to follow. All of these artists would eventually become popular in England, and the hipper musicians such as Lennon and McCartney were already listening to their discs.

But most British pop fans were not rockin' around the clock. The big stars in England in the mid-fifties were mostly old-timers and mainstream balladeers like Gary Miller, Shirley Bassey, and Edmund Hockridge, all of whom Joe Meek recorded while he was working at top recording studios in London. There were attempts at copying rock and roll, but the vast majority of them resulted in music that Americans would not have identified as such. In much the same way that "safe" American singers such as Pat Boone recorded cleaned-up "cover" versions of black records, British singers sought to appeal to popular tastes with emasculated rip-offs of American songs. By 1959, as Joe Meek was preparing to depart the tight confines of the British studio world in search of independence, the British charts were largely dominated by lifeless covers of American hits, and records by squeaky-clean teen idols such as Adam Faith and Cliff Richard.

And speaking of squeaky clean, in the fifties and into the sixties British recording studios resembled electronics laboratories, and engineers were scientists dressed in white coats with pocket protectors. Every aspect of recording was carried out with the intention of producing the cleanest possible product, and there were specific procedures, strictly adhered to, for nearly everything. Engineers did what they were told to do, the way they were told to do it. They didn't make "suggestions," much less insist on having them carried out, and recording and music were only functionally related. It's not that the engineers were unintelligent or incompetent—quite the opposite—but everything was tightly organized and highly regimented. Creative decisions were left to the record company A&R men, who wore suits and ties, not lab coats. A creative soul with lots of innovative ideas such as Joe Meek was naturally a round peg in a square hole.

But Joe's creative ideas were not the only thing that set him apart from most of his peers. Another was his homosexuality. These days most people, at least in the music and recording industries, think no less of a man or woman because of their sexual preference. But that was far from the case in England in the fifties and sixties. At that time homosexual acts were theoretically punishable by up to life in prison, though fortunately the law was not often enforced. According to eyewitness accounts Joe routinely experienced discrimination and humiliation as a studio employee, which is in itself a form of imprisonment.

Joe Meek was also mentally ill. He experienced extreme mood swings, sometimes accompanied by violent outbursts of anger, and suffered mild to intense bouts of paranoid schizophrenia. According to a common definition, paranoid schizophrenia is a type of schizophrenia involving feelings of being persecuted or plotted against and affected individuals may have grandiose delusions associated with protecting themselves from the perceived plot. While the exact causes of paranoid schizophrenia are still under debate, a chemical imbalance in the brain appears to play a major role, and stress can severely exacerbate the symptoms, which may explain why Joe got worse as the problems in his life intensified. His abuse of stimulants also could not have helped the problem. Unfortunately, attitudes regarding mental illness were no more enlightened in the mid-sixties than attitudes regarding homosexuality, and modern drugs were unavailable. Consequently Joe never received adequate treatment—treatment that might very well have saved his life.

Given these two significant obstacles to contend with, Joe Meek's many accomplishments appear all the more remarkable. Of course, it is possible to argue that the struggle to overcome these handicaps is what in fact drove Meek to such creative heights, but that is like telling someone forced to suffer poverty and perform grueling labor that their conditions "build character." The fact is that at times Joe Meek experienced guilt and shame as a result of his homosexuality— particularly the fear that his mother would find out about it—and that his paranoia and uncontrollable fits of anger continually disrupted, and in many cases destroyed, his personal and business relationships. One is hard pressed to explain how he benefited from either of these things.

Despite the many challenges that working with Joe entailed, those who knew him personally generally liked him, and they speak of him with genuine affection. Joe Meek was a very

charismatic person who touched others deeply and brought inspiration and motivation into their lives, and when his light went out many of them felt the darkness acutely. Joe Meek was a "nice guy" who loved to laugh and have fun, who cared deeply for the few people who were truly close to him, and who was capable of great generosity. As Joe's good friend Adrian Kerridge once said quite wistfully, "Joe was a great dreamer." Indeed!

[1] BBCTV *Arena* doctumentary *The Very Strange Story of Joe Meek*

[2] Joe Meek's philanthropic work is generally overlooked. He was very much involved with local charities in the village where he grew up, particularly those for people with physical and mental handicaps, and he sponsored the rehabilitation of an undetermined number of prison parolees.

[3] My primary sources when researching Meek's childhood and teenage years were his own accounts, those of his two brothers presented in the *Arena* documentary, and most significantly that of Meek biographer John Repsch.

A Few Words about Stereo and Echo

To understand Joe Meek's recordings it is necessary to listen to them. This may seem like a truism, but *understanding* does not necessarily follow from hearing. One approach is to attempt to imagine how he thought about the recordings as they were being made. For example, with the very notable exception of *I Hear a New World* all of Joe Meek's major recordings were mixed to mono. Unless you were born before the sixties, mono simply means that the same sounds are coming out of both the right and left speakers, with no stereo separation. But Joe mixed on *one* speaker [1], and during his entire career most people listened on one speaker as well. Meek's records were targeted largely to teens, the vast majority of which listened through inexpensive phonographs and even less expensive transistor radios. Consequently, if you want to hear the recordings the way that they were intended to be heard you should listen to them on a single speaker.

But what kind of speaker is best? We know that regardless of the fact that most people listened to his music on inexpensive systems Joe Meek mixed using a Tannoy "Red" driven by a Quad preamplifier and a Quad power amplifier, all of which were state of the art at the time. The best way to glean his intent is therefore to listen to his recordings played on the highest quality speaker available to you, preferably a "flat" studio monitor, and preferably in a relatively neutral listening environment. An acoustically treated control room in a professional studio is ideal, but a good system in a decent room should be fine.

Beyond the question of listening environment is the question of the actual recordings. Unless you are a serious Meek collector with thousands of dollars worth of rare vinyl records you will probably be listening mostly to CD re-issues. Some of these appear to be straight transfers from the records, with varying amounts of restoration done to them—old tapes and acetates almost always need some help—while others have obviously been "enhanced" so that they will sound better on stereo playback systems. A simple test to sort out which are which is to run them through a stereo mixer and collapse the output to mono. If the image shifts at all the recordings have been processed in some way.

I listened to hundreds of Joe Meek's recordings in my personal studio. Some of the recordings were on commercial CD compilations, and the others were out-of-print records transferred to CD by private parties. The CDs were played on a Tascam CD-RW5000 professional recorder digitally connected to a Yamaha 03D digital mixer (via S/PDIF I/O) and routed to JBL LSR 28P professional powered monitors. Occasionally I also monitored using Sony MDR-V4 headphones.

ECHO, REVERB, AND DELAY

The terms echo, reverb, and delay are often used interchangeably when describing Joe Meek's sound, but they are not synonymous. These days we are used to seeing these effects listed, along with hundreds of others, on the preset menus of even the most basic multi-effects processors. In these digital days we generally think of "reverb" and "delay" in terms of time, with reverb representing a range of very short delay times, and delay as representing all delay times longer in duration than reverb. The term "echo" is sometimes substituted for delay, and defined the same way, though "echo" is more commonly used to represent digital delay with some high frequencies rolled off to make it sound more "analog."

But in the late fifties and early sixties there were no digital processors. "Echo" was an effect achieved by employing an echo chamber, which is a highly reflective room with a speaker on one side and a microphone on the other. Sound was "sent" to the echo chamber by amplifying it and playing it on the speaker; the sound then "echoed" around the room and was picked up by the microphone, by which means it was "returned" to the mixer and blended with the original dry sound. Some echo chambers were scientifically constructed so as to produce a specific range of sounds, and a few included baffles of various sorts that were used to adjust parameters such as dampening, regeneration, and early reflections. But any room with reflective surfaces could be converted into an echo chamber by simply placing a microphone and a speaker inside it, and many ad hoc chambers were created that way, using stairwells, closets, automobile garages, and even bathrooms. When I use the term "echo" in the context of Joe Meek's recordings I am referring to an acoustic echo chamber.

"Reverb" was not a common audio term in the fifties, and by the early sixties meant more or less one thing: spring reverb. The term was sometimes used to describe the sound produced by an echo chamber, and technically most echo chambers had short enough delay times to be more accurately called "reverb chambers." But echo chamber stuck, and so for clarity when I use the term "reverb" in the context of Joe Meek's recordings I am referring to spring reverb units. Plate reverb technology had been developed by the late fifties, but Meek certainly never had a plate system, and most likely none of the independent studios that he worked in did either.

Delay in the fifties and early sixties meant mechanical delay, and it was most commonly achieved by using a 3-head tape recorder. On a 3-head machine there is a gap between the record head and the playback head, so if you record a sound onto the tape and then play it back there is a short delay while the tape travels from one head to the other. The delay time can be adjusted by changing the tape speed, say from 7.5 to 15 inches per second, or by using a variable speed control if one is provided. Joe Meek had a 3-head Vortexion tape recorder that he used specifically for this purpose, though he had several other 3-head machines throughout his career, any one of which could produce the same effect. By 1958 the first commercially available dedicated tape echo units were being developed, and Binson had produced an "echo" unit that recorded onto a metal disc rather than magnetic tape, but it is unclear whether Joe used either type of device. Dave Adams says Joe built his own "endless-loop" tape delay back in 1958 or 1959, but his is the only account of it, there are no details, and the unit is not extant. Whatever it was that Joe showed Dave, for now it is shrouded in mystery. For clarity, when I use the term "delay" in the context of Joe Meek's recordings, I am referring to tape delay.

[1] When you think about it, mixing in mono should be a lot less difficult than mixing in stereo for any number of reasons. But when you do it, you discover that it isn't. True, there are not the same kinds of phase and polarity problems that you encounter with stereo, but there's also not the $180°$ soundstage within which to place your sounds. There's no spreading anything out, or putting pairs of instruments opposite each other; every sound will be coming to the listener's ears from a single speaker, a single point in space. You have literally eliminated an entire dimension from the soundscape. In fact, you have done away with the soundscape, because you have eliminated the "scape." In mono you are left with just the sound.

Joe's Been a Gittin' There

Robert George "Joe" Meek was born at No.1 Market Square in the small English farming village of Newent on the fifth day of April in 1929. At that time his parents and their first son, Arthur, were living there as guests of his paternal grandmother. Young Joe would soon find himself responding to and participating in an extraordinarily complex family dynamic.

Joe's father, Arthur George Meek, went by his middle name. George was one of nine children, and just before he was born his father abandoned the family, leaving his mother to raise the children. While serving in the Royal Field Artillery in Belgium during World War I, George watched his three brothers die before having his horse blown out from under him and suffering severe shrapnel and other wounds. He spent five years in a military hospital without ever fully recovering and was forced to rely heavily on his mother for several years after his discharge.

His condition, then termed shellshock, left him susceptible to unpredictable outbursts of violent rage, sometimes lasting for days, in which he would scream wildly and smash nearby objects. Something as simple as a sharp rap on a door could trigger the response and often his doctor would have to administer a pill or shot to calm him down. Once he recovered he would be fine until the next incident.

George had difficulty sticking with a job—particularly one that required taking orders—and consequently the family moved a lot. By all accounts he had considerably less trouble giving orders than taking them and ruled over his household as a benevolent autocrat. In 1950 a piece of shrapnel that had been lodged in his brain since the war came loose and he died.

Joe's mother, who was nicknamed "Biddy," was relatively reserved and quiet. She had been a schoolteacher before marrying George and taught all subjects. She had also played the piano before getting married, but was unable to continue doing so as the Meeks never owned one.

When Robert was born his grandmother called him "Joe," after one of her lost sons, but Biddy would have preferred that he not be a son at all. She wanted a little girl, so she dressed Joe up like one, let his hair grow long, and gave him dolls to play with. This continued until Joe was four, when he caught on and began dressing like a boy [1]. Even afterwards, though, Joe's behavior wasn't that of a typical English country lad. For the most part he preferred the company of girls, and didn't participate in the usual "boys" activities. He did, however, take a precocious interest in audio recording.

As Joe himself would later recall: "I was about five years old when I first wanted a gramophone; it was one of those toy gramophones with a celluloid soundbox and a key to wind it up. I remember I'd seen it in a shop window and I asked for it for Christmas, and as quite often happens, my wish came true and I got the gramophone, with some children's records. Well, I used to play this all the time, and it was quite obvious to my parents that this fascinated me. And when I was seven years old they bought me a proper gramophone, a portable one that used to be popular...well, 20 years ago."

Thomas Edison made the first recording of a human voice ("Mary Had a Little Lamb") in 1877, and a year later was granted a patent for a phonograph that used cylinders wrapped with tin foil; it had a two to three minute recording time capacity. In 1885 a second type of phonograph was invented by Chichester Bell and Charles Tainter. The "graphophone" used wax-coated cylinders incised with vertical-cut grooves. In 1887 Emile Berliner developed yet a third type of phonograph, the "gramophone," which used a non-wax disc photoengraved with a lateral-cut groove. That same year Edison introduced an improved phonograph using a battery-powered electrical motor and wax cylinders–but neither he nor the graphophone inventors were able to mass-produce copies of their recordings.

In 1888 Berliner demonstrated an improved gramophone that used a flat seven-inch disk with lateral-cut grooves on one side only, manually rotated at 30 rpm with a two-minute capacity. He also developed a process for mass-producing hard rubber vulcanite copies of records from a zinc master disc. Meanwhile, a record standard for cylinders had emerged: they were a little over two inches in diameter, four inches long, and made of a brittle wax-like substance. (It took considerably longer to agree on a standard for speed, which ranged from 90 rpm to 160 rpm, but by 1902 most cylinder machines ran at the latter speed.)

In 1889 the Columbia Phonograph Company (originally called the American Graphophone Company) was organized and obtained the right to market a treadle-powered graphophone. Rather than developing devices to be used for dictation, Columbia focused on selling music, and produced the first "record" catalog in 1890: a one-page list of Edison and Columbia cylinders. A year later the list had grown to ten pages–including 36 songs by popular whistler John Yorke Atlee–and to 32 pages by 1893. The Edison-type cylinders played on low cost spring-motor machines such as the 1897 Eagle model that sold for only $10.00. The first "juke box" was also introduced in 1890. It was a coin-operated cylinder phonograph with four listening tubes, and it earned over $1,000.00 in its first six months of operation (in San Francisco's Palais Royal Saloon).

By 1894 Berliner's U.S. Gramophone Company had sold over 1,000 machines and 25,000 seven-inch hard rubber disc records. Two years later the company switched to shellac discs, and developed a manufacturing process that used a glass disc to create a negative master, and acid to etch grooves on a copper or zinc disc. In 1900 Eldridge Johnson perfected the first popular disc phonograph, and in 1901 merged his Consolidated Talking Machine Co. with Berliner's company to create the Victor Talking Machine Company, using the "little nipper" dog as trademark. The Victor IV phonograph, and then

"At this time, I used to be fascinated with making things out of shoeboxes, like puppet shows, slot machines, and all sorts of things. I used to try and experiment with my gramophone, and I discovered that if you played the record at the end—on the run out groove—you could shout down the sound chamber, and the sound would be imprinted in the grooves. I thought that I'd discovered something marvelous when I was really doing just what Edison had done years before. This became not only a hobby; it used to take up most of my time. I used to go around old record shops in Gloucester, and old sales rooms, and buy up lots of old gramophone records, a lot of which I still have at home in my attic."

The "puppet shows" Joe refers to were mere precursors to the much more elaborate theatrical productions that he would soon present to the unsuspecting neighborhood children. His father had switched jobs a few times, with subsequent moves, but by the time Joe was eight the family—which now included a sister, Pam, and a second brother, Eric—had moved back in with the elder Mrs. Meek. She let Joe have the use of a small shed at the edge of her garden, which he immediately wired for electricity and converted into a workshop and base of operations. Eventually, he also began staging Sunday afternoon shows there.

Along with his brother Arthur, Joe had played a pixie in a church play. Afterwards he decided that not only could he act, he could also write scripts, choose a cast, create a set and properties, and produce and direct his own shows as well—which he did. He even DJ'd by playing records on his gramophone between acts, and catered by providing the refreshments that were included in the price of admission. At first he held shows in his little shed, and then later at the Market Plaza across the street.

Joe's shows didn't always have a lot of structure, and sometimes the cast mostly improvised; but when they did have themes murder and mystery were consistent crowd pleasers, the scarier the better. Also, Newent is located on the edge of the legendary Forest of Dean, long known for strange goings on—so ghosts, witchcraft, and magic shows were also surefire winners. But no matter what the theme, the action nearly always included Joe dressing up in girl's clothing—actually, usually that of his grandmother—and he is said to have made a convincing and impressive "girl."

The "rougher and readier" boys in the neighborhood, including Joe's brothers, didn't really care for Joe's shows. It was bad enough that Joe was an "inside boy" who didn't like to hunt and play sports like they did, but to have to sit there and watch him prance around in his girlie getup was more than they could bear, and they routinely broke things up. That was one of the reasons Joe liked to keep tight security around the shows, and why he went so far as to swear cast members to secrecy after rehearsals.

In addition to his theatrical exploits Joe continued to expand his understanding of the electronics of sound. He got his first copy of *Practical Wireless* for Christmas when he was nine and built a crystal radio set shortly thereafter. Soon he became adept at basic electrical repair and began filling his workshop with all sorts of old electronic gagetry. He also showed some ability with drawing and painting at Picklenash Primary School, where art was his best subject. Joe even sang in the church choir, which has got to be difficult to imagine for anyone who heard him sing, or attempt to sing, later in his life.

Young Joe was totally dedicated to whatever it was he was working on. After school or work he didn't play with his brothers and the other kids, he went directly to his shed where he would work alone, tinkering away. His brother Eric remembers: "Joe was a dreamer. I mean, he'd sit and be miles and miles away, and the world was in oblivion to Joe. You could talk to him and he didn't take no notice. Joe tended to live and think in the different world he'd be in. He didn't live in our reality world as far as getting up to go to the fruiting. Joe lived for his little shed at the top of the garden, and as soon as we came home from work—it didn't matter whether it was 4:00 in the afternoon or 7:00 at night—he never came into the house. He went straight up the garden to his little shed, and that was his world." [2]

Joe eventually accumulated so much gear that it completely filled the shed and spilled into the outer room. At his mother's request, George Meek officially agreed to let Joe have exclusive use of the shed. At that point barricades were erected and Master Meek made it clear that he didn't want anybody in "his" room "interfering with anything." Given the relative instability of Joe's family environment, especially his father's unpredictable emotional outbursts, he would naturally have valued having a place of his own where nothing happened unless he wanted it to. His studio provided sanctuary from the uncontrollable forces outside and contained tools he needed to fulfil his many creative aspirations. Little did he imagine at the time that he would continue to live much the same way throughout his entire life.

Joe was basically a "good" boy who didn't get into much trouble. He liked to play practical jokes and get up to some mischief, but he never did anything so heinous as to warrant a caning, as did his brothers. He did, however, share some of his brother's other qualities, such as the legendary Meek temper. According to Arthur and Eric all the Meeks were fitted with short fuses—fuses that were attached to powerful egos and the stubborn belief that whatever the issue they were always right. Eric summed it up thusly: "All the Meeks thinks they'm pretty clever at theirselves."

When he was 11, Joe had an accident that nearly led to his having his hands amputated. The Home Guard had been demonstrating phosphorous bottle bombs in the Market Plaza, and not all of the phosphorous had been cleaned up afterwards. Joe found some and discovered that when he put the mysterious substance on his hands and clapped them together it created a cloud of gas. Figuring that it would be perfect for his magic show he gathered up quite a bit. But when he clapped his hands again while holding a larger amount it exploded and burst into flames, and his hands were burnt down to the bone. Despite predictions that he would never use his hands again they were saved by the family physician, Dr. Johnson, who spent several hours a day with the boy for a year.

The injury didn't keep Joe from attending school, but he was unable to use his hands, further hindering his already poor progress. According to his brothers and some of his schoolmates Joe found it difficult to pay attention in class, and he often daydreamed and drew pictures of radios. He failed his most important tests and was barely graduated to grammar school. Evidence of these failings can be seen in Joe's pitiful attempts at spelling. His letters to his mother and others, and reports from artists attempting to read his lyrics, indicate that he misspelled even the most common words and had very little command of grammar and punctuation. According to some accounts, Joe was dyslexic. He left school at age 14.

Meanwhile, George Meek had bought a farm about 25 miles from Newent and when Joe left school he went to work there with his brother Arthur. They shared many of the chores, but apparently Joe mostly handled the cooking and cleaning. Joe's brothers felt that he was a pretty good cook—a claim unsubstantiated by those who sampled his cooking in the future—but their view was mostly based on how he prepared sausages. Arthur recalled that "Joe was mighty fond of sausages," and that he and Joe ate about twenty pounds of them a week! Before long George sold that farm and began buying and selling others, including one that was home to over a thousand pigs. Whether Joe's love of sausages was a contributing factor is unclear, but he reportedly did a remarkable job of managing the pigsty. According to Eric, Joe took his work quite seriously, which is ironic given the descriptions of the mess he would later make in his studio!

The Meeks also had a cherry orchard, and during cherry season Joe's brothers used to shoot starlings to keep them from eating the cherries. Joe didn't like shooting birds so he placed speakers in the trees and blasted the birds with intimidating noises instead—such as the sound of banging on a large sheet of corrugated iron. He had assembled a small public address system by building a microphone and a one-tube amplifier, and combining them with his radio and gramophone. He would also use the system to play music for the entertainment of the cherry pickers. "They used to love that," remembered Eric.

However, the cherry pickers weren't the only ones who appreciated Joe Meek's DJ skills. "By the time I was about 14, I'd sold my most treasured possession, a cine-camera, and I'd bought my first amplifier. The war was on by this time, and I used to play records for dancing, mainly Victor Sylvester and different records that were very popular then. I think this was when I began to get an ear for the type of music that the public liked: something with a good, solid rhythm and a tune forced home. I also, naturally, began to collect a lot of radio gear. I soon found that my entertaining with records became very popular around Gloucestershire, and I was in pretty big demand: at one time to such an extent that I used to have to employ some other friends of mine to operate gear. Say, on an August Bank Holiday they would be in Huntley, I'd be at Gloucester, and somebody else would be at Newent."

A couple of years later Joe combined his theatrical and DJ interests and began acting as musical director, music supervisor, and sound effects engineer for local theater groups. "By this time I was about 16, I used to provide music for amateur dramatic societies. I remember plays like *The Ghost Train* and *The Poltergeist*…lots of plays. And I used to go out of the way to provide the right sort of music for them and the right sound effects." It must have been quite entertaining watching 16-year-old Joe manning his gramophone and collection of records, while at the same time creating special effects. Just think, if they had filmed the plays and recorded Joe's soundtrack along with the images he would also have been Newent's first, and likely only, Foley engineer. [3] And speaking of first and only, Joe built a small television set from the chassis up before anyone else in

Newent had one. Unfortunately, he was unable to demonstrate it because television signals were not being broadcast to Gloucester yet. In this case Joe Meek was *well* ahead of his time. When the first broadcasts did finally begin, the Meeks watched them in style on another and larger television that Joe had also built for them.

After the Second World War ended, George Meek sold off all the farms. He bought a dairy and put Arthur and Eric in charge of it, while he conscripted Joe to office work as an estate agent in a real estate office. Joe had absolutely no interest in realty, and he found working in the office torturous. Nonetheless, he suffered through it for about a year before he received notification that he must begin his compulsory National Service. He could have opted out on a farm-worker exemption as Arthur had done, but he chose instead to sit for an exam in radar. He and one other young man were selected out of a group of 2,000 applicants.

Joe did not fare too well during the intense physical training—including tackling an "assault course"—that comprised the first two months of his stint in the RAF. He was made fun of by his instructors, and harassed by bullies, but he rolled with the punches—sometimes literally. From there, after two months of technical training, he began working in the field. That entailed travelling to remote radar shacks, usually on the tops of high hills, and spending long hours monitoring the screen as part of the aircraft early warning system. Joe would later recall being lonely in those days, but also having had a lot of time for self-reflection and gazing at the stars. He also said that it was during that time that he began to become fully aware of his homosexuality. Whatever went on during those 18 months, Joe must have found being isolated in a shed full of equipment oddly familiar, even if he was sharing it with one or two others.

When Joe returned home from the service in 1950 he found that his father had recently died. Among other things, that meant that he no longer had to think in terms of the estate office and the dairy. "When I came out—in the meantime my father had died—I decided that I must take the plunge and move to London, and take a job connected with recording. During my time in the services I'd experimented with wire recording and disc cutting; this really fascinated me more than anything else."

But Joe didn't go to London immediately. Instead, he took a job repairing televisions "under the counter" at a small shop called Curry's. His boss, Mr. North, recalls: "He was ambitious, and made known his interests in advanced electronics and noises." [4] One bit of advanced electronics that he was interested in was a hand-built tape recorder, which he would stay up until all hours working on, often causing him to be late for work the following morning. Late or not, the management was sorry to see Joe go when he told them he was heading off to London to take another job.

In reality Joe didn't head immediately to London then either; he instead took a job with the competition, a much larger company called MEB. The Midland Electricity Board's repair facility was located off-site from the main store, far enough away from the supervisory eye to afford the three technicians who worked there a little autonomy. Joe's boss, Geoff Woodward, apparently a very liberal fellow, allowed him to bring his new tape recorder to the workshop and spend part of his time working with it instead of on televisions. "He was more interested really in sound effects than repairing tellies, because he always said to me, 'It's a dead-end job,' but he didn't mind mixing the two. He'd tape music and edit it as if he was a disc jockey. And he did it very, very well. In fact he lent me for a couple of dos some of his recordings he'd made up. He used to get the hits from the radio." [5]

In fact, Joe had assembled an entire mobile DJ rig and formed his own sound reinforcement company. He painted its name, RGM Sound, on the sides of the two huge speakers that served as his mains. RGM, which happened to be his initials, was his adaptation of "MGM," a company that would be one of his clients a few years later. For nearly four years Joe used the MEB facility as *his* workshop, where he assembled complex comedy and dramatic recordings, complete with all manner of sound effects. He used multiple recorders to create layered performances—sometimes playing all the roles by himself— by bouncing mono tracks back and forth from the two machines while adding overdubs. Professional recording studios in England, let alone amateur recording enthusiasts, were still years away from that kind of experimentation; and perhaps not surprisingly, Joe would play a pioneering role there as well.

And as if being one of the first mobile DJs, multi-track engineers, and honorary Foley artists were not enough, Joe Meek also assembled an extensive sound effects library. He was constantly on the lookout for new sounds, and frequently employed his family members and friends to help out. According to Eric, "He was always interested in weird sounds and he had us doing all sorts of things to get them. He used to get up at 3:00 a.m. and put microphones out on the walls so that he could record the early morning birds singing; he'd have me spinning round the corners, ripping on the brakes and smashing glass to sound like a car crash. The shop was full of literally everything under the sun and he was never happier than when he could get somebody in to make a noise in there that he could record. The local people quite possibly thought that he was a nutter." [6] In the summer of 1953 Joe built a disc-cutter at MEB—no small feat—and cut his first record, a disc of sound effects.

Unfortunately, as Joe began spending more and more time working on recordings, he began to arrive at work later and later, and eventually he was told to show up on time or get another job. He wasn't about to let up on recording, so he fed his habit by working a perfunctory job at yet another shop, called Broadmeads, while expanding his DJ and recording activities. In the summer of 1954 he took a major step by recording Marlene Williams—a Newent schoolgirl who would later marry his brother Eric—singing "Secret Love," probably to a track he had recorded earlier by the Melody Dance Band. He cut a disc from the recording and played it at dances, as well as sending a copy to a record label (who obviously turned it down). The recording was not only significant as being his first "record," but also because he treated the voice with delay, reportedly created using a modified tape recorder. [7] If that account is accurate, Meek must have figured out how to rig his recorder with a third head, which is staggering to say the least!

Shortly after that Joe accidentally drove a television repair truck into a telegraph pole, scattering television sets all over the road, but leaving him unharmed. It is possible that he interpreted the incident as an omen of some sort, because shortly thereafter he decided that the time had finally come to head for the big city in search of fame and fortune. He saw an ad for a job in London that sparked his imagination, and when he applied for it he was offered the position.

[1] The Meek family has consistently denied that Joe was ever dressed as a girl, and Joe himself is the only source of this story. An anonymous source in Newent said that there was a boy in the town who had been dressed as a girl, but it wasn't Joe. It is possible that Joe adopted this story as his own in an attempt to explain his homosexuality to others.

[2] *The Legendary Joe Meek*, by John Repsch, 1989, pg.14]

[3] Jack Foley was a technician at Universal Studios in the 1950s. He developed the method of adding sounds and sound effects to films that bears his name.

[4] *Legendary* pg. 22

[5] *Legendary* pg. 22

[6] *Arena*

[7] *Legendary* pg. 25

CHAPTER 2

IBC

At the end of the summer of 1954 Joe Meek headed for London. He'd taken a job in a film dubbing room, but apparently the work failed to capture his imagination because within a couple of weeks he was fixing televisions at Stones radio shop. Two months later fate smiled on Mr. Meek and he got a job in the projection room at Television Commercials (TVC) screening American commercials for the education of British advertisers. Operating film projectors wasn't much more prestigious than repairing televisions, but TVC was part of the International Broadcasting Company (IBC) [1], the largest and most advanced recording studio in the country.

Figure 2.1:
The tape assembly room at IBC. The man is standing in front of an EMI BTR1 (or possibly BTR2) tape recorder, a second machine is mounted in the cabinet to his left, and there is what may be a third machine behind him and to the right. Note the window looking down on the studio control room, where there is another BTR1. The assembly room is where the compressors were kept.

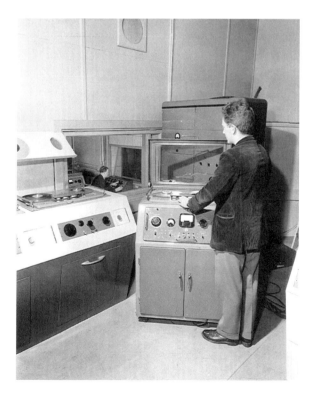

Photo courtesy of Denis Blackham

Figure 2.1a:
Another shot of the assembly
room at IBC in 1955.

It didn't take long for someone at IBC to figure out that Joe could handle more challenging tasks than that of projector boy, and after just three weeks he was offered a job as Junior Engineer on *People Are Funny*, one of the most popular Radio Luxembourg road shows. As Junior Engineer Joe would unpack the gear, set up the microphones and recorders, and then pack it all up when the show was over.

A typical weekly road show schedule went something like this: Saturday afternoon was spent travelling to wherever the show was being recorded, usually by train, and setting up the equipment. Rehearsals were held Sunday morning at 10:00, with the show in the evening. On Monday you returned, and if there was time edited the tape. On Tuesday the final editing was completed, and Wednesdays you would be back in the studio doing odd jobs. It was at this point that Joe learned how to professionally edit tape for broadcast, which would have meant simply expanding and refining the skills that he had already developed.

A week after his first trip Joe was promoted again, this time to Chief Recording Engineer. He brought a higher standard of professionalism to the job than was usual, and made some waves while doing so. "Of course, this was a great honor for me and I really did work extremely hard to keep the standard of recording up, which at times was extremely difficult," Joe recalled. He took his work very seriously, and by all accounts achieved excellent results; other members of the crew, however, didn't appreciate being pushed so hard. One of Joe's assistants, Jimmy Lock, recalls: "It was nerve racking to work with Joe because his demands of his expertise were so good—his ability to be able to keep the atmosphere of that show alive. If you didn't punch the music in at the right time you'd have a hell of a night at dinner because he would never let you forget it. But although his moods were sometimes Purgatory to go through, it did set one's standards for the future, which at the time I didn't appreciate so much, but I certainly do now on reflection. I did go on other shows with other engineers and it was a much more easy, laisser-affaire with them." [2] For most of Joe's associates it was a gig, not an artistic endeavor, and they wished that Joe would simply chill out—the one thing he was not likely to do.

That notwithstanding, at least one of Joe's assistants, Adrian Kerridge *[see Sidebar 2.1]*, developed a good working relationship with him. Kerridge understood the trade-off involved in weathering Joe's tricky temperament for the opportunity to share in his creative adventures, and accepted the challenge. "He was an artist, a pure artist, temperamental, impossible to work with. I could work with him because he used to shout at me and I used to shout back, and we had a very close, mutual understanding. I learned an enormous lot from this man, primarily because there was so much in the guy."

Sidebar 2-1: Adrian Kerridge

Adrian Kerridge met Joe Meek while working at IBC Studios in 1955. They worked together closely for several years, both as a team recording road shows, and on many recording sessions, particularly those produced by Denis Preston. Later, after Kerridge had served his two years of National Service, he and Meek reunited to join Preston at his newly opened Lansdowne Studios. Since then Kerridge has gone on to become one of the most significant figures in the British recording community, and is currently the managing director and a co-owner of the CTS-Lansdowne organization. He also serves as Chairman of the Association of Professional Recording Services (and recently received its Professional Recording Association Award for Lifetime Achievement), as well as being a participating member of the Association of Motion Picture Sound, the Audio Engineering Society, and other trade organizations.

Meek may have made heavy demands upon others, but according to Kerridge he set the standard himself by often going far beyond the official call of duty. For example, Joe used to act as an ad hoc Music Director and DJ. "He'd choose the music; he'd spend hours dubbing off records. Tremendously artistic, and the only man in that company that had that capability—to do that sort of thing on the road in those days. Remember, it wasn't very technical; it was a few microphones, and a few old drums of cable that would fall apart."

Joe was also a strict adherent to the maxim that "the show must go on," and to that end he could be extremely resourceful. On one occasion a theatre's PA amplifier failed mid-show and Joe, keeping his cool, troubleshot the problem in a couple of minutes. On another occasion Joe went considerably further to save the show. Kerridge recalls: "I remember vividly, one year he was sent—and this was just a mobile recording job—to Scotland to record Jimmy Shand. And in those days we used to have a tape machine called a (EMI) BTR2—and there was a portable version of the BTR2, and it would be in three boxes. And they'd put it on the train at King's Cross to go into Scotland, and he gets there and the machine is damaged—how, I don't know. But he worked all night, repaired that machine, recorded the material—quite extraordinary—and came back with the show, finished; and that was something."

Apparently Meek was similarly impressed with Kerridge and his work, and they became fast friends. Kerridge says that Joe's homosexuality was never an issue, and that in all the time they worked together, on all the road trips and then for years after-wards, Joe never approached him as he reportedly did others. But Joe didn't try to conceal his homosexuality either; he joked about it and made it obvious as to what he'd likely be getting up to when he went "out" after dinner on Saturday evenings.

Joe Meek recorded over 115 *People Are Funny* programs, and worked on lots of others as well, including *This Is Your Life, Strike It Rich, The Winifred Atwell Show, The Petula Clark Show, The Candid Microphone,* and *When You're Smiling.* A show called *This I Believe* replaced *People Are Funny,* and Joe worked on it too.

The hundreds of train trips to and from the shows left Joe, and Adrian, with lots of time on their hands. "He (Joe) would sit on the train and he'd write songs, he'd write down technical ideas, he would dream of the future. He would talk about his RAF days, when he used to sit on transmitters on the tops of hills, and how lonely it was doing the work." One of the songs Joe wrote while riding a train was "Put a Ring on Her Finger," a song that would later play a pivotal role in his career.

In addition to working as Chief Recording Engineer on remote recordings, Meek was quickly elevated to Junior Engineer on studio sessions. So if the weekly road show had been fully edited and was turned in by Tuesday, he would spend Wednesdays, and sometimes even his days off, helping out around the studio as a "tape monkey." This got him closer to where he wanted to be, a Senior Engineer in charge of recording, but there were some obstacles in his way.

Figure 2.2:
The control room at IBC.
This is the area visible
through the assembly room
window in the previous
photograph. Note that the
large monitor is placed in the
corner of the room, and that
the lid on the EMI BTR1
tape recorder is closed. The
client appears to be doing a
voice-over.

Sidebar 2-2: London Recording Studios

By the late thirties the London recording community included EMI/Abbey Road, Decca, Star Sound, IBC, and a few others, all of which were owned by or associated with large broadcasting and record companies. The first truly independent studios– Advision and Philips–appeared in 1956, followed by CTS in 1957, Lansdowne in 1958, and Pye in 1959. The earliest studios were constructed within existing buildings rather than designed from the ground up.

For the first 40 years the studios operated in virtual isolation from one another, and given the scarcity of pro audio manufacturers at the time, studios designed, built, and maintained most of the equipment they used. Decca, Pye and particularly EMI were all renowned for the quality of their in-house gear. Around 1950, EMI introduced the BTR1 full-track professional reel-to-reel tape recorder, and began producing tape stock. The BTR1, and later the BTR2, became staples of the London studios, and served as something of a common denominator; but equalizers, compressors, mixers, and most other gear was proprietary. That meant that engineers at each studio developed engineering techniques based on the particular equipment they were using–techniques that may or may not have been developed elsewhere–and those techniques were considered to be company "secrets."

But it went deeper than that. The big studios operated in the spirit of Fraternal Orders, each centered within its own Lodge, and privy to the sonic secret grips and passwords. A team of people working together under one roof, with lots of secrets, can reasonably be viewed as a de facto secret society. And as is often the case with secret societies, once you're initiated into one, you may find it difficult to leave and join a rival team. There was an unwritten law–and in the cases of Decca and EMI perhaps an actual arrangement by management–that made it extremely difficult for engineers to switch studios. In spite of this, or perhaps because of it, studio employees often exhibited passionate allegiance to their own "lodge."

Here are some descriptions from people who worked in the early studios:

"Abbey Road resembled a hospital, with orderlies in white coats."–Bruce Welch (The Shadows)

"Decca's Number One studio looked like a hospital–this massive room, probably 18-foot walls and 24-foot high ceilings, 50 feet long, 40 feet wide. A four-piece rock band would go in there and get totally lost. They'd just spread us out a little bit and leakage was no problem."–Peter Miller (Peter Jay and the Jaywalkers)

"I shall never forget EMI in those days; I mean it was a sort of bare wooden floor and a canteen where you've got a cup of tea and there was a spoon on a piece of chain to stir your tea with, I mean that was it! Really, and it was a big joke. And people used to always walk around in white coats up there."–Adrian Kerridge (IBC/Lansdowne)

"They stood up. The engineers in those days actually stood up, which amazed me. Where you see them…a big symphony hall, and they're playing in it, and you go into the control room and the guy is sitting there with whatever he had–a small, little, dinky mixer–and a smock on. And the son of a bitch is standing up there looking out of this tiny little window, to look at a hundred-piece orchestra out there, doing their thing, yeah."–Les Paul (Guitarist)

"We (EMI) had a manufacturing center upstairs and all the RS60s, limiters and things, they were made there. We later made those into cutting rooms, when we formed a thing called REDD, which was Record Engineering Development Division. The REDD 1 was the first sort of stereo gear. The REDD 17 mixing console used 40 dB (V72s) amplifiers made in Germany–to my knowledge, that was the first-ever recording console, rather than a sort of box. It had eight inputs and two auxiliaries. You had sum and difference transformers on channels 1 and 2, and on 7 and 8; and at the next stage you could plug in either pop or classical EQ."–Ken Townsend (EMI)

"All the mixing consoles (at Decca) were pretty bloody awful. I'm thinking of the mixing console in Number 1, which was 'Heath Robinson.' There were ten channels, so if you wanted the bass–and we're talking about 4-track recordings–to be on Track 1 you had to be in a particular place in the studio. You actually had to physically move people around in the studio to get them on different tracks. It was awful."–Jack Clegg (Decca)

"Almost to the end of Wilkie (Arthur Wilkinson) retiring, if you did anything that was slightly different you were considered to be not one of the real Decca people. It wasn't on."–Mike Mailes (Decca)

"I can remember going to EMI studios in those days…the engineers had to wear white coats. They all had to walk around in white coats with pencils in their pockets–all rather like that."–Tony Kent (Joe Meek's Assistant)

The primary obstacle was a man named Alan Stagg, who had recently taken over as Studio Manager. IBC was not only a production studio, it was one of the foremost training grounds for young engineers, and it was Stagg's responsibility to instill the proper respect for tradition in his charges. Stagg liked to do things by the book [3], which by itself put him on a collision course with Meek. In addition, Stagg disliked Joe right from the start, and initially he blocked his advancement to Senior Engineer status.

Figure 2.3:
Another shot of the control room at IBC, but this time with a much larger mixer.

That didn't sit well with Joe, of course, so he began asking various producers to petition Stagg on his behalf. One such producer, Arthur Frewin, finally prevailed; when Stagg gave Meek his first assignment, however, it was in the spirit of, "I'll show you," not as a supportive mentor. "When we had this big session at Conway Hall, Joe turned up to do it. We had a very expensive orchestra there. It was for an LP called *Film Themes*, arranged and conducted by Alyn Ainsworth. We had a complete show-band brass; we had top rhythm. Bill McGuffie was on piano; we had really top people on it, and a 20-piece orchestra led by Freddie Sverdloff who was recognized throughout the country as the top string leader."

It was a beautiful orchestra, and Joe had never engineered a session in his life. I think that Alan thought it would stop Joe dead in his tracks. It was fantastic! Joe's job of balancing was out of this world and the musicians applauded the playback. Joe was over the moon. We all went out and got drunk. We just talked and talked about every track all over dinner. And Joe was so really pleased, not bumptious or anything like that, but he was really humbly pleased that he'd done it. His first one, and it was a big one, and it was a good one." [4]

As a result of this success Meek got his promotion and a raise, and he began engineering other sessions. By his account his first recording of any importance, and also his first classical recording, was by American pianist Daniel Abrams playing a work by Chopin—a record that became a minor hit in the United States. Meek recorded all sorts of music, from accordion records to Western movie themes, on sessions ranging in size from soloists to small orchestras. His first pop session was recording Canadian baritone Edmund Hockridge. Early the following year (1956) Joe would record Hockridge's "Young And Foolish," which would chart at #10. Joe also demonstrated his sound effects skills by, among other things, simulating the twang, whoosh, thwack and sproing of an arrow on Gary Miller's hit version of "Robin Hood" in October 1955.

Figure 2.4:
Publicity still taken at IBC for Dennis Lotis's "There's A Kiss And A Place"/"The Extra Day" (1956). Back to front: Smedley Aston (producer of the film The Extra Day*), A&R Man Michael Barclay, Dennis Lotis, and Joe Meek. Record Mirror Feb 4, 1956.*

Meek engineered lots of notable recordings from the very beginning, one of the earliest of which was "Georgia's Got a Moon," sung by jazz vocalist Betty Miller. For many years Meek felt that it was one of his finest recordings, and listening to it today it is still striking in its richness and clarity, as it perfectly balances the rhythm and brass sections, while still allowing the warm vocal to sit right on top of the mix. Frankie Vaughn's version of "Behind the Green Door," Marion Ryan's version of "Cry Me a River," and Shirley Bassey's version of "Burn My Candle (At Both Ends)" share many of those same qualities.

Speaking of "versions" and sharing the same qualities, in England in the 1950s it was commonplace for artists to do "cover versions" of American hits *[see Sidebar 2.3]*, and it was not unusual for there to be several versions of the same song competing for space on the charts simultaneously. Since IBC was an independent studio, with several labels as clients, engineers would often be asked to record the same song for different artists. That might have been fine for most engineers—a record's a record—but Meek would create a special sound to best put across a particular song, and understandably he would not want to do it more than once. Kerridge recalls the situation: "It was odd working for Philips and working for Decca: we'd do one title with one artist and one major company, and then the following morning, or the following afternoon, we'd have another session with another arranger and a different artist; but the same tune, and with the same team of engineers often. And of course, Joe would refuse—he'd get very upset. It happened fairly regularly." A prime example occurred after recording Gary Miller's version of 'Garden of Eden,' for which Joe had devised a thunderstorm effect. He was asked to add the exact same effect to another version by Frankie Vaughn, and he hit the roof."

These days we think of "cover versions" as one artist or group recording a song that is clearly associated with, and usually written by, another artist or group. For the last thirty-five years it has been common for artists to write much or all of their own material, and we naturally associate the two. But in the fifties, songs were still most often written by "songwriters" and performed by "singers," and record company A&R men (they were always men) decided which songs would be sung and by whom. Sometimes a song would have "hit written all over it," and two or more labels would rush to see who could get their version of the song in the shops first. At other times one artist would have a hit with a song and others would "cover" it as quickly as possible to cash in while it was still hot. This phenomenon occurred worldwide in one form or another.

In the United States cover versions were of two types: white artists covering songs originally recorded by black artists for black audiences, for consumption by white audiences; and "safe" covers of rock and roll songs, whether originally by black or white artists.

The former more or less ended when white DJs such as Alan Freed began playing the originals on white radio, black labels began to "tone down" their records to match white tastes, and in particular when black singer LaVern Baker complained to her congressman. Similarly, once listeners had access to the original versions of rock and roll songs, and could judge the relative merits of each for themselves, it didn't take long for records like Steve Lawrence's cover of "Party Doll," Andy Williams's "Butterfly," and Pat Boone's covers of Chuck Berry and Little Richard classics to elicit laughter rather than adoration.

In England the situation was similar, but the racial and class distinctions, though present, were defined differently. On the one hand, the "whiter" American rock and rollers and pop singers seemed to fare best with the general public. On the other hand, American rock and roll ignited an entire generation of young British musicians who tended to seek out the original (mostly black) artists, including blues and other "roots" artists dating back to the thirties and forties. In fact, many young British music fans were more knowledgeable about American music than Americans, which is, of course, what made the British Invasion possible.

But there were also big differences, not the least of which being that the state of British pop music was relatively dire during the mid-fifties and early sixties, and British labels counted on cover versions of American pop records for nearly half of their sustenance. They didn't wait until the American records had reached England; they sent agents to the United States to search out nascent hits so that British artists could release versions of the songs before the American discs had arrived. Record companies would typically record a song (plus B-side), and have it cut, pressed, and delivered to the shops within 48 hours.

And, they not only tried to scoop the American labels; they tried to scoop themselves—often resulting in multiple versions of the same song appearing simultaneously. For example, on July 1, 1955 Jimmy Young, Al Hibbler, and Les Baxter all had versions of "Unchained Melody" on the chart at numbers one, two, and twelve respectively. On the same Top 20 chart there were also two versions each of "I Wonder," "Stranger in Paradise," and "Cherry Pink." In other words, slightly under half of the twenty available slots were filled with just three songs. Similarly, in October of 1960 Don Costa, Manuel and Music of the Mountains, Lynn Cornell, and Makadopoulos and the Greek Serenaders all had Top 30 hits with "Never on a Sunday."

One of the most fateful meetings in Meek's career took place in April of 1956, when he was assigned to work a session with the great jazz and world music producer Denis Preston, [see Sidebar 2.4] recording an EP for trad jazz trumpeter Humphrey Lyttleton. The recording took place in Studio B rather than the larger main studio, because Preston preferred its less diffused sound. (Adrian Kerridge, who assisted on the session, described Studio B as a "small room, big rotary knobs, old BTR1 [see Sidebar 2.5] tape machine with the heads faced the wrong way—the heads faced inwards—the tape with its coating out, running at 30 inches per second.")

They needed four tunes for the EP, but the sax player had to leave for a gig before they could record a fourth song, and Joe or Denis, depending on which account is correct, came up with the idea of improvising on a blues. Lyttleton wound up building the piece around a rolling boogie-woogie piano bass line, pushed along by a snare drum played with brushes. Meek took advantage of the fluidity of the situation and began tweaking the sound to his tastes. First of all, he used compression and limiting very aggressively in order to tighten things up and get as much sound on the tape as possible. He squashed the dynamic range of the individual instruments far more than was usual on jazz records at the time, and then pushed them all up against a limiter. But more importantly, he made two major production decisions that changed everything, and turned "Bad Penny Blues" into a hit.

Sidebar 2-4: Denis Preston

Denis Preston was Britain's first independent producer and is usually associated with the "trad jazz" movement that occurred there in the mid-fifties and early sixties, though his work extended far beyond that genre. The Grove Dictionary of Jazz credits Preston with coining the word "fusion" to describe the meeting of jazz with other forms, such as pop, rock, and Indian raga. Preston brought Indian violinist John Mayer and American Joe Harriott together in 1966 to record *Indo-Jazz Suite* and *Indo-Jazz Fusions*, two pioneering world jazz albums. Preston also worked with Josh White, Big Bill Broonzy, Alan Lomax, Ramblin' Jack Elliott, Shawn Philips, and the Grandmaster of Calypso, Lord Kitchner. Preston began in 1947, inspired by American jazz producer Norman Granz. His production company was called Record Supervision.

Humphrey Lyttleton explains [5]: "In jazz, the general idea was to stick a mic up and get as natural a sound as possible without mucking about. Joe over-recorded the drum brushes, and he also did something very peculiar by distorting the left hand of the piano. The [left-hand] octave rolling up sounds very peculiar on the record, and it's very difficult to recapture that live, because that's not the actual sound that comes out of the piano. Had I not gone on holiday, had we all gathered 'round and listened to playback, I would have had a fit. I would have said, 'That's dreadful!' And I would have thrown Joe into one of his sulks. I would've said, 'You've over-recorded the drums, and I don't want that. And you've distorted the piano, and I don't want that either.' But in fact I wasn't there, and so it all came out like that, and became a hit—I think for those reasons."

Denis Preston shared Lyttleton's view: "I don't think, with due respect to the musicians, that it was the music we made. I think it was Joe's concept. He had a drum sound—that forward drum sound—which no other engineer at that time would have conceived of doing, [and] with echo. And it was the sound that

Joe Meek created that made that record for Humphrey. And Joe created this at a time when other people were still—when I was [being] told that the rhythm section should be felt and not heard. And Joe's concept—he was the first man to use or utilize what they then called distortion. I know what they call it now; now you build it into your equipment. And that made a hit out of what would otherwise have been another track on a jazz EP. And it was purely a concept of sound. [However] the idea of a sound engineer not doing what you tell him, but actually twiddling the knobs and distorting things, was a totally new world for me."

Sidebar 2-5: EMI BTR1 and BTR2 Tape Recorders

At the end of World War II it was discovered that the Germans had developed tape recorder technology that was far beyond anything known elsewhere. German Magnetophon recorders were captured and analyzed by the Americans and the British, both of which built their own versions of the machines. American engineer Jack Mullin, financed by Bing Crosby, built a machine that Crosby used to record and broadcast his radio shows on ABC. In Britain, EMI built the BTR1, which became the staple recorder in British studios for many years. The early tapes ran at 30 ips and shed oxide with each pass.

The BTR1 was eventually replaced by the BTR2. Stuart Eltham began working at EMI/Abbey Road in 1948 and recalls that, "It (the BTR2) was still a mono machine, but it had been redesigned and it was pretty good. One of the big things was that somebody at the factory designed a way of getting bias on the tape—the previous method used to give quite a few harmonics that caused distortion. Somebody there had designed a push-pull method of making an oscillator, so it just gave out more pure frequencies and no harmonics, and all the harmonics were killed, and you got a pure source of bias in the tape, and it didn't distort."–London Calling, www.prostudio.com

"Bad Penny Blues" made it into the Top 20 on the pop Hit Parade, which was extraordinary because at that time jazz records were generally EPs or LPs that didn't sell in large numbers, much less make it into the charts.

Shortly after that Meek pulled another rabbit out of his hat. When Anne Shelton was recording "Lay Down Your Arms," a song with a military marching beat, the producers wanted to add the sound of actual marching soldiers. As Shelton recalls, Joe came up with a more economical solution: "I had the most beautiful Christian Dior suit on for the recording session, a beautiful black one. I stood by the microphone and there was this lovely man (Adrian Kerridge) close by who had a box with stones in it to give the effect of marching feet by shaking it backwards and forwards. My whole suit was covered in gray dust and I could never get it out." [6] The recording also features a beautiful fade at the end, where Joe brings the music down and the echo returns up, leaving the voice suspended in a wash of echo. The record was a massive hit.

Robert George Meek had become the most sought-after engineer at IBC, which suited him just fine; as before, however, everyone didn't welcome Joe's success. According to Kerridge: "Joe was the best engineer in the place, he was a big client-puller. He was a talented guy, I mean Alan Stagg was jealous of this, I'm pretty sure of it." It didn't help that Denis Preston had gone to Stagg and threatened to pull his sessions from the studio unless Joe worked them all.

Figure 2.5:
A low-resolution photograph of the tech shop at IBC, showing two "technicians" and some of their gear.

Figure 2.5a:
Another low-resolution
photograph of the tech shop
at IBC.

Stagg and some of the others, perhaps because they too felt
threatened, took pot shots at Joe because he was gay. By nearly
all accounts Joe conducted himself in an entirely professional
manner, but he also powdered his nose, went a little heavy on the
aftershave (he shaved several times a day), spent an inordinate
amount of time combing his hair, and on at least one occasion
showed some photos of his hunky live-in lover around the
studio. This was more than enough in the staff's eyes to
warrant harassing him. According to Kerridge: "There were
some horrendous things that used to take place at IBC. Every
month there used to be a staff meeting, where all the staff were
put together in Studio A, and the studio manager used to make
particular comments about performances; and usually they'd
have a go at Joe, because of the way he was. I used to see Joe
reduced to tears at some of these meetings, and in fact they had
me reduced to tears at one stage. A lot of them are now men
who are contemporaries of mine, running studios. I mean this
has never come out before because no one has ever asked me;
but it's quite interesting."

On the other hand, dealing with Joe wasn't always a romp in
the daisies. He experienced significant mood shifts, which when
combined with his hot temperament were problematic even for
allies such as Denis Preston: "This was a great problem [when]
working with Joe. He was in a sense a split personality. When
things were going well, he was the most marvelous person to
work with. But if there was a crisis, he'd blow up, and he
became impossible." Meek also began exhibiting signs of what
would develop into acute paranoia, and he became livid when

others spoke about him behind his back. He was becoming increasingly afraid that his co-workers and others within the industry were conspiring against him, and it angered him. "When it came to what was being said behind his back, that's the one thing that he couldn't tolerate," recalls former IBC engineer Jimmy Lock. "There's no doubt about it that there was a certain madness always within Joe—there's no question." [7]

One thing that routinely angered Joe was the incompetence of certain A&R men [8] (in the role of producers) who had no understanding of recording. They were used to calling the shots and didn't like being told what to do, particularly by a lowly engineer. Joe made suggestions, sometimes insisting that they be acted upon, and those suggestions routinely led to success. It was bad enough that he would insist on having his own way, but it was particularly irritating that his suggestions so often turned out to be right.

"He got on very well with the artists," says Kerridge. "He gave short shrift to some of the producers, because Joe was very much a man that, well, when you're recording you can take direction—well I suppose it's like acting: if you're really into a character, that has got to come from within. There's a certain amount of direction you can take, and then it's got to be you. And Joe always latched on to the job precisely right, in the pop field. It would sound right, it would feel right, and it would *be* right. And if somebody criticized that, they were, you know— because he knew it was right. Hence the way he would sometimes go off."

Joe was also seen as demanding special privileges. For example, there was a policy of rotating second engineers, but Joe only wanted to work with certain engineers, and would sometimes entirely ignore the others. At least one person has suggested that Joe only wanted to work with those that he "fancied," but a simpler and more likely explanation is that he preferred to work with those who were the most competent, or at least those who didn't hassle him. Joe would also request that the control room be locked up whenever he took a break from a session— just like his shed back home—so that other engineers couldn't examine his setup. Though his requests were always denied,

Joe's fears were not entirely unreasonable. Adrian Kerridge explains: "Secretive yes, about everything; about the EQ, about the echo that he would use, about his microphone techniques. [He used to say] 'Those rotten pigs gonna take my secrets.' I mean quote, unquote. It was something that grew over years as his engineering capabilities grew in stature. With his success, people wanted to know what he was doing, naturally."

This attitude enraged Alan Stagg, who regarded Joe as a selfish prima donna unwilling to be a team player. But the lack of teamwork went both ways, and reportedly some engineers and producers went out of their way to cause Joe problems, such as taking a piece of gear that he needed and had reserved. "And therefore he would create an artistic scene because, in my view, he didn't have the tools of the trade, which were very limited in those days. Those are the sort of scenes I remember," says Kerridge. Ray Prickett, a Senior Engineer that worked alongside Meek at IBC, summed it up this way: "The main problem with Joe, he was a bit before his time, in many ways. I mean today, the gay side is looked at much more liberally than it did in them days. Plus, all his experimental ideas and the things he wanted to play around with, you know, which everybody basically did later on. And it's always the same: anybody's out of step, they just rub up people. So many people just can't stand something a bit unusual."

One unusual thing that people couldn't stand was the way Meek would tweak the gear in the studio totally off-spec during a session and then just leave it that way for whoever came along after him. "Oh yeah, that was a nightmare," says Prickett. "If you had a session you used to [have to] find out if Joe had been in there before you; because if he had you made sure you had an extra half-hour, and got the workshop up to check everything out. There was no guarantee that everything was going to be working at a basic standard."

When asked if Meek was an inveterate tweaker, Adrian Kerridge replied: "Oh, absolutely. He would upset everybody. Somebody would set a machine up and he'd tweak; that was Joe. He would adjust the tape recorders to get them more within the parameters that he was recording to. He'd drive the tape fairly hard, and perhaps he would take specific precautions to either increase the level going onto it, or take it down as the case may be. It would either avoid [distortion] or increase it; knowing Joe he'd pile as much level as he could on the tape. He used to tweak with the high frequencies on the tape machines. He would never trust anyone except himself to tweak it up." Kerridge felt that it was more of a management problem, and that rather than blaming Meek, someone not making hit records should have been assigned to put things back after Joe's sessions. "Why not? It doesn't matter what you do as long as you get the results, and Joe's results were commercial and he used to sell records. That's what counts at the end of the day."

Figure 2.6:
Joe Meek in the disc-cutting room at IBC circa 1956.

Photo courtesy of Denis Blackham

Figure 2.6a:
The same room in 1957, with
a new Lyrec cutting system.

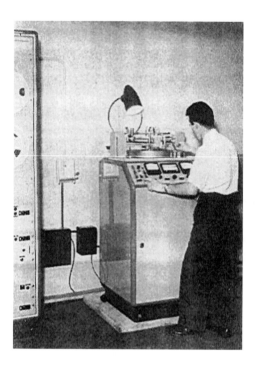

Just what *were* Meek's secrets anyway? "Microphone technique, basically," says Kerridge, "And the type of microphone that he used. He was so far-sighted. Engineers in those days had very funny ideas about microphones. There was an instrument here and a microphone over there, and you didn't do it any other way. The companies that made the microphones wouldn't quote a distortion-free output figure for a given sound pressure level, so naturally engineers would put a microphone well back, particularly on [loud instruments like] brass, and they'd get a lovely clean sound. And Joe said, 'Don't want that.' His concept was to place the microphone close—and the sound was like a trumpet in your ear."

And not just figuratively. "One day Joe had a big session with four trumpets—we used to use these old STC pencil micro-phones—and Joe said 'I'm not gonna put four trumpets and a mic up there. I want two microphones, and they're gonna be *that* far away, two feet away from the bells of the trumpets. I'm gonna put two in parallel, into one mic socket.' That was unheard of, really, and it was a tremendous trumpet sound. [9] It was the same with drums. Engineers would use maybe one microphone on the drums suspended one-and-a-half meters above the kit. Joe would say, 'No, right on the snare drum, right on the cymbals.' Two microphones, or three if necessary. Our engineers would be frightened to do this. Joe would get hold of it by the balls, as it were, and get in there and get the sounds. That was the forerunner of pop technique. He really was, I suppose, the father—or the mother—of modern recording techniques." Additionally, engineer Arthur Frewin credits Meek with being the first British engineer to remove the front head on a bass drum and place a microphone inside, a technique that became common many years later.

Figure 2.7:
STC 4038 microphone. The STC 4038 is considered to be one of the greatest microphones ever produced, and it has been used on thousands of recordings in England, Europe, and the US.

Another hallmark of Joe Meek's recordings was his use of limiting and compression. Ray Pricket: "He used to use limiters a lot, heavily, you know, to create some of these effects—breathing and pumping effects, things like that. It features quite strongly on most of his records of that period. [They were] all fairly heavily limited to create a good, solid sound. If you ever look at the meter on those recordings, it just stays up there, because the limiter or the compressor holds the level. See, if you use the limiter properly you shouldn't hear it. It compresses the dynamic range, so that when it goes on to disc you've got a record which has a nice level all the way through, so that you don't get any quiet bits; you know, it holds the level up. That's the technical way to use a limiter. But Joe used to do the reverse—and a lot of other people have done it as well—but he practically always used it as a tool to create part of the sound that he wanted—a pumping effect."

But there were only two limiters at IBC, and both were located in a separate room from the studio. Adrian Kerridge recalls: "It was a funny set-up in those days—very much like, I suppose, the Americans now—if you had extra equipment you paid extra money. So if Joe was doing a session, we used to tie up what we used to call the Assembly Room, which had various machines in it for assembling and editing radio shows. And he used to tie up the limiters in that room so the client would get charged another five pounds for the use of that room for the limiters, which Joe always wanted. So if there were two studios working, there'd be fights over who'd use the two limiters, and usually Joe won. That was his sound. Tight sounds, 'lot of reverberation, limiting. [*slaps hand emphatically*] It was all punchy, and, you know, tight."

The third element in Meek's bag of production tricks was artificial acoustic ambience, which at that time came in the form of echo and reverb. "He was an echo man. He used to use a lot of echo—that was Joe—because it sounded commercial," says Kerridge. "We had two very good natural echo chambers at IBC in those days and recordings up until then—pop recordings—were usually "roomy." They didn't have a tight sound with artificial reverberation; they had a room sound with some reverberation. But Joe's approach was very tight, punchy, forward sounds with reverberation and compression (and) limiting."

Figure 2.8:
A poor photograph of the legendary echo chamber at EMI/Abbey Road studios in London. Note the microphone on the left and the large speaker on the right behind the column.

These days it's difficult to comprehend how moving mics closer to sound sources, beefing up sounds using compressors and limiters, and adding echo and delay could have ever been considered revolutionary. Nobody mikes instruments from several feet away unless they are intentionally trying to capture the sound of a particular room; compressors are routinely used on bass, drums, vocals, and nearly everything else (not to mention the millions of guitarists and bassists who use stompbox compressors); and if a record was made using no reverb or other ambient effects *that* would be considered revolutionary.

But to simply credit Meek with devising clever new applications for gear misses the most important point. Certainly he used the tools at his disposal in creative ways, and he was a technical innovator, but the reason that his recordings sounded different than the ones that everybody else was making at the time was that Joe Meek was a visionary; he knew in his own mind what the recording *should* sound like. In fact, viewed from another perspective, Joe was mostly using technologies that were in their infancy, limiting his efforts as much or more than assisting them. Meek made great records in spite of the limits of the tools he was working with.

According to Arthur Frewin: "He loved music, he loved sound and creating new sounds. And very often in the studio after a run-through you'd say 'That's great Joe.' He'd say, 'Look, I've just had an idea, can we have another run-through?' And he would create it there and get a wonderful sound. All of a sudden something clicked in his mind and he'd get, say, twenty strings sounding like sixty strings. And he'd come out with ideas that nobody else had at the time—well ahead of his time, Joe. Sound-wise, well ahead of his time. He'd have all sorts of ideas: throwing echoes in, but he knew how to control echo and make it work for him. He loved to put a microphone next to every instrument, but it couldn't always work, though; he loved to pick out instruments in the orchestra. A most creative man."

"He'd get a sound in his head and he would work and work until he got that sound. Some producers at that time didn't like it; they wanted bang, bang, bang—in and out. They couldn't understand what the man was after because half of them didn't know what the bloody hell they were doing, quite frankly. But he knew what he wanted. If you had the patience with Joe he'd get the most marvelous sounds for you. If you wanted the regular, routine stuff as most producers did he'd get it but he didn't like doing it. He'd need one or two run-throughs then he'd play it back—'What do you think of that?' Sometimes you had to say, 'No Joe, that's not what I'm looking for.' It *usually* enhanced it." [10]

Denis Preston recalls things similarly: "He was slightly ahead of what the equipment could do for him. That's why I say it's a tragedy, in a sense, that he died—or was born when he was, not later. Because I think if he'd have worked with 24-track equipment and all the ancillary things we now have today, he'd have made Phil Spector look like a specter, if you know what I mean. He was anticipating (the future), in a sense, aurally, but without the equipment to do it, because it didn't exist (yet). Joe had a concept of sound I really and sincerely think ten years ahead of its time."

Be that as it may, Meek worked intuitively as much as he did technically, and by most accounts he was not even a particularly "technical" engineer. He had learned a great deal about basic electronic circuitry, and he was certainly capable of repairing and modifying much of the gear that he used, but when it came to the hard science aspects of engineering he was partially in the dark. Some of the other engineers found the combination of Joe's lack of technical chops and his "know it all" attitude to be an annoyance, and they were particularly irritated when in spite of those perceived limitations his recordings routinely went on to be hits. Adrian Kerridge summed it up this way: "Joe was very funny. He used to think he was technical, and he wasn't really technical, but he was technical, but not *technical* technical. He'd say, 'We're gonna do this.' He wouldn't really know why. He couldn't give a technical explanation why, but he'd do it, and it would work, and it would cut, and the results were, for those days, enormously progressive. He sat down behind a console and he'd make the right results for people. He used to sell records, and I reckon that's pretty good engineering."

Ray Prickett was also amused by Meek's attitude: "See, in them days recording was a lot different from today; you had to be very careful about, you know, you have overload points and things like that. I mean, these days a desk (the British term for a mixing console) is built in with what they call an overload factor. It means you can overload the early stage of the desk, because you've got various stages of amplification. In them days you couldn't. If you had to start pulling back here, oh, 10 dB at the most, you had to do something about it. And one of the things you had to do was to get an attenuator, which is like a little plug, and you had to go down and unplug the microphone and stick it in, to give you 10 dB of padding. I mean, it was as critical as that. Well Joe didn't want to know anything about that, because he wasn't worried about that, because his mind was on the creative side, not on the little technical aspects, and them sort of things."

And in those days tape distortion posed more of a problem than it would years later when the technology had been improved. Prickett continues: "There's a law. If you've got a tape, and you copy it, you always increase the distortion—it's a fact of life—there's no system that is 100% distortion-free. So what happens is, every time you copy something you create more distortion. But if you've got a clean tape to start with and can't hear (the distortion), it's fine, because you've got about 2% distortion before it becomes noticeable to the human ear. But if you've got a tape, and it's crunchy, and it's just the sound you want, but (there's) a lot of distortion there, (even on) a one-generation copy there's terrible problems. But Joe didn't want to know anything about that—that's the tape—and he wouldn't, you know, want to understand those sorts of things. Those are the sort of things that probably upset other people."

Prickett goes on to give a third, less charitable, example: "On some occasions when he was recording he'd alter the EQ—the record EQs—to get the effect. Then if he'd already got a take and he wasn't happy with it, and he was going to have it cut or copied, he'd tweak the replay EQ curve to make it play back differently, until he got what he wanted. But then that particular tape might not play back right in every machine, if the tape's being sent to another place. Well what it boiled down to was that if he'd produced a tape that way, for it to be played back properly the EQs on those machines would have to be…see what I'm getting at? He wasn't that technical. (But) he was there and he was creating, and he was doing a better job than some of those producers he worked with (laughs), to be quite honest."

Technical limitations or not, Meek was reportedly one of the first British engineers to experiment with sound-on-sound recording. According to Kerridge, "He and producer Michael Barclay used to work what they called 'composites,' which they made track by track by track by track. They'd make a rhythm composite, add something else to it and then put the voice on top, so it ended up (being) three or four generations removed from the original. But what they were in effect doing was multi-track recording via the composite method. And nobody else, to my knowledge, in London, in fact in Europe—I don't know about America—was working this way at that time. Well advanced." In fact, American guitarist Les Paul *[see Sidebar 2.6]* had used the same technique to record what he called "multiples" while creating his New Sound in the forties and mid-fifties. However, it is extremely unlikely that Meek and Barclay knew what Paul was up to at that time, as he was every bit as secretive about his methods as they were.

SIDEBAR 2.6: Joe Meek And The Wizard Of Waukesha

When Joe Meek was asked to name some of his favorite artists, he listed Les Paul and Mary Ford second, just after Judy Garland (who happened to be a close friend of Les and Mary's). Meek was quite familiar with Paul's work and had enormous respect for him, and it is easy to understand why. For one thing, Les Paul is credited with inventing sound-on-sound recording, Joe's primary recording technique.

Sometime around 1934 Les Paul began experimenting with "multiples," which he created using a homemade disc cutting lathe made from a Cadillac flywheel, dental belts, and a turntable. He would record a track onto the acetate, then play it back on the turntable while simultaneously adding another

"track," both of which were mixed down to the disc cutter and recorded on a second acetate. At first he only used the multiples to accompany himself while rehearsing.

In 1945 Les Paul began using the sound-on-sound technique to create what he came to call his New Sound. He spent two years secretively experimenting with recording techniques, guitar pickups, effects, and other devices, and by late 1947 he had amassed 22 multiples, all recorded in his garage studio. One of these recordings, an extremely futuristic version of Rodgers and Hart's "Lover," was released in February of 1948 and quickly rose to #21 on the charts. "Lover" was a tour de force employing all of the playing and recording techniques that Paul had developed thus far including delay, sped-up sounds, and muted guitar. Paul even says he invented phasing and flanging at that time, using identical recordings played on two turntables. By combining all of his tricks on one record, and doing some fancy tape editing, Paul created an uncanny masterpiece that sounds nearly as startling today as it did over 50 years ago.

Les Paul effectively invented electronic delay when he attached a pickup behind a disc cutter-head, and delay effects are one of the hallmarks of his recordings. He is also generally credited with being the first person in the United States to employ sound isolation and close-miking techniques, including close-miking drum sets. These are all techniques that Joe Meek is said to have originated in England, and it is impossible to know to what extent Meek was influenced by Paul. Meek was certainly familiar with Les Paul's recordings, but since Paul never divulged his secrets, even to his wife Mary, Meek would have had to have figured out what he was doing simply by listening.

Two other characteristics common to Joe Meek and Les Paul's recordings is their limited dynamic range and relative "hotness." This is partially due to close-miking the instruments and the voices, but in Meek's case it primarily had to do with his overt use of compressors and limiters, while in Paul's case no electronic dynamics processors were used. Les Paul explains: "The way we did that was that Mary recorded in the same room with me, and we kept our eyes right on the VU meter. If I picked a note and I got my 0 level, and the next note was +3 (dB), I would find a way of adjusting as I played. Mary did the same, so we were our own built-in compressor/limiter. That's why on our records everything is coming out 100%." According to Les, the first electronic compressor/limiter was developed by RCA (and modified by Columbia Records) in an attempt to emulate the Pauls' "compressed" sound.

When asked about Joe Meek, Paul said that he didn't really know anything about him. When I told him that Meek wrote

"Put a Ring on My Finger," that he had used the royalties to found his own record label and recording studio, and that apparently Meek had stumbled onto several of the same techniques as he had while working independently in England, Les replied: "I'll be darned; that shows you how close someone can be, and yet so far away." Indeed!

Figure 2.9: The Columbia 45 of "Put a Ring on My Finger" by Les Paul & Mary Ford. Note that the song is credited to "Duke," meaning Robert Duke, one of Meek's songwriting aliases.

Other similarities between the two audio pioneers include:

Both were extremely precocious youngsters who were simultaneously fascinated by electronics and music at an early age, and remained passionately focused on their work to the exclusion of nearly everything else.

–Both built their first crystal radio sets at around age ten.

–Both had no formal education beyond the high-school level.

–Both lost the use of their hands due to tragic accidents, just avoided having limbs amputated, and recovered miraculously.

–Both began their careers working within the established recording industry and later built home studios where they produced hit records rivaling those made at major recording facilities.

–Both licensed their recordings to major record labels before the practice became common.

The differences between the two men are equally striking. Les Paul once said his greatest God-given gifts are perfect pitch, a love for music with the ability to learn it quickly, and the curiosity and persistence of an inventor who wants to know how things tick.

Joe Meek had enough electronics knowledge to build and repair televisions and radios, to operate military-level radar systems, and to customize, maintain, and in some cases even build recording gear. Les Paul invented the electric guitar and the multi-track tape recorder.

Both men deeply loved music, but Les Paul was (and still is) a virtuoso guitarist, and though he never learned to read music, he had a fantastic ear and an extraordinary ability to conceptualize and work musical ideas out in his head. He mastered the guitar at an early age, worked as a session and backup musician for major stars (including the Andrews Sisters and Bing Crosby), and was able to pull entire arrangements seemingly from mid-air. Meek, in contrast, failed to learn to play any instrument at even the most elementary level, and was incapable of communicating his musical ideas in any sort of standard form. And while many adjectives have been employed in attempts to describe Meek's sense of pitch, perfect has never been one of them.

Throughout 1957 and 1958 Meek's association with Denis Preston continued to flourish, and together they made many interesting recordings, some of which became major hits. One of the most consistent hit-makers they recorded was Lonnie Donegan, who, along with Chris Barber, launched the "skiffle music" [11] craze almost by accident. Donegan had recorded a few folk songs during the sessions for an otherwise instrumental Chris Barber record, and one of them had made it onto the disc. The songs from the album were released as singles over a period of time, with the lone vocal number, a cover of Leadbelly's "Rock Island Line," released last. The song sold three million copies in three months! Donegan neglected to credit the original writer—the beginning of a tradition later continued by the Rolling Stones, Led Zeppelin, and other British groups—but he also didn't make any money on it, as he'd been paid a few pounds as a session musician. [12]

Donegan had already chalked up a few more hits by the time Meek began engineering his sessions, but he had two #1 songs with Meek at the board and Denis Preston producing: "Cumberland Gap"/"Love Is Strange" and "Gamblin' Man"/"Puttin' on the Style." From a recording standpoint, "Love Is Strange," a Micky and Sylvia cover, is by far the most interesting. The instrumentation is double bass, at least two guitars, either a bongo or a snare with the snares muted, and what sounds like an ashtray or some other glass or metallic object being played as an incidental percussion instrument. Donegan's voice has a warm presence suggesting he worked the mic at close proximity, and the song has a spacious and haunting feel to it—though oddly there's relatively little echo.

Meek also recorded Donegan live at Conway Hall in early 1957. He recorded the show from the audience with the recorder on his lap, but only four songs survived because the audience was worked into a frenzy by the wild skiffle sounds and wrecked the recording setup as they rushed the stage. Another Donegan song with a story is "My Dixie Darling," which was recorded at a British Legion Drill Hall, where Joe converted the Men's bathroom into an echo chamber using a speaker and a microphone.

Skiffle madness was still going strong in England in mid-1957, and Joe Meek decided that he wanted to get in on it himself while there was still time. He had co-written a song with teenage arranger Charles Blackwell called "Sizzling Hot," and he was in search of the right group to record it. He found what he was looking for in the Station Skiffle Group, whom he promptly re-named Jimmy Miller and the Barbecues. Meek had recently relocated to an apartment in Arundel Gardens, where he had set up a makeshift studio, and he rehearsed the band there for several weeks. Once they were sufficiently prepared he brought them to IBC, on Denis Preston's dime, and "Sizzling Hot" backed with "Freewheeling Baby" made history as the first record entirely produced by an engineer. "Sizzling Hot" opens and closes with the unmistakable sound of a spring reverb being given a good whack, meaning that either there was a spring reverb at IBC, which is unlikely, or Joe had already built his famous "black box" spring reverb. *[see Sidebar 2.7]*

Joe Meek built several pieces of gear that became known as "black boxes," the most famous being a spring reverb unit. The first stories regarding the black box reverb sprang up in 1957, and according to Adrian Kerridge: "He (Joe) used to carry it around with him in a case, taped-up. Joe's 'black box' was in fact an old HMV-manufactured fan heater! These were used then at Lansdowne to heat various offices. The fan heaters were made from fairly tightly coiled suspended wire that twanged when you moved them. Joe got hold of a broken one and made what is known as a spring echo unit, using transducers—I can't remember which they were. It worked very well and Joe was, as you know, very secretive about it. To my knowledge this was most probably the first spring echo unit of its kind. It produced a very twangy and reverberant sound that he used to great effect on many of his recordings. Reverb (reverberation) is actually a modern-day term, not used at that time in Audio."

Figure 2.10: Joe Meek's "Black Box" equalizer. It was modeled on the Pultec.

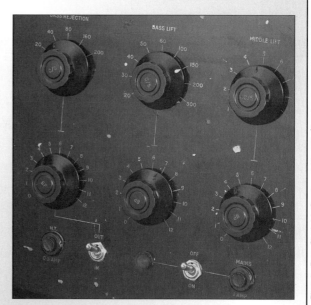

Figure 2.11: Detail of the Black Box Equalizer's controls.

Photo by and courtesy of Adrian Kerridge

Figure 2.12: The compressor that Joe Meek designed and built while he was at Lansdowne, circa 1958.

Dave Adams recalls that Joe's reverb unit was an ongoing experiment: "The 'black box' existed at Arundel Gardens and went through various transformations and springs. The only time I saw the inside of it I was just a kid who didn't know my AC from my DC, but the spring itself was wired at both ends. I always assumed that the sound actually traveled down the spring but it's anybody's guess."

Another of Joe's black boxes was a compressor/limiter (pictured) that is now in Adrian Kerridge's possession. Meek also built a black box equalizer (pictured) that Nigel Woodward, its current owner, describes as "Probably the warmest, smoothest, most transparent equalizer ever made."

Photo by and courtesy of Adrian Kerridge

Figure 2.13: Side view of the compressor showing a sidechain circuit added by Adrian Kerridge.

Joe Meek had become England's first independent producer-engineer, and he had done it while recording a song he had co-written, played by a group that he had chosen and prepped for the session. He was becoming increasingly interested in expanding those new roles, and increasingly disinterested in suffering what he believed to be continuing harassment at IBC by Alan Stagg. Of course, from Stagg's perspective Joe was a selfish megalomaniac with a bad attitude and a streak of paranoia a mile wide who "wasn't worth the trouble." [13] So when Meek finally decided to leave "the rotten pigs" at IBC in September of 1957, few of them were sorry to see him go.

Denis Preston, however, had come to rely on Joe as an essential member of his team, and his take on the situation at IBC was decidedly different than Alan Stagg's: "Joe was enormously sensitive—he'd be hurt by, you know, the slightest thing. And no one, in those days, seemed to have any sympathy for him, or understanding of his particular situation, or make allowances for his particular personal problems, as opposed to his talent." Nobody, that is, except Denis Preston.

Preston made Joe an offer: "We'll get some equipment and set up an editing suite for you next door to my office. And I want you to engineer all my stars. And we'll take the tapes back, and you edit them—because I don't want to lose you." The plan also called for Joe to continue engineering Preston's sessions at IBC, now as his personal engineer, but they hadn't counted on Stagg and the others taking the hard line. IBC's management didn't acknowledge "independent engineers," least of all Joe Meek, and he was informed that he would not be permitted to use the facilities unless it was as a producer. [14] Rotten pigs or not, there were certainly a lot of sour grapes at IBC.

Despite this significant impasse, Denis Preston was determined to have Joe Meek continue to make his records. Short-term, he bought an old Magnaphon editing machine and put Joe to work editing tapes in a small room on Newman Street. Beyond that, Denis had decided to open his own recording studio as soon as he could find the right location, so he was delighted when Joe told him about a studio that he'd found. "It was not a professional studio, but it was a recording studio with a license to record. And some amateur guy, a cellist, very nice guy, had the place, and he just made records, or recorded for fun. And he had the basement here. Joe discovered the place, told me about it, and I went in like a shot."

[1] On a tape recording made circa 1957 Joe Meek refers to it as the International Broadcasting Corporation, a view shared by British recording industry veteran Peter Harris, who recalls it being the only corporation in Britain other than the BBC.

[2] *Legendary* pg. 31

[3] Alan Stagg later became the studio manager at Abbey Road, where he also became an obstacle to Pink Floyd while they were recording *Dark Side of the Moon* in 1972 and 1973. Martin Benge: "There was a battle between the artists and the management, to shut down the sessions at 10 o'clock. And Pink Floyd had absolutely no intention of going along with this. And on one session Stagg came in and turned the power off." [The Abbey Road Story—Independent Television, UK]

[4] *Legendary* pg. 32

[5] *Arena*

[6] *Halfway to Paradise: Britpop 1955-1962* by Spencer Leigh and John Firminger, 1996. Interview #28.

[7] *Legendary* pg. 44

[8] "Artist & Repertory" men were staff employees at record labels who were responsible for matching artists with songs, and supervising recording sessions.

[9] Joe also pioneered the technique of recording brass by having them play facing a reflective wall, so that the early reflections were recorded along with the direct sound, adding thickness and depth.

[10] *Legendary* pg. 37

[11] According to Chris Barber, he and Lonnie Donegan took the word skiffle from a record by Dan Burley, a black "rent party" pianist. They felt that some of the music they were playing was reminiscent of rent party music found in poor black American neighborhoods. In fact, Donegan's skiffle music was a scrappy blend of bluegrass, New Orleans jazz (via trad jazz), country blues, and outright hillbilly. Donegan had far more in common with Bill Monroe than with, say, Muddy Waters or even Dan Burley. Skiffle instruments were largely impromptu: comb-and-paper, washboard, guitar, maybe a banjo, and what was literally a "string" bass: a broom handle stuck through a large upside-down wash bucket with a single string attached to the bucket on one side, and the top of the broom handle on the other. Pulling on the broom handle tightened the tension on the string, raising and lowering the pitch. In England they substituted a "tea chest" for the bucket.

[12] Skiffle may have been a simplistic DIY music based on three chords, but Donegan was no musical simpleton, and skiffle wasn't the only three-chord music he was familiar with—he was a skilled musician who had previously played jazz banjo in Chris Barber's Jazz Band. Born Anthony Donegan, he lifted the name "Lonnie" from the great American jazz/blues guitarist Lonnie Johnson—the same Lonnie Johnson that legendary bluesman Robert "Johnson" had lifted his last name from. Donegan's "skiffle band" was comprised of top musicians, and there were no washboard or tea chest bass players among them (though Beryl Bryden did play washboard on the studio version of "Rock Island Line").

[13] *Legendary* pg. 55

[14] Meek actually did return to IBC as a producer shortly after leaving. He recorded Jackie Davies with His Quartet performing a schlocky ballad that he co-wrote with Charles Blackwell, "The Land of Make Believe," backed with a cover of "Over the Rainbow." The record stiffed.

C H A P T E R 3

Lansdowne

The studio that Joe had found was actually little more than an empty basement that happened to be licensed for recording. Denis Preston wanted to turn it into a state-of-the-art stereo recording studio that would not only provide him with a place to record, but would also attract professional clients of all sorts. He hired three extremely bright men for the task: Ian Bradbury to design the studio, Sandy Brown to engineer the acoustics, and Joe Meek to assemble all of the equipment, including designing the main mixer.

Meek's job was considerably more challenging in 1958 than it would be today. For one thing, if you wanted a nice new recording mixer it would have to be custom built. According to Preston: "Joe Meek's thing was always, 'I'm technical,' which he was to a degree. He designed the original equipment. Now, it's not like today, where you've got multitudinous firms. Joe designed the original mixer we used in the studio. I went with him to EMI. He saw to the installation, and literally, I'm not kidding, he worked—and Adrian will confirm it—24 hours a day."

The reason that Adrian can confirm it is that he had wound up at Lansdowne through an odd twist of fate. He had left IBC to do his compulsory two-year National Service and hadn't seen or spoken to Denis Preston in nearly as much time. Preston was cajoled into helping the army with some jazz broadcasts, and when he arrived at the radio station he found none other than his former Junior Engineer. Preston told Kerridge about the new studio, that Joe was working with him, and that he should come see them once he was out of the service. He did.

Figure 3.1:
Joe Meek in the Lansdowne control room, 1959.

It took about a year to design and build Lansdowne, and before long the studio became so renowned for the quality and clarity of its sound that the engineers at IBC started calling it "The House of Shattering Glass." Joe Meek probably earned more respect from the London recording community for his role in creating Lansdowne than he would for any other accomplishment in his post-IBC career. Apparently, non-technical Meek was technical enough in this case.

Adrian Kerridge recalls that, "During the first year of Lansdowne's operation Joe Meek had EMI/Hayes design and build a twelve-channel valve mixer with built-in EQ in each channel. It was maroon in color with gold edging: very posh and typical Joe! It was very well built. It was a mono board, the idea being that a stereo control room should be built upstairs overlooking the [mono] control room, but this didn't happen while Joe was there. The recorders were valve stereo and mono TR50s built by EMI/Hayes. [1] The other processing was very limited: just a limiter/compressor that Joe had made, which I still have, and some of his black boxes—the spring reverb for example. The only box he took from Lansdowne was his spring reverb. We also had a natural echo chamber *[see Sidebar 3.1]* and this was used on many of the early hits and indeed by me for some years—a very good-sounding chamber."

Before the days of electronically produced ambient effects, the only way to get "echo" was to use a physical echo chamber. Though there were slight variations on the design, they basically consisted of an empty room with a speaker placed at one end, and a microphone placed at the other end. Sounds would be amplified, played through the speaker, and "echo" around the room before being captured by the microphone and returned to the mixer. Several of the larger British studios had them, including the BBC's Maida Vale studios (where a BBC AXBT ribbon microphone was used) and Studio 2 at EMI/Abbey Road. Veteran EMI/Abbey Road engineer Stuart Eltham recalls: "One of the big things that we got going was the echo chamber, and it took quite a time persuading the research department that we needed a mixer–they thought you could just put echo on everything. We had to try to explain to them that you needed more echo on violins and voices, and you didn't need any on the drums...which means you wanted to select which microphone circuits you were going to inject echo on and be able to adjust the level. The trouble was they used to give us what they thought we ought to have–you thought, 'For God's sake, why doesn't one of you sit in on a session and see what we're trying to do?'"

When the echo chamber at Lansdowne was first built an amusing incident took place. Dave Adams, who began working with Joe Meek in 1958, recalls: "That was in the cellar where we painted the stone walls ceiling and floor with high gloss paint. A speaker stood in one corner and a microphone in the other. Sound would be played through the speaker, bounce around the room then into the mic which relayed it back to the mixer. One day a lady from the top floor of the building came and complained that music was coming from her gas stove. We all, including Joe, trooped up there while a tape played in the control room and sure enough, open the oven door and here came "Bad Penny Blues" or the like! It turns out her gas meter was in the corner of the Echo chamber and the music was travelling the pipes. Joe thought it was a great joke, which tells me that his paranoia had not yet begun."

"He also had built a valve EQ similar to a Pultec. For flanging we used two tape machines and varied the speed of one against the other by slowing one down by the tape flange hence the name flanging. It was very successful and we used it a lot together with expansion, compression and limiting. [2]

"After some early mono recordings we used to record not what I would call stereo as we now know it but it was very fashionable to record ping pong stereo—left and right with a hole in the middle. [3]

"After the first year we went stereo exclusively; we were the only studio in London at that time to do so. Lansdowne was also the first truly independent London recording studio."

The long hours didn't stop once the studio had opened. Denis Preston would later joke that Joe worked 26 hours a day, and Adrian only 25, but the joke wasn't far from the truth. According to Kerridge: "We worked six days a week. We were very dedicated people and we *worked*. We used to finish at midnight sometimes, but Joe was so dedicated that he worked right 'round the clock if necessary. That's the way this industry was. Joe was totally dedicated to his work—*absolutely* dedicated to his work." Meek often worked on his day off as well. "That was his problem," said Preston, "He did every bloody session."

According to a letter Joe wrote to his sister Pam, he felt sick as well as tired when he arrived home after working 18-hour days. He also mentions that he found it necessary to monitor at very high levels, and that by the end of the day not only was he exhausted, he couldn't hear. What Joe didn't mention in the letter was that he had begun using over-the-counter diet pills as stimulants, and had quickly become addicted to them, at least psychologically. This was the beginning of a dependence on stimulants that would span his entire career, and very likely contributed to its end.

The long hours notwithstanding, for the time being things were going pretty well for Joe, and the sessions he was working were mostly good ones. Denis Preston had been one of IBC's biggest clients, and when he opened Lansdowne lots of his clients followed him there. Many if not most of them were jazz artists, but there were also some major pop stars. In fact, since some of the jazz records he had produced with Joe at the board had made the pop charts, he was being asked to do more pop sessions, an irony that greatly amused him. Dickie Valentine, Red Price, Lita Roza, Cherry Wainer, Petula Clark, Lance

Fortune, and other British pop luminaries all recorded sides at Lansdowne during Joe's tenure there. Maintaining distinctions between "jazz" and "pop" production styles must have been tricky for Preston and Meek, and indeed there were some problems.

British jazz musicians in the late fifties were after a very "pure" sound, and some of them, including heavyweights Chris Barber and Humphrey Lyttleton, complained about Denis Preston's tendency to put a pop spin on their records. Presumably Joe Meek sided with Preston, and probably offered lots of advice while he was twisting knobs and providing Preston with options. However, purity notwithstanding, Barber's dislike of commercialism probably didn't stop him from cashing the hefty royalty checks he collected when his Jazz Band's "Petite Fleur" went to #9 in February, re-entered the charts again in July, and eventually became the largest selling British record of the year. Mr. Aker Bilk, Kenny Ball, and other top traditional jazzers were also regular clients.

Figure 3.2:
A mid-sixties EMI/Columbia Records EP by popular trad jazz clarinetist Mr. Acker Bilk, the first British jazz musician to have a #1 hit on the pop Hit Parade. The songs were originally released in 1959, 1960, and 1961; three of them on Columbia's Lansdowne Jazz Series. Joe Meek, Philip Clark, and Adrian Kerridge are credited as engineers. Denis Preston is credited with supervision.

But apparently not all of the artists who recorded at Lansdowne were so concerned about the music. Many of the session players in particular used to annoy Meek when they failed to put heart and soul into their parts. He would try all means of coaxing more feeling out of them, sometimes even going so far as plying them with alcohol. But it really shouldn't have been all that surprising that the musicians didn't pour their emotions into every song that they recorded. Top-drawer session players worked *lots* of sessions, sometimes from ten o'clock in the morning until well into the evening, often at more than one studio. They were routinely expected to sit down "cold" in front of a sheet of music or a chord chart and be doing a fine job of playing the tune a few moments later. Sometimes the muse was present and sometimes not—and in many cases the players didn't find the music particularly interesting or even enjoyable. Considering the circumstances it's probably more remarkable that so many performances *were* inspired than it is that many were not.

Another thing that must have influenced the musicians was the producer's mindset. The jazz musicians may have wanted to take the time to get a good sound, and Joe Meek no doubt lobbied for license to explore creative possibilities, but many if not most of the A&R men who brought their artists to Lansdowne took the opposite tack. According to popular recording artist Joe Brown: "Few people in the business really cared about creativity and if you said that you wanted to spend some time getting a decent sound, the managers wouldn't consider that important. No one really looked at sound as being a crucial part of what was going on because the whole emphasis was on getting the song on tape. As long as they could tap their foot, or tap their wallets, the managers would be happy. Back then, it was just a record."

And they had a point. Jazz EPs and LPs may have been played on high-fidelity phonographs, but most singles were played on inexpensive machines, such as the ubiquitous Dansette. In the United States a large part of the production strategy was creating records that would sound good coming out of transistor radios; very little pop music was actually broadcast on British radio, however, so record marketers there focused on making the sound leap out of what were little more than children's "record players." This didn't go down too well with the disc-cutting engineers, as EMI's Harry Moss recalls: "We made records so that they could be played on a Dansette, and we used to argue that instead of making our records inferior to suit an inferior machine, we should tell Dansette to make better players or just go out of business. The arm was too light, there wasn't enough volume in the speakers, and the whole mechanism was too stiff. With a few pounds in the making they could have made a great deal of difference to the actual product." [4]

At the same time that pop records were being mixed with Dansette specifications in mind, another trend was simultaneously headed in the opposite direction: records were being produced for an increasing number of "hi-fi" audio enthusiasts, and the up and coming thing was stereo. The concept of stereo was not new— stereo recordings of various sorts had been made as far back as the early thirties—but it wasn't until improvements in disc cutter-head technology in the mid-fifties that it became feasible to mass-produce stereo records. The earliest stereo records were orchestral, perhaps because of consumer preference, and were recorded using only two or three microphones. For example, in early 1954 RCA recorded a performance at Symphony Hall in Boston using an RCA RT-11 2-track tape recorder and two Neumann U47 microphones. At about the same time, EMI made their first "stereosonic" recording at Abbey Road Studios. In May Decca entered the game in a big way when ace recording engineer Roy Wallace devised the now legendary "Decca Tree" microphone array: three Neumann KM-56 condensers mounted on a cross-bar suspended eleven feet above and just behind the conductor's platform. The mics, which were directional with a cardioid pick-up pattern, were mounted close together and facing down at a thirty-degree angle so that they "heard" the music from just above the conductor's position—the truly sweet spot. The signals from the three mics were mixed and recorded onto an Ampex 350-2 running at 15 inches per second.

By the time Lansdowne was being designed, stereo was well enough established [5] that there would be no sense in building another mono studio. The transition from one primary recording format to another is always a tricky matter for studio managers; they must decide well in advance if they are going to invest time and money in the new technology so that they may be "in place," and hopefully ahead of the competition, if and when the trend takes off. Only eight years earlier EMI had been the first to develop a professional tape recorder (the BTR1), and consequently theirs was the first British studio to complete the transition from disc [6] to tape recording. (Other studios reportedly rented BTR1s from them at first, while they waited to see if the trend would continue.) The switch to stereo didn't require changing media—they were still recording onto tape—but it wasn't just a matter of adding another monitor or two either. At the very least it would involve purchasing a new recorder, drastically modifying or replacing mixers, adding power amplifiers, and possibly even altering the acoustic design of the monitoring environment. Of course, multitrack was just around the corner, and there would be new equipment to buy at that point, too; but at least that stereo half-track recorder that they'd just finished paying off would still be of good use!

The next major format crossroads was the advent, or near advent, of "quadraphonic sound," something Joe would very likely have taken an interest in. Four-channel sound had originally been developed back in 1953 for the 4-track stereo soundtrack to the first CinemaScope film, *The Robe,* which featured effects such as Roman soldiers marching from one side to the other, storms moving around, and off-screen voices. Perhaps unfortunately, the technology was never used again after that [7], which certainly resonates with quad. Though the public never embraced it, numerous manufacturers were at least researching and planning quad products, and studio owners, once again, had to ponder the possibility of equipping their facilities to handle the potential work. Those that did discovered lots of interesting things—for example, it is a *very* bad idea to pan low-frequency sounds around in a circle—but they may not have considered the knowledge satisfactory compensation for the trouble and expense of re-tooling their facilities—and then having to put everything back! It is somewhat frivolous to speculate as to what Joe Meek might have done had he survived into the seventies, but assuming that at some point he had switched from mono to stereo mixes, and acquired a multi-track recorder, it is easy to imagine him mixing in quad.

Back to stereo: "Those were some of my most adventurous days," recalls Denis Preston, "because Joe and I were at the beginning of stereo. It was an experiment that no one fully understood, but Joe was the sort of guy who said, 'Mmm,' and he went in and took a chance with a technique that he didn't fully understand—that no one understood at that point. And many of those early records, many of which have been reissued with great success, certainly had technical problems, phasing problems, but that was not Joe's fault. It was that he was slightly ahead of what the equipment could do for him."

Be that as it may, the "problems" with Joe's recordings were not always the unintentional consequences of primitive technology; often Joe deliberately pushed the technology beyond the breaking point. "Joe was a man with great foresight," says Adrian Kerridge, "He'd go all outside of the book, totally outside of the book as an engineer. For example, Joe made this 'commercial record.' I mean, he used to say, 'It's commercial!' And Denis always used to say, 'Well, Joe, it's not commercial until it sells.' But Joe kept saying it was 'commercial,' with his gesticulations—and they took this record to EMI. EMI said, 'We can't cut this; it's distorted.' So Joe said, 'I know it's distorted; it's commercial! If I put it on the tape, and I can record it, you cut it!' And they did."

Despite Meek's technical transgressions, or perhaps because of them, many great recordings and even a few hits consistently flowed from Lansdowne. Denis Preston, who had lots of experience dealing with quirky and temperamental jazz artists, was temporarily able to keep Joe at least partially pacified by allowing him considerably greater creative freedom than other engineers typically enjoyed, and by bankrolling his gear craving. The "company" even awarded Joe an automobile (perhaps hoping among other things that he would use it to take a much-needed holiday), but Joe took no more interest in his new red and white Sunbeam Rapier than he did any other object unrelated to recording. Adrian Kerridge remembers: "The company bought him a car, a Triumph, and from the day that he had it, until I think the day he left here, he never put a drop of oil in it, and he never had it serviced. And the tools that were with the car, he brought them into the studio, and they were used in the studio and never on the car—now that's a funny little story. He used to get in and if it didn't start he'd leave it."

But Joe's attitude towards the car was a microcosm of his overall attitude. He might ride along for a while, as long as things were going his way, but unless he was convinced that he was heading in the direction that he ultimately wished to be going, sooner or later he would get out and walk away. Working at Lansdowne was a great opportunity for Joe, but after a few months his ambitions began to outgrow his position, and he became increasingly disinterested in simply being an engineer and studio manager, albeit a highly appreciated and nearly unrestricted one. For one thing, he felt that he had more to do with Preston's successful records than Preston himself. For another, he felt that he knew more about how to make hit records than most of the A&R men that he had to serve and answer to as an employee of the studio. He could do all of their jobs and probably some others too: scouting out new artists, choosing their repertory, producing and engineering their records—maybe even writing the songs. Why not, wasn't he was already half the way there? But he wasn't ready to make a move just yet.

Along with everything else, Joe had continued to write lyrics and songs, and he had stepped up his search for talent to perform them. Several months before, Joe had hooked up with Joy and David (Adams), a teenage brother and sister act that he felt could be marketed as a wholesome, squeaky-clean pop duo. Though they were siblings, and Joy had a young son, the songs they did together often presented them as a couple, or were at least ambiguous on the point, and Joy's son was kept out of the public eye. Joe got them an audition at Parlophone, which they passed, but for some reason Denis Preston didn't want them to record at Lansdowne, so they went to EMI instead. Sir George Martin, who supervised the session, was reportedly unimpressed. They recorded a near-novelty song that Dave had written called "Whoopie," which featured a gimmicky "smooch," more than a little reminiscent of the "pop" on "Lollypop," which was a hit at the time. However, unlike "Lollypop," "Whoopie" didn't chart. Joy and David continued to record for Joe for several years, both as a duo and as backing vocalists, until Joy moved on. Dave Adams decided to stick around, and became an important part of Joe's team, working closely with him on hundreds of demos and records, right up until Joe's death in 1967.

Figure 3.3:
The acetate of "Whoopie," a
Dave Adams song that he
and his sister Joy recorded for
Joe Meek the first time they
visited him at Arundel
Gardens. Joe cut the disc for
"the Kids" on his portable
disc-cutter.

A few months later Joe "discovered" another new act, this one already fairly well established. The West Five were a skiffle band from Ealing who had cut their teeth playing the US Air Bases circuit, and had done several television appearances by the time they met Meek. The group combined rock and roll and country and western with an original flare, and featured a "Hawaiian" steel guitarist [8], giving them a highly unusual range of sounds for a band in 1959, particularly a "skiffle" band. Joe sneaked them into Lansdowne when nobody was around, and the audition tape demonstrates that besides having a tight, crisp sound and impressive vocal harmonies, they were capable of playing convincingly in a wide variety of styles. They ran through seven tunes, presumably from their usual set: "Please Don't Touch" by Johnny Kidd and the Pirates; "('Til) I Kissed You," the Everly Brothers' current hit; steel-driven arrangements of country standards "Alabama Jubilee" and "Blues Stay Away From Me;" Frankie Ford's "Sea Cruise;" a rocking up-tempo rendering of Gene Vincent's "Be Bop A Lula;" and a bluesy "Don't You Know."

The West Five passed the audition and Joe signed them to a deal making him their recording manager. He also changed their name to the Cavaliers, though for their first record they were called Rodd, Ken and the Cavaliers, for reasons probably only known to him. They returned to Lansdowne, once again clandestinely, to record two of Joe's songs [9]: "Happy Valley" and "Magic Wheel." The former has a very up-front hi-hat part, nice steel work (including a very expressive double-tracked solo) providing string-like textures, tight vocal harmonies, and Meek's ridiculous lyrics. The latter begins with the sound of a train leaving a train station and a faint "announcer's" voice that sounds very much like Joe's. From there it moves into a sprightly march, eventually becoming a stomp, and ultimately ending with sped-up voices that are supposed to be the "happy" passengers arriving in Happy Valley. [10] Considering what the Cavaliers were capable of, these two songs fell far afield of their natural musical inclinations. But Meek would take them *much* farther afield later when he recast them as the Blue Men, and had them perform his lunar-life fantasy *I Hear a New World*. The Blue Men would also back one of Joe's other new artists, Peter Jay (Peter Lynch). [11] Jay's "Just Too Late" (written by Duke) opens with a dry steel-guitar riff placed up-front in the mix. The steel also takes a tasty solo, featuring a striking combination of creamy tube-distortion tone, and processed (compressed?) tape echo. "Friendship," the flip side, has so much echo chamber and spring reverb on it that it could easily just be the reverb returns going directly to tape—and who's to say it isn't? The lyrics, written by Jay and his mother, are as sappy as any Meek ever wrote. These two records would be the first releases on what would soon be Meek's Triumph label.

Figure 3.4:
The "Magic Wheel" 45 by Rodd, Ken and the Cavaliers, on the Triumph label (1960). The song was recorded at Lansdowne. Rodd, Ken and the Cavaliers were the same band as Rod Freeman and the Blue Men.

In the meantime, Joe had written a song called "Put a Ring on Her Finger" for English singer Eddie Silver, and though the song had flopped in the UK, somehow Les Paul and Mary Ford had gotten a hold of it. They changed the title to "Put a Ring on

My Finger," and had a Top 40 (#32) hit with the song in the United States. After that, English pop star Tommy Steele also decided to cover the song, and his version charted back in the UK. (Interestingly, Steele's version features an up-front brush snare drum part very similar to the one on "Bad Penny Blues.") Joe's writer's share of the publishing amounted to a tidy sum, and provided him with the resources he would eventually need when it came time for him to go independent—a time that was approaching more quickly than he imagined.

While at Lansdowne, Joe was also the de facto producer of a side by Emile Ford and the Checkmates called "What Do You Want to Make Those Eyes at Me For." Michael Barclay, the official producer, had left the session after the first side had been completed, with little time remaining, leaving Joe to take over. The recording is bathed in Lansdowne's great-sounding echo chamber, and features a big, warm, and slightly distorted vocal, along with a crisp and very prominent snare drum part (though the kick drum, if there is one, is inaudible). The record has a great feel, and quickly shot to #1 in October of 1959. Another interesting record from that period was "A House, a Car and a Wedding Ring" sung by Jack Davis, who had changed his name to Mike Preston after being "discovered" by Meek. It didn't chart in England, but reached #57 in the US.

In hindsight it appears clear enough that Joe Meek and Denis Preston were two trains racing towards each other on a single track. Denis had rewarded Joe's work by granting him virtual producer status on many sessions, and inevitably that led to instances where the two "producers" came to loggerheads. Additionally, Meek had placed a number of his songs with Preston's publishing company, and he was lobbying hard for him to accept more.

As Denis Preston recalls, at about eleven in the morning on November 4, 1959 the two trains ran out of track: "We had a most difficult session for America: Kenny Graham with Joe Harriot—'Jazz Cha Cha.' It was a very difficult album, big orchestra, with all brass and saxes and a big rhythm section, and we were working in a tiny control room with the temperature probably about 85 degrees, because we didn't have air conditioning at that time. And the mixing facilities were inadequate really for the sound we were aiming to make.

"And Joe's written a song. He'd scrawled something on the back of an envelope, and I'm trying to get this session through for MGM and Joe keeps saying, 'Look, I've written a marvelous song. I think that my song is much better than what you're recording now.' He keeps showing me. And I said, 'Joe, for Christ's sake, if you want to talk about songs—later. We're trying to make a record.' 'Oh, rotten pig,' he said, and he got up and walked out." [12]

The next day Meek received a telephone call from Preston telling him not to bother coming back.

[1] Shortly thereafter the studio upgraded to EMI TR90 twin-track recorders.

[2] Dave Adams also recalls two of Joe's other innovations at Lansdowne: "Joe had some Lucite (what we now call Plexiglass) screens made which were about seven feet tall and three folding panels each. He would place these around the studio in different configurations depending on the musical lineup, to liven the sound of a very dead room. One other innovative thing he did there was to have us make the exhaust fan duct in the shape of a giant S, the plan being that any outside sound trying to find its way in there would be minimal by the time it reached the studio."

[3] One of Joe Meek's office assistants, Tony Kent, described another form of pseudo-stereo that was used in the early sixties: "It's not what I would call 'stereo' in the strict sense of stereo today [1983]. It wasn't pure. What they used to do— what they did with the early Beatles stuff—was they would pan the backing tracks high-bassed on one side, and high-trebled on the other, with the voice equally. So if you listen to it, it doesn't sound like true stereo. If you listen to one side it sounds fluffy and bass-heavy, and on the other side it sounds bright."

[4] *Halfway* pg. 475

5 In 1931 Alan Dower Blumlein, also credited with inventing the cross figure-eight stereo miking technique, filed a patent application for stereo recording in Britain. On March 12, 1932 a stereo recording of Scriabin's "Poem of Fire" was cut directly onto a vinyl disc at Bell Labs in Philadelphia. The stylus cut separate grooves for the right and left tracks, effectively halving the total record time. On January 19, 1934 Blumlein recorded another orchestral performance in stereo, this time at EMI/Abbey Road using a vertical-lateral stylus that vibrated in two directions, simultaneously cutting one channel vertically and the other laterally.

6 Before the introduction of tape recorders the professional recording method of choice was "direct to disc," which involved cutting grooves into a disc—much like a record cutting lathe. This technique had been around for decades, but was highly refined for military purposes, and by the fifties produced recordings of great clarity, with surprisingly wide frequency response.

7 More than thirty two-channel stereo films were released that year, but the format failed to catch on, partly because only Fox and Todd-AO were willing to record effects in stereo. Stereo films reemerged in 1975, with the introduction of Dolby optical stereo sound. Similarly, Disney Studios created a proprietary "interlocked dual-system format" in 1940, used to play the stereo soundtrack of Fantasia, but no other Disney films with stereo soundtracks in that format were produced after that, and the system was never used again.

8 According to Ken Harvey, the steel double-neck guitar was homemade.

9 Attributed to "Robert Duke," one of Meek's several pseudonyms.

10 The sped-up voices gag may have stemmed from the runaway success of the "Chipmunk" records made by David Seville (Ross Bagdasarian). He and chipmunk friends Alvin, Simon, and Theodore had multiple #1 hits, and by 1970 had sold over thirty million records. Bagdasarian's first #1, "The

Witch Doctor," also featured sped-up voices.

[11] Not to be confused with another Meek artist named Peter Jay, the drummer for Peter Jay and the Jaywalkers.

[12] *Legendary* pg. 75

CHAPTER 4

I Hear a New World

According to Dave Adams, Joe Meek was "over the moon" when he heard that Les Paul and Mary Ford had recorded "Put a Ring on My Finger." But Joe had been well on his way to the moon for years, and to hear him talk, already knew quite a bit about it. For several months Joe had been writing music for what he called "An Outer Space Music Fantasy" about life on the moon, the existence of which he was apparently convinced. "Long before it began to be recorded Joe would describe these moonscape situations, Glob Waterfalls, Bublights, etc., and I would politely listen and wonder what I was doing there," relates Adams. "In retrospect I think he did have some kind of vision about it. He would tell us about the way the water ran up there and collected in a ball, and it fell down. I forget which ones are which, but the Saroos and their little hovercraft...when you think about it, it's quite amazing that he would see these people hovering about in hovercrafts, which came a long time after he did. And the idea of the gravity being different enough to ball the water up—we don't know that exists, but somewhere out there maybe it does. That is strange, that stuff." [1]

Figure 4.1:
The RPM CD cover.

Strange stuff? "Yes! This is a strange record; I meant it to be. I wanted to create a picture in music of what could be up there in outer space. I can already see and hear in my imagination from the studies I have made on outer space what wonderful new sights and sounds are in store for us. I must admit that most of the ideas on this record were to please myself, at the same time hoping it will please you, after all you buy records for entertainment not often for education. This I hope you will find entertaining and different.

"There is another reason for making this record, that is to show off stereo, and as you will hear on this record things actually move, and makes it ideal for demonstrating the abilities of stereo equipment. At first I was going to make a record with music that was completely out of this world; but I realized that it would have very little entertainment value, so I kept the construction of the music down to earth and wrote tunes that I hope you will grow to like." [2]

What inspired Joe to create *I Hear a New World*? To begin with, he had been interested in outer space, and the new technologies that were bringing people into closer contact with it, from an early age. By November 1959 rocket science had been around for thirty years and the Soviet Union's Sputnik 1 satellite had been in orbit for two years. Flying Saucer movies were the rage, and there had been hundreds of UFO sightings reported. Millions of people throughout the world opened their minds not only to the possibility of inter-planetary space travel, but also to the likelihood of encountering intelligent aliens along the way. And there was something else. While he was living at Arundel Gardens Joe still took the time to listen to music for relaxation, and his favorite album at the time was Gustav Holst's *The Planets,* with "Mars: The Bringer of War" being his favorite track. "I think this is probably where the spark of things to come sprang from—the thundering drums in 'Mars' are very reminiscent of the later Joe sounds," says Dave Adams.

It's only a short step from UFOs to séances and Ouija boards, and Joe took that step at about this time. After Joe's death, stories began circulating about his "occult" interests, and the strange goings-on at his studio. Some accounts even presented

Joe as a wand-carrying lodge member of one or more secret magical societies (other than IBC, of course!). [3] Most of the stories have turned out to be just that, but we do know that Joe enjoyed holding seances, and that they were a fairly regular event at his Arundel Gardens flat. Dave Adams recalls the circumstances in less-than-transcendental terms: "I always believed that the seances around the Ouija board were manipulated by Joe, albeit subconsciously. He never received an answer *he* didn't want to hear and so the glass would slide effortlessly to the desired letters, since we all knew that to let it do otherwise would bring up a tantrum and an enjoyable evening would be over. But Joe got a lot out of it; it told him things that he needed to hear."

One of the most sensational stories in the Meek Mythos is the account of a prophetic Tarot reading given by Jimmy Miller in John Repsch's Meek biography. [4] Miller describes how he and Joe and Faud—Joe's mysterious "Arab friend"—were suddenly gripped by a supernatural force, and Faud, through a feat of automatic writing, channeled the words: "February the 3rd, Buddy Holly, Dies." Joe is said to have attempted to convey a warning to Holly via his record and publishing companies, and then even after February 3rd passed without incident, to have gone to London to hand-deliver the message to Holly while he was on tour there. Holly is said to have accepted the warning graciously, without appearing particularly alarmed. The following February 3rd Holly's plane crashed, killing him, the pilot, Ritchie Valens, and the Big Bopper. Whether or not the tarot card story is true [5], the fact is that Joe *did* believe in "spirits" in some sense, and he believed that Buddy Holly's spirit, in particular, visited him regularly—a belief that persisted his entire life.

Why is Joe's interest in outer space, the moon, Oujia boards and seances relevant? Besides telling a good tale, gaining deeper insight into what made Meek tick aids in understanding his creative motivations, his methods, and his music. Joe Meek had high hopes for *I Hear a New World* while he was recording it. He had just been booted out of the recording establishment, and he was determined to show them a thing or two more about innovative engineering and production—and he was going to do it in stereo! As usual, Joe needed someone to help him translate the music that he clearly heard in his imagination into actual musical arrangements. He worked out a deal with Rod Freeman, of West Five/Cavaliers/Blue Men fame, and appointed him musical director. Rod would listen to "demo" tapes of Joe's pitchless vocal caterwauling, or worse, sit with Joe looking over his shoulder as he picked parts out on the piano or guitar. The challenge was formidable, but judging from the results Rod met it heroically.

Not surprisingly, Freeman chose members of his own band for the session. Joe was particularly interested in Roger Fiola's steel guitar and it features prominently on the album, often processed in highly imaginative ways. Two other primary instruments on Meek's sonic palate were his recently acquired Clavioline *[see Sidebar 4.1]*, and a modified player piano.

SIDEBAR 4.1: The Clavioline

M. Constant Martin designed the Clavioline in Versailles, France in 1947. It was a small monophonic keyboard instrument that produced brass and string sounds using a tube oscillator as a tone generator. The oscillator covered a frequency range of one octave, but it was extended to five octaves using a tube-powered frequency divider. A switch on the front shifted the three-octave keyboard one octave up or down. Eighteen rocker switches located along the front of the keyboard adjusted the timbre via multiple low-pass and high-pass filters, as well as attack and percussive characteristics. The unit could be used with a small stand, or it could be attached to an organ so that its keyboard protruded just below the main organ keyboard. The overall volume was controlled with a knee lever on the underside of the unit.

The Clavioline was quite similar to Laurens Hammond's Solovox, which appeared at about the same time. Like the Solovox, the Clavioline consisted of two units: the keyboard/sound module, and a tube amplifier/speaker section. The instrument was licensed to Selmer in the UK, and Gibson in the U.S. Martin also made a duophonic model of the Clavioline in 1949, but it never went into production. Variations on the Clavioline appeared from time to time up until the mid-sixties, and the instrument was used by the Beatles, Sun Ra, and others.

Figure 4.2:

An advertisement for a version of the Clavioline marketed for the Electronics Division of Gibson by Chicago Musical Instruments circa 1955.

The Clavioline was one of the earliest electronic keyboard instruments. It produced a nasally organ-like sound and had a variable pitch control that allowed it to produce sweeping portamento effects. The sound of the Clavioline would later be showcased on the Tornados' "Telstar," and was principally responsible for its distinctive sound.

Meek's player piano had the "player" part removed, leaving a big cavity where microphones could be conveniently dropped in. Thumbtacks were placed in the strikers to produce a sharper attack, and a slightly metallic sound. Dave Adams recalls the weekend that he and Joe spent pushing thumbtacks (called drawing pins in England) into the felt hammers of Joe's piano, and says that he got the idea from his father, who had done the same to his uncle's pub piano. But the concept was not entirely unfamiliar to Joe, as Adrian Kerridge explains: "You know he had a piano he put tin tacks in? Here (Lansdowne), we have what they used to call a "jangle piano," and you push the middle pedal, and all the tabs come down. So the tabs go in front of the hammer, and when you hit it, it makes a jangly sound. I don't know if you can buy jangle pianos today…this one's 25 years old and it still works, and you de-tune it and it's smashing. You can de-tune it, say from the middle C to two octaves up, so that some notes sound in tune, and other notes sound out—you just de-tune the middle string. [6] You've got three strings on every note and you take them down slightly; or you de-tune every fifth note or something, so you can get specific sounds. The Joe Meek [piano] sound was the jangly piano that was the drawing pins in the hammers; that was it—with the echo, always the echo." The modified piano became one of Meek's staple sounds, and was featured on hundreds of recordings.

Besides the steel guitar, the Clavioline and the piano, Meek used lots of what Brian Eno would later call "found" sounds, though in some cases Joe had to go pretty far out of his way to find them. In their liner notes to the RPM CD of *I Hear a New World*, R.W. Dopson and A.D. Blackburn list a number of sound effects created by Joe and the Blue Men, presumably as recalled by Rod Freeman. The sounds include: "Running water, bubbles blown through drinking straws, half-filled milk bottles being banged by spoons, the teeth of a comb dragged across the serrated edge of an ashtray, electrical circuits being shorted together, clockwork toys, the bog being flushed, steel washers rattled together, heavy breathing being phased across the mics, vibrating cutlery, reversed tapes, a spot of radio interference, (and) some, well-quirky percussion." All of these sounds were likely processed to some extent, with the usual EQ, compression, reverb, delay, and possibly even echo (at an outside studio or via a converted bathroom or other reflective space). After they were on tape they could be manipulated in various ways, including being slowed down or sped-up, played backwards, or made into tape loops. Then, of course, the edited tape could be processed again as many ways and times as necessary.

It has been suggested that some parts of *I Hear a New World* were recorded at Lansdowne—something Adrian Kerridge doubts—but exactly which parts remains unclear, and almost certainly none of the mixing was done there. Most if not all of the tracks were recorded in Joe's tiny "studio" at Arundel Gardens, using whatever gear he had on hand at the time. His black box spring reverb was definitely present, and he created tape-delay effects using a 3-head tape recorder—but beyond that it's impossible to tell what sorts of devices he used. [7]

How Joe Meek was able to record, much less mix, a stereo album in his apartment is one of the most perplexing of the Meekian mysteries. By definition Joe must have recorded *I Hear a New World* on a stereo machine. Dave Adams recalls there being three mono recorders at Arundel Gardens, and there is good reason to believe that two of them were the EMI TR50 and TR51 full-track recorders that Joe had when he moved out in 1960. The latter was a 3-head machine, and so would have made a fine tape delay, but neither machine could record in stereo. Perhaps Adams was wrong, and the third machine was stereo; it might even have been the Lyrec TR16 twin-track, though all available evidence suggests otherwise. That would still leave him needing a second stereo machine to mix down to, unless he mixed at another studio. Joe had done a good bit of work at Star Sound, so he could have gone there.

Another possibility is that Meek simply borrowed a stereo machine for the sessions. At least one of the Blue Men recalls there being a Grundig recorder at Arundel Gardens, along with the two EMI machines. Grundig did manufacture a "semi-pro" stereo recorder at the time, and it would have been good enough to do a decent job in the hands of an engineer of Joe's caliber.

Another possibility is that Meek synchronized the two EMI mono machines using a variable-speed oscillator (VSO). He almost certainly used his Advance oscillator to control the motor speed of single machines [8], and so he *could* have connected the sync signal to the two EMI machines to achieve a very rough synchronization. That way he would have been able to record the left channel on one machine, and the right channel on the other. While theoretically possible, such an arrangement would probably have resulted in serious phase (and other) problems, and therefore is not a likely explanation. For now, Meek's Arundel Gardens stereo recording setup will have to remain a mystery.

As to the circumstances surrounding the recording, it was apparently pieced together over several months, presumably as Joe had time to devote to it. Rod Freeman and his fellow musicians were reportedly unimpressed with the project as they were working on it, a view shared by Dave Adams, who helped out here and there. "*I Hear a New World* was sparked at Arundel (Gardens). I did a few rough demos of little bits of tunes that I—as a rock and roll fan—thought trite and a waste of time, but I had quickly learned to humor Joe's idiosyncrasies. Bits were added along the way and before I realized what was happening the finished thing emerged, which I still thought trite. It is only in recent years I have come to understand the enormity of the techniques used in achieving its completion."

The same could be said for a number of other works dating from roughly the same period, like Barry Gray's pioneering electronic scores for television programs like *Supercar*—created in 1959, at the same time as *I Hear a New World*—*Fireball XL5, Stingray, Thunderbirds,* and others. Gray had a home studio in North London and made use of the Ondes Martinot—a French electronic keyboard related to the Theremin—in much the same way as Meek used the Clavioline: combined with acoustic instruments and processed using echo, delay, and other effects. On the other end of the musical spectrum technical comparisons can be made to Karlheinz Stockhausen's "Kontakte," the original version of which was a four-track tape collage created about the same time. Comparisons to earlier composers working with tape-manipulation and electronic processing can also be made: the Musique Concrete devised by Pierre Schaeffer, Jacques Poullin, Otto Luening, and Vladimir Ussachevsky; Ottorino Respighi's use of recordings of nightingales in his "Pini di Roma;" and even Darius Milhaud's experiments with altering the pitch of voices by changing the speed of phonograph recordings in 1922.

Joe Meek might have found the comparisons flattering, but more likely he would have simply been amused. When *I Hear a New World* was released in 1960 he tried to downplay any serious intentions that he no doubt had by presenting it as a recording useful for demonstrating stereo phonographs, and of interest to teenagers. "I have always had a special interest in this record. With stereophonic playback equipment, quite often one can sit through a whole symphony, or through a whole excerpt from a show, and get very little impression of stereophonic sound. As a matter of fact you could be walking around a room and not realize that it's happening. I've tried—and I've had to do it rather carefully—to create the impression of space, of things moving in front of you, of a picture of parts of the moon. At the same time I didn't want music that was impossible to under-stand, and I wanted it to appeal to the younger generation; after all, they are the people that will be concerned, very much, with interplanetary exploration. So, I composed different tunes, that, to me, different parts of the moon would have in common (sic)." [9]

Unfortunately, due to distribution problems related to another record (dealt with in the next chapter), the album was never released. A four-song EP version called *I Hear a New World Part 1* was released in February 1960, with *Part 2* and the LP to follow in March, but other than printing up some sleeves the records were never made. A "white-label" demo of the LP was pressed, and some demos of both the EP and the LP were supposedly circulated, but how many copies of either release exist is unclear. It has been said that only 99 EPs and 20 white-label LPs were ever pressed, but Meek experts R. Dopson and A.

Blackburn question both assumptions, saying that far too many copies are still around for those numbers to be accurate. Rod Freeman apparently told them that only 99 copies of the EP had been *sold,* which may be the source of that number. Regardless of how many were actually produced, it was a small number, and few people ever heard the music. It is interesting to note that the number of reel-to-reel copies is never given, but that Dave Adams and Tony Kent both have recalled seeing 7- or 5-inch tapes, in printed boxes, rather than records.

RPM Records in England released a remastered CD version of *I Hear a New World* in 1991. It was assembled from various sources, some of them not particularly good, and "enhanced" to make it more presentable to modern listeners. The masterfully executed restoration process eliminated a great deal of the surface noise, brought out previously obscured sounds, and added overall clarity. However, it changed the stereo balance as well. Also, in some places (digital?) delay was added to conceal some serious problems. In addition to the sonic changes, the original sequencing of the songs was altered, disrupting the programmatic flow envisioned by Meek. These changes may have improved the package from an aesthetic standpoint, and made the recordings more palatable to the average listener, but they rendered them largely useless to those seeking to understand the record from a technical and historical standpoint.

The CD of *I Hear a New World* included with this book was created using a different source than the RPM version, and presents it more or less "warts and all." Very minimal restoration was done, and the clicks, pops, and other surface noises are there to prove it. However, the natural deterioration caused by aging and the distortion in some sections notwithstanding, this is the original version of the recording, as Joe Meek intended it to be heard, presented for the first time since its original limited release. Also presented for the first time is an alternate mix of the title track, which appears at the end of the series. It differs from the official version in several important respects.

I have gone into greater detail in dealing with this recording than with any of Joe Meek's other works because it is a long-neglected recording of great historical value that deserves to be brought to the attention of more listeners, particularly those in the professional audio community. Of particular interest is how it represents Joe Meek's attempt to come to grips with the challenges and opportunities offered by stereo, which in 1959 was in its infancy. It should be obvious to anyone listening to *I Hear a New World* that Meek understood many of the implications of the new technology—including phase relationships, imaging, and the juxtaposition of dry and effected sounds—in a way that was years ahead of anyone else working at the time. Remember when listening to *I Hear a New World* that it was recorded in Joe Meek's apartment, probably on marginal equipment, in 1959. Everything else follows from those facts.

GENERAL REMARKS ON I HEAR A NEW WORLD

In his liner notes Joe Meek provided descriptions of some of the scenes he was attempting to convey musically. Those notes are presented in italics.

Meek employs several different mixing setups, all of them bordering on what Adrian Kerridge refers to as "ping-pong stereo," where the sounds are mostly on one side or the other, with a hole down the middle and maybe a thing or two in the hole. What makes Meek's mixes different than most ping-pong mixes is his use of reverb and delay returns. He often places a sound on one side, with effects on that side too, but bleeding over to the other side as well, in a way that the dry sound does not do. These are sometimes criss-crossed, with the effects returns for one sound on one side, and those for another on the other side. There are a number of exceptions to this basic setup, where sounds are moved around from one place to another, particularly on "March of the Dribcots," where almost every-thing "marches" from one side to the other.

The bass sound throughout is also less defined and solid than on most Meek recordings. The reason is that Meek typically recorded electric bass direct, but the bass on *I Hear a New World* is an acoustic double bass, which had to be miked. It's hard to say why the bass sounds so weak. It certainly wasn't because Meek was unfamiliar with recording the instrument, given all of his successful trad sessions, though his microphone selection may have been so limited at that point as to force him to use the best mics on other things. The recording may also have suffered at the hands of the cutting engineers, who were struggling at the time to come to grips with cutting stereo records with a wide dynamic range.

In addition to the instruments and special effects listed previously, many of the sounds were created with a processed test oscillator (used to maintain his tape recorders and other equipment), and tape delays pushed into self-oscillation with regeneration. There are usually sounds on the tape when he cranks up the regeneration, but they become layered and distorted so quickly that it is almost always impossible to identify them. Variations on these two sounds are used throughout the entire album: and they are the two sounds used to create the introduction to the first song.

1. I Hear a New World (2:44)

The arrangement of this piece is deceptively simple, but becomes more interesting the more carefully you listen to it. The intro consists of three basic sounds: a track playing backwards with what sounds like a combination of compressed cymbal (played with a mallet?) and low piano notes (played with the sustain pedal down?), those sounds played through a tape echo with the regeneration increasing and decreasing, and an oscillator rising and falling in the background.

The next section is built up around a repeating three-note "bass" line that is either a tape loop or a *really* steady bassist; and though the sound—much less the pitch—is not well-defined, it resembles a double bass more than anything else. Bassist Doug Collins played double bass, so that makes sense, but he also played one-string "tea chest" bass and either instrument could have made the sound. (If the bass line is looped, then add Godfather of Electronica to Meek's many honorific titles.) The bass line acts as a de facto sequencer, with the drummer following along. Also, the bass part gets panned from side to side a few times towards the end.

The vocals, which sound more like chanting than singing, consist of three sets of two voices organized in rounds, with each set repeating each line once. For example, the first line, "I hear a new world," is sung once by two voices in very tight harmony. The same line is then repeated four beats later, but this time the EQ and effects are much different. The phrasing in the two sets is almost identical, and there are what could be faint punch-in sounds each time the second part begins, suggesting that the first part was transferred to another machine, processed, and then manually "flown" back in.

A similar effect could have been achieved using tape delay, with the delay time set to fall precisely on the beat. That would require synching to a steady pulse, and certainly would explain why Meek might have chosen to use a bass loop as his "clock." On the other hand, there *are* a couple of very subtle phrasing differences between the two parts, raising the possibility that the second part is an overdub; but the differences might just as likely be the result of sonic shifts in emphasis induced by EQ and compression.

The voices comprising the third part are sped up to double time, so that they are pitched an octave higher. This is obviously the result of recording at, say, 7.5 ips, and playing it back at 15 ips. However, the rhythmic and harmonic phrasing of the sped-up part follows that of the other two parts, meaning that it must have originally been sung at half time, and probably recorded onto one machine while listening to the backing track playing at half-speed on another. Then, when both tapes were sped back up and combined, they would have been in sync. (Just imagine being the vocalist on that session!)

One can easily imagine the synchronization issues involved here. You record onto one track on a two-track machine and then transfer the track to another machine. There it is either slowed down or sped up by changing the playback speed of the machine, usually doubling or halving it. Unless he was slaving two machines together using a VCO, they would tend to fall out of synch after a few moments. Perhaps because the verses are so short there's not enough time for that to happen.

2. Glob Waterfall (3:11)
This may contradict the belief that there is no water on the moon;
I still hope there is, if it's not external then it's inside the crust.
Gravity has done a strange thing, and has formed a type of over-
flowing well. The water rises to form a huge globule on the top of
a plateau, and when it's reached its maximum size it falls with a
terrific splash to the ground below, and flows away into the cracks
of the moon; then the whole cycle repeats itself again and again.

This is basically a simple call and response arrangement using a single-note piano melody followed by combinations of other instruments repeating the line, sort of. The piano line itself is an ascending four-note pattern that repeats six times before each crescendo. Bits and pieces of that line, played by several different instruments, comprise the response sections. Something that might be a double bass (or a slowed-down piano) often plays the first two of the four notes in each pattern—though not always—and a drum-like thud tends to fall on the final two beats. But this is by no means a consistent arrangement, and various elements fall in and out of the blend haphazardly. And that's just the rhythm section on the verse!

When the crescendo arrives the drummer pounds away, the piano is given a good whack, and a gong or cymbal is hit once (three times at the end), probably with a mallet. Immediately after that everyone stops playing and the fading gong blends into the decaying reverberation of the piano's sound board—vibrating freely with the sustain pedal down—processed through who knows what. The subtle echoing of the piano chamber must have sounded great when Meek and crew were recording it, but it is only barely audible above the surface noise of the record, and not well-defined. It would be nearly a quarter of a century before compact discs offered consumers the sort of dynamic range and noise specs needed to adequately render sounds of that subtlety.

On top of all this are several layers of sounds so deeply layered with reverb and echo as to be unrecognizable. According to several sources, one sound on the album is water bubbles made with a straw, and one of the main sounds on this piece is a likely candidate (it certainly sounds very sub-aquatic).

Whatever the source sound, the post-processing sound has a distinctly synthetic quality to it—recalling sounds synthesized by Eno on his album *On Land*. Also very Eno-like are the sparse piano notes played with the sustain pedal all the way down and processed through multiple echoes. The effect results in a sonic and emotional atmosphere remarkably similar to those found in the ambient piano works of Harold Budd. There are also little bits of tapping "percussion" sounds and tiny fragments of guitar and piano.

There is a fairly wide dynamic range, beginning very subtly and working towards sudden crescendos marked by loud cymbal crashes and pounding on some drum-like object—followed by enough silence to make you wonder if the piece has finished. There's not much going on stereo-wise. When the image is collapsed to mono it doesn't change much, and when you throw the two sides out of phase there is a fairly dramatic shift.

3. The Entry of the Globbots (3:17)
This is one of the tracks where you can almost see the type of people that live on one section of the moon. They are happy, jolly little beings and as they parade before us you can almost see their cheeky blue-coloured faces.

This song has two sections. In the opening section Meek once again "plays" a test oscillator as a tone generator, or ad hoc synthesizer. In this case the tones he generated were reminiscent of those emanating from the laboratories of mad scientists in '50s sci-fi flicks, an image that almost fits Joe's studio!

Accompanying the oscillating waveforms are clouds of rumbling noise and distortion (perhaps using a slowed-down recording as one source?) that slowly becomes louder, eventually building up to a pretty good "rocket taking off" effect.

At the very end of the first section there's a snippet of sped-up voice, which could have been intentional (e.g., a mock count-down) or simply a rough edit that he decided to keep. The sped-up "alien" voices combined with the spaceship taking off emerge again seven years later on "EXP," the gag that opens Jimi

Hendrix's second album. (One can only imagine what might have resulted from a Meek/Hendrix collaboration.)

There is what *might* be called a crossfade between the two sections, where the oscillators merge briefly with the martial drumming that forms the core of the second section. Accompanying the drums are a two-note "bass" line, multiple sped-up voices (the Dribcots?) and additional percussion sounds produced by rubbing a comb across an ashtray.

But that's not all. The mix employs the simple but effective technique of panning a mono recording to one side, while simultaneously delaying the signal and panning the delays to the other side. Meek uses the same setting for both sections, creating a *very* interesting effect with the oscillator, and adding cacophony to the clamoring drums. There are several layers of voices, not all of which are run through the delay, indicating a fairly complex signal routing arrangement. There is also what sounds like echo chamber on a few sounds.

4. The Valley of the Saroos (2:54)
These are rather sad people being cut off from the rest of the moon. They live in a valley which has some vegetation, but it is a hard struggle for them to live and they have a form of rationing which is a strain and they seem always to be sad. They live and love each other but never leave the valley, for if they did they would surely die. They are green in colour.

The piece opens much like "Entry of the Globbots," with a low, rumbling noise and oscillator sounds processed through a short delay and lots of reverb. But this time the sound fades up gradually, the oscillator tones are lower in frequency (producing a watery, gurgling sound), and the whole section only lasts about 20 seconds.

The second section is organized around a four-bar bass figure in 6/8 time that repeats continually throughout the song. The bass part is played so consistently that it sounds looped, though there is one apparently telltale clam note in the last bar. Instruments are introduced one at a time every four bars, beginning with the bass on one side, then a cymbal on the other side, then a shaker along with the bass, and an out-of-tune piano with the cymbal.

The piano plays a simple two-note-per-bar melody, eventually being joined by a guitar, at which point it shifts up an octave, dropping back down again later just before the end. The guitarist plays muted harmonics through a slap-back echo, forming a bizarre harmonic texture as it interacts with the out-of-tune piano. Then, a very tentative steel part creeps in weakly on the other side, joining the bass and shaker.

Figure 4.3:
A 45 of "Entry of the Globots" and "Valley of the Saroos" from I Hear a New World *(1960). Both songs appear to be on the A side, suggesting that two more were on the flip. If so, the "45" is essentially an EP. Note the catalog number RGX ST5000; ST is probably the code for stereo.*

5. Magnetic Field (3:10)
This is a stretch of the moon where there is a strange lack of gravity forcing everything to float about three feet above the crust, which with a different magnetic field from the surface sets any article in some sections in vigorous motion, and at times every-thing is in rhythm.

The recording setup appears to be the same as the one used on "Valley of the Saroos," with bass, percussion, steel and echo returns on one side, and drums, guitar and keyboard (this time Clavioline instead of piano) on the other. The opening section is another story. It is a one minute and twenty-six-second masterpiece of musique concrete formed from snippets of backwards tapes processed with delay and reverb. By reversing this section you can hear its components. Most of the sounds are made by tapping reverb springs, presumably those within the black box. They are unprocessed, plain as can be. There's also another tapping sound, which might easily have been made by simply touching the end of a live jack or bare cable. It, and all the sounds other than the spring taps, are run through a regenerating tape delay. A high whistling sound is also prominent, though less easily identifiable. For a brief period there are what sound like bits of compressed and muted snare drum, run through the tape delay.

The second section, in sharp contrast, is a bouncy pop ditty lasting only about a minute and a half. The main melody is played on the Clavioline, with steel chords backing it up harmonically.

6. Orbit around the Moon (2:48)
This has a definite Russian trend, they were the first to tell us what was on the other side of the moon! This conjures up the more exciting possibilities and has a strange musical content.

Basically the same recording set up as on the previous song, but with voices added, and with the steel taking the melody at one point. The bass is very indistinct and the "shaker" (could this be the washers on a string?) more muffled and echoed than before—obviously a few passes down in the sound-on-sound process. The arrangement is fairly complex given the simplicity of the music, with guitar, steel, Clavioline, and voices interweaving in ever-changing combinations.

The piece begins with about 25 seconds of bursts of taped feedback and distortion played in reverse. That leads into some Clavioline bleeps shifting from one side to the other, doing a call and response bit with the guitar. A melody eventually emerges, played first by the Clavioline and backed by the guitar, then they switch, then the steel takes it, then the guitar again, and then all three play in counterpoint. In the final section the voice joins in.

One of the voices is horribly off-pitch (Joe?), with the other dubbed over it, apparently in an attempt to salvage the first take. (Perhaps Joe recorded his own voice at some point in the layering process and was too far along to go back once he realized, or was told, how bad it was.)

7. The Bublight (2:43)

This is a wonderful sight—a great patch of the sky becomes filled with different coloured lights, almost I should imagine like the end of a rainbow, except that each light takes on a shape. People travel from great distances to dance in the coloured rays, and about every five minutes the different lights all mix up, take on different shapes, and settle down to shimmer for another five minutes; then the shuffle takes place again. This lasts in our time about ten hours. This strange sight only happens about once every six months, and to dance in its coloured rays gives people the belief that it casts a magic spell over them for the next six months, and safeguards them from evil.

This composition is recorded differently than the previous few, utilizing more sound-on-sound layering, and therefore sounding fuzzier and less clear overall. And speaking of fuzzy, there is some super-hot distortion on the guitar and nearly as much on the steel. It's the type of distortion that you get by overdriving a tube preamp: fat, warm, and rich in harmonic overtones. At one point the overdrive is so intense that were he to have been listening in 1959, it would have given James Marshall Hendrix pause.

There are clusters of sound effects at the beginning and end, just as on most of the other pieces, but in this instance they sound like short tape loops and they are running *forward*. The editing is pretty odd in some spots, but in a charming sort of way, with parts clicking in and out, starting and stopping, etc.

The sounds on each side are richly layered. On one side the bass and the piano are the two main sounds—actually, at least two pianos, but one is prominent—along with (washer) shaker, and distortion that sounds like bleed-through from the guitar on the other side. Half of the sound effects are on this track too. On the other track there is also bass—meaning that the part sits just off to one side in the mix—and another piano track, as well as a second shaker track. The featured instruments, however, are the guitar and the steel guitar.

8: March of the Dribcots (2:18)

All of the elements in this piece center on a rapid-fire (slightly sped-up) snare drum playing a scatter-shot marching-type rhythm. It begins and ends with the snare, and the arrangement, such as it is, is a simple A/B/A/B/A with the two parts being only slight variations on the same simple melody. The "de-do-be-dum" (and dumb) melody is sung by sped-up voices.

The mix changes in some interesting ways. At first the drums are mostly on the right side, with their echo returns on the other, creating a pseudo-stereo wash. About a minute in, the dry drum sound begins to shift to the left side, while the drum sound on the right becomes increasingly distorted and thin. Similarly, the voices begin on the right, with their echoes on the left, and as they move across to the left what's left of them on the right gets thinned out totally using EQ. Meek creates the sense of the chanting and drum-playing Dribcots marching from left to right mostly by tricking the ear.

The overall levels of the two sounds do not change dramatically, but their sonic "weight" does. The other instruments stay basically the same throughout, though there are slight level changes. As usual, the steel is on the left side and the guitar and piano on the right, but this time the bass sits near the middle. All of the sounds other than the drums and voices are almost entirely dry.

9. Love Dance of the Saroos (2:31)
Once again we find the Sarooes [sic, this spelling appears on the original record liner notes, and in some press clippings, while "Saroos" appears in others] *in a sad mood as they twist and turn in this almost Eastern dance. This dance is performed every eight days when the light is only half as bright, and a strange purple haze* [!] *seems to cover their Valley. They dance for almost four hours non-stop, and then fast for three days. Perhaps it's a superstition; anyway it is a means of saving their valuable food rations and to watch this dance is a beautiful sight.*

This is another unique mix, using a very different setup than the others. Almost all of the low-mid and low frequencies are panned hard left, while the high-mids and highs are on the right. This method was used on some mono recordings in the sixties to create a wider, pseudo-stereo sound when played on a stereo phonograph; but I'm not aware of anyone employing it on an actual *stereo* recording.

The bass, drums, and a guitar are mostly on the left, and what there is of them on the right is equalized as described above. The drums are very unevenly recorded, with a snare (snares off) and cowbell being the most prominent sounds, and no kick until the last beat, when it gets hit once along with the hi-hat. Bits of Clavioline and steel bleed through from the right side as well.

On the right side there is a *very* peculiar percussion sound that sort of "swishes." The Clavioline plays the melody at first, then the steel joins in, and on a few sections there is a heavily modulated, Theremin-like, "whistling" sound that lends a sci-fi edge. (Perhaps Barry Gray stopped by with his Ondes Martinot?) There is also considerable distortion of the undesirable variety at around 2 kHz and 4 kHz, producing a coarse rasp. At about 1:45 the rasp turns into feedback.

10. The Dribcots Space Boat (2:20)
This looks rather like an egg, and it floats about 100 yards from the surface of the ground. It glides along at about 20 m.p.h. and is built and owned by the Dribcots. It is driven by huge inductance coils that set up a magnetic field with the same polarity as the moon. Therefore, when the magnetic field is strong enough, it is repelled by the moon and rises into the air. By varying the polarities and their direction, the space boat is driven along. By reducing the magnetic field the boat can gracefully settle down on the ground. Its disadvantage is that it follows the shape of the ground below, and with a few odd craters around the Dribcots have a few 'ups' and 'downs,' but the big disadvantage and the reason for drifting 100 yards from the surface is that if a passing satellite of opposite polarity came by, it would whisk the space boat, Dribcots and all, away and perhaps into orbit around some other heavenly body!

This composition is highly programmatic, and consists of three distinct sections: take-off, flight, and being whisked away, as Joe says, "perhaps into orbit around some other heavenly body."

Meek creates the feeling of rising by having the steel guitar slowly slide up the neck, in time with a fantastic creaking effect, almost like the sound of a door opening. The effect sounds a lot like a pick being scraped up a guitar string, but it might also have been created using a (very) heavily processed test oscillator.

These two sounds are accompanied by cymbal washes in the background, and a minimalist bass part. At the end of the twenty-second opening section the steel guitar plays a series of four very interesting chords, and then there's an abrupt tape splice into a completely different and entirely unrelated section.

The middle section is quite interesting from a mixing perspective. On the left side there's relatively dry bass and drums, a quiet and dry Clavioline, and eventually a muted guitar with lots of echo playing in unison with the Clavioline. On the right side there's a trace of bass, a crispy high-frequency version of the drums (mostly cymbals), the Clavioline with heavy echo, and steel towards the end. By equalizing the drums so heavily, Meek has in effect created an additional percussion part that plays in perfect time with the drums. Also, it sounds as if the same delay—a fairly quick repeat—was applied to both the Clavioline on the right and the guitar on the left, suggesting that they were processed simultaneously.

The main melody is as simplistic as they get, and it's played in unison on the Clavioline(s), guitar, and steel guitar. The Clavioline voicing is both edgy and silly sounding, and is reminiscent of a small battery-powered Casio keyboard. It does, however, convey the feeling of little Dribcots bouncing along merrily in their space boats, in a *Jetsons* sort of way.

The final section is a fantastic collage of edited and processed tapes that opens with a wrenching blast followed by a symphony of sped-up and slowed-down sounds, speeding up and slowing down in real time. [10] The source sound seems to be mostly steel, but there are also plenty of hisses, feedback squeals, and miscellaneous clicks, pops, and buzzes. So long Dribcots!

11. Disc Dance of the Globbots (2:15)

The opening 16-second bit of musique concrete is a logical sequel to the sounds at the end of the previous piece. The opening wash of sound is very likely just that; when played in reverse it is either a recording of waves on a beach, or the best damn fabrication of that sound on record. Other sounds are extremely difficult to identify. Crowd noises from a sporting event? Chickens? Whining dogs? Steel guitar? It's anybody's guess. The wave sound is used again at the end—a piece of otherwise entirely unrelated tape edited on with the subtlety of an elephant—but this time it is accompanied by frantic banging on drums, and distorted electrical noises.

On the left side of the mix are bass, a shaker sound that could have a muted snare and other drums mixed into it at a very low level, steel, piano, and what must almost certainly be a banjo. The banjo and steel play in unison over the rhythm section at first, then the piano joins in, with its sustain pedal pushed to the floor as usual. On the right there is a faint trace of bass, a raspy percussion sound, and a piano. (The piano playing is brilliant or inept, depending on whether the dissonant notes and rhythmic irregularities were intentional or not.) At the head of the track, before the piano comes in, you can hear the banjo part on the other track, but it is delayed slightly. It may be what's left of a previously recorded track several dubs back, but given the uniformity of the delay offset it is more likely the return from a tape delay on the banjo panned hard right. As the piece goes on it very gradually increases in speed, once again suggesting a VCO was used to control the recorder's motor speed.

12. Valley of No Return (2:48)

This extraordinary composition begins with a noise not unlike the one that opens "The Overload" on the Talking Heads' *Remain In Light* (1980) album, co-produced by Eno. An oscillator sweeps languidly across the speakers, creating a sense of gazing out onto a vast expanse. The basic backing track is very similar to the one on "The Valley of the Saroos," and employs the same 6/8 bass and drum figure, but the harmonic and melodic development is richer and more complex.

The stereo imaging sounds as if it may have been created all at once; that is to say, recorded directly to a stereo machine with no overdubs. The steel and most of the bass are panned left, and the guitar is on the right, but there is some bleed between sides, perhaps from effects returns. A cymbal and what may be a bottle being tapped on are near center, as is the main keyboard part. The Clavioline voicing is similar to that of a harmonica, and the sound is given a nice treatment, creating a lush spread across the stereo field.

"Valley of No Return" is an example of what Joe Meek could create when he got serious and put his mind to composing, as opposed to "songwriting." It is quite unfortunate that this piece and the others on this album have been so long in finding their way into the world.

13. I Hear a New World Work Tape (2:23)
There is an alternative "mix" of this piece that may in fact be a work tape representing some particular point in the development of the final or official mix.

On this recording the rhythm tracks are almost entirely on the right side, but short bits of bass pop in and out on the left side about 1:09 in. The main—or first and clearest in the cycle of three—vocal pair are on the right, the second on the left, and the ultra-high vocals are spread across both sides (and therefore panned towards the middle). Three guitar parts follow the same panning pattern as the voices. If this is actually an alternate mix it is a "ping-pong" mix, with hard left and right panning, and a few things right down the middle.

[1] Interview with Dave Adams conducted by the JMAS Midlands Branch on November 10th, 1995.

[2] From the sleeve notes written to accompany the original LP.

[3] Just kidding, but maybe not: "He used to always tell me about the ghost at IBC, about the footsteps. He claimed—I never heard this tape—that they had a recording of footsteps at IBC, coming up the staircase to the control room, and they had recorded this without anybody ever being there. He would tell the story to me quite often. He was convinced that it was true. He did believe in the spiritual world, definitely."—Dave Adams

[4] *Legendary* pg. 60

[5] Dave Adams says that he first encountered the story when reading the book, and that as far as he was aware, Joe never met Buddy Holly.

[6] Note that this is essentially the acoustic equivalent of the chorus effect, which combines a modulated pitch with an unmodulated original.

[7] Joe may also have used some sort of stand-alone echo unit, and if so it was probably homemade. According to Dave Adams: "Joe had built himself an endless loop tape echo unit (at Lansdowne), a thing which was not to be a marketable product for many years. If he had heard of such a thing through the grapevine, or whether it was a product of his own electronic genius, I could not say, but at the time it was just another miracle he had performed." Adams goes on to say that neither Adrian Kerridge nor Denis Preston was aware of this experiment.

[8] This is accomplished by generating a 50 Hz waveform, amplifying it, and using the voltage change to control the motor speed. Peter Miller says that he actually used a Fender Twin Reverb for this purpose!

[9] From a tape recording made at the time of the record's release.

[10] These drastic speed changes strongly suggest that the recorder motors were being controlled via an external VCO, as described previously.

CHAPTER 5

Triumph

When Joe Meek left Lansdowne he was still living in his small flat at Arundel Gardens. For several years he had used the flat for auditions, rehearsals and to record demos; and big fifties stars like Lonnie Donegan, Shirley Bassey, and even Petula Clark had spent time there. Now that recording at Lansdowne was no longer an option, the flat became his base of operations.

Joe decided that he would start his own record label, where he would be in charge of A&R and production decisions, and where he wouldn't have to work for anybody. There was only one problem: even with the money that he had made from "Put a Ring on Her Finger," he still didn't have enough to bankroll the entire operation himself. He began contacting record companies and publishers, but he soon found that his reputation preceded him, and none of them were willing to take a chance on becoming the next "rotten pigs." The frivolous lawsuit he brought against Lansdowne alleging wrongful termination didn't help either.

But Joe didn't have to wait too long before opportunity knocked. Saga Films, a classical record label that despite the name was no longer involved with films, was hoping to enliven its sales by expanding into the pop market. After several discussions, label head William Barrington Coupe decided that Meek was the man to head up the new pop label—Triumph Records. The deal was a 50/50 split, with each man contributing half the start-up costs. Coupe would handle the publicity, his specialty, and Meek would be in charge of A&R and production. They would use Saga's existing distribution network, and contract with various pressing plants. The actual recordings would take place at London studios other than IBC or Lansdowne, such as Star Sound and Olympic.

All of these arrangements are fairly typical for an independent record label, and if they had been located in America they would have been just one more "indie" out of hundreds, but in England at that time they were attempting something that was almost unheard of. A glance at any British pop chart from the period will quickly confirm that other than records imported from America, all slots were filled with discs from the British majors: Pye, Decca, Columbia, Parlophone, HMV, Philips, and Top Rank. Despite the odds, Triumph was determined to press on.

One of the first artists signed to Triumph—or rather to Joe himself, as Coupe would later discover—was an actor named John Leyton. John didn't have much of a voice, but he was a handsome man, and British pop stardom had always been as much or more about looks than about singing talent, so Joe signed Leyton right up. Another "looker" that Joe quickly added to his roster was Ricky Wayne, a super-buffed West Indian bodybuilder who would go on to become first Mr. World, and then Mr. Universe. Ricky wasn't a great singer either, but his voice was no worse than popular American teen idols like Fabian and Tab Hunter, and he had built up a local following with his reportedly rocking nightclub act.

In February of 1960 William Barrington Coupe conjured up a storm of publicity for the official launch of Triumph, and the release of its first two records. He threw a big press party at a fancy restaurant, placed display ads in papers and magazines, and even plastered posters all along an underground public transit line. "Records with Teenage Appeal" and "Records Made for the Hit Parade," they read. And Joe wasn't above bending the truth a little to add credibility to his role as pop A&R man. A news article from that time quotes Meek: "Because we're young we know what the pop fans like. I'm a pop fan myself, so I should be able to tell. I don't think the big companies do know what the youngsters want; it's more a case of hit or miss with them." In the article, Meek claims to be 28 (He was 30 at the time), and to have been in the record business for "eight years." If both things were true that would have him making records in 1952 at age 20, which would have come as a shock to the residents of Newent!

But Meek and Coupe were no fools, and they knew their potential market. According to a Triumph press release: "These records are being planned with the teenage market well in mind and the 45s will introduce some new teenage stars. They will receive top publicity in the 'pop' press, as well as special additional exploitation." Indeed, a newspaper article trumpeted: "Triumph To Tour Pop Package Show," and said that, "Triumph discs will be plugged from the stage during every performance, and advertisements will be placed in the concert programs." The label even purchased a short program on Radio Luxembourg, "It's A Triumph," which ran on Wednesdays from 9:15 to 9:30 p.m. for thirteen weeks. The show was hosted by Ricky Wayne, and must have been quite interesting, with Wayne spinning discs ranging in style from his own rocking "Chick A' Roo," to Joy and Dave's silly "Let's Go See Gran'ma," to the Blue Men performing tracks from *I Hear a New World*. ("The Entry of the Globbots" was featured on the first show!) Exactly which teen market the latter was expected to appeal to is unclear, unless Joe was hoping to cash in on what was left of the Chipmunk craze.

Teen appeal or not, Triumph sent out a few four-song EP versions of *I Hear a New World* at the same time they were plugging the first two singles. An official Saga Records Press Release pitches the EP to record shops: "Among the first releases is a very unusual record—a stereo E.P. RGX5000—an Outer Space Stereo Fantasy—which we feel sure will prove a big hit. It is suggested that you use this record in the first place as a demonstration disc for selling your stereo equipment as the weird gimmicky 'outer space' sounds give an unusually interesting stereo effect." At the time, "record shops" sold record players alongside the actual discs, so if the retailers could be convinced to play the EP whenever they demonstrated the latest "stereophonic" sound system, the problem of arranging in-store play would take care of itself. It was a clever ploy, though unfortunately it didn't work.

But in-store play was the least of Triumph's concerns; they would actually have to get the records *into* the stores before being afforded the relative luxury of that problem. Saga Films had record distribution, but the network they were connected to specialized in classical recordings and had little understanding of the pop market, much less the nascent teen pop market. In the pop world, the majority of retailers only stocked the Top 50, almost all of which were releases by the Big Seven major labels. Getting independent releases into the stores is one of the biggest obstacles that any small label must face, be it in the past or present—but in England in 1960 it was particularly daunting. After awhile Joe did what dozens of American indie record men had done before him: he got on his phone and into his car and contacted the most important shops in the larger metropolitan areas directly, particularly those reporting sales figures to the charts. You had to sell records to get into the charts, and you had to get into the charts to sell records.

Another big obstacle to indie endeavors is matching manufacturing runs to market demand. If you have a runaway hit, ideally you should have a warehouse full of discs ready to rapidly meet the mad rush of orders. If not, and the hit catches you with your trousers down, by the time you can manufacture another batch and truck them all over the country and into the stores, your record may not even be on the charts anymore. Then you are still stuck with a warehouse full of unwanted records, just as sure as if you had mistakenly manufactured a warehouse full of stiffs to begin with. And that's not all. Cash flow plays a major role, as it does in any business, but in this case with a nasty twist. Unless they are dealing with a label that is obviously healthy and steadily generating cash, disc manufacturers insist on being paid on delivery. Record distributors—or in this case the retailers themselves—generally insist not only on having several months to pay, but also on the right to return unsold records. The dangers implicit in this arrangement should be obvious enough.

Once the word got out that a new label was signing artists, flocks of them began appearing at Triumph's doors. The label roster soon expanded to include an instrumental combo called the Fabulous Flee-Rakkers, and three more singers: Yolanda, George Chakiris, and Michael Cox. The Fabulous Flee-Rakkers supplied Triumph with its first hit: an almost surf-punk adaptation of Henry VIII's "Greensleves." "Green Jeans," backed with "You Are My Sunshine," was released in April 1960, meaning both songs were recorded during the Arundel Gardens period, perhaps even at Joe's flat. One indication that they may not have been recorded at the flat, however, is the unmistakable presence of echo chamber on both. There's also the fact that when compared with recordings made by the Flee-Rakkers backing Ricky Wayne, made at the flat at about the same time, the sound is quite different, and does not include echo chamber. "Green Jeans" may have been the hit, but the flip is far more interesting compositionally. "You Are My Sunshine" opens with a syncopated electric guitar figure that is joined two bars in by a second, interlocking guitar figure. Both guitars are heavily treated with reverb, tape delay, and tremolo; and produce the sort of sound you would expect to hear if Duane Eddy were leading a gamelon guitar orchestra. In both songs crunchy, ultra-fat saxophones (double-tracked?) honk out a simple melody over percolating rhythm sections, pushed along by a nicely defined and fairly prominent bass, with lots of echo and tape delay.

Figure 5.1:
The "Green Jeans" 45 by the Fabulous Flee-Rakkers, on the Triumph label (1960).

The Flee-Rakkers were an accomplished outfit led by tenor saxophonist Peter Flee-Rackers (a Dutch name), and featured not only two saxophones (three at one point), but also the innovative guitar work of Dave "Tex" Cameron, who was a Duane Eddy fan. The band performed on television numerous times, and was a staple on British package tours. Meek may have been partially drawn to them because of their country flourishes (members had belonged to fifties groups called the Ramblers and the Statesiders), and also their stylistic similarity to Johnny and the Hurricanes, who were quite successful at the time. Their second single for Joe, "Sunday Date" backed with "Shiftless Sam," was released in September 1960, and sounds as if it was recorded at a studio with a really good echo chamber. "Sunday Date," a Tex Cameron composition, opens with a single drum (sounding like, and played in the style of, a Middle-Eastern dumbec) and bass, providing an opportunity to hear the processing on those sounds apart from other instruments. The echo chamber sound is dense and rich—and possibly compressed, as it blooms and quickly fades—while the bass is *huge,* combining a sharp attack with a full low end. Cameron's guitar is processed through all of the above, and some sort of *major* modulation set-up, yet the effects are kept back in the mix, allowing the bright and clear tone of the instrument to shine through. This juxtaposition of densely layered effects against lots of the original dry sound was one of Joe's most frequently used techniques. The difference in sound from the first Flee-Rakkers record to this one suggests that in the intervening five or six months Joe's skills had evolved considerably.

The Flee-Rakkers, in the guise of "the Off Beats," also teamed up with Ricky Wayne for Ricky's debut. "Chick A'Roo," combines a typically vapid Robert Duke lyric with a spirited performance by the Flee-Rakkers, and a plausible vocal from Wayne. Most of the sounds, but *particularly* the drums, are compressed so heavily that at times the original signal fades entirely. Meek uses the pumping and breathing sounds musically, instead of thinking of them as undesirable compressor artifacts, a commonly held conception at the time. The flip, "Don't Pick On Me," is less memorable, and sounds hastily arranged and executed. Both songs were recorded at Meek's Arundel Gardens flat, and feature lots of spring reverb (but no echo chamber). The sound of the spring reverb can be heard perfectly clearly on the demo of "Chick A'Roo," where Ricky is accompanied by acoustic guitar and someone, probably Joe, stomping his foot (?) along in questionable time.

Yolanda was a Senegalese jazz singer signed to Saga who decided to switch over to pop. As a rehearsal/demo tape (on which she is accompanied by an accordion, or perhaps a harmonium) shows, Yolanda actually knew how to sing, and did not require heavy effects or tape editing to produce a good take. "With This Kiss" (by Robert Duke), and "Don't Tell Me Not to Love You," are arguably two of the first "classic" Meek recordings, by which I mean the sort of recordings he is most often associated with. Both songs are melodramatic and somewhat plodding (almost Phil Spectorish) ballads, with arrangements by Charles Blackwell that include harp, violins, vocal chorus, and solo soprano—the latter two now often referred to collectively as the "heavenly choir." All of the tracks are awash in multiple types of reverb and delay (and possibly echo) likely added at various stages of production, making it practically impossible to distinguish one from another. Whenever Yolanda suddenly stops singing or the music stops entirely for a moment, the multiple reverb tails and decaying delay repeats can be heard clearly.

George Chakiris was another Saga artist that transitioned over to Triumph, and his "Heart of a Teenage Girl" and "I'm Always Chasing Rainbows" disc has as much to do with Charles Blackwell's arrangements as it does with Joe Meek's production. "Heart" substitutes an eighth-note percussion pulse—cleverly performed on cowbell, wood blocks, and tambourine—for drums, and would not be out of place in a Hollywood musical. "Rainbows" has lots of romantic orchestral flourishes and nice bits of harmonic coloration, but could easily be mistaken for an Andy Williams record. There is, however, an amazing tremolo guitar part played and mixed tastefully throughout, and there are some subtle touches, such as Joe's adding additional echo to the voice on sustained notes at the end of certain phrases. These sorts of things were no doubt quite impressive to people observing the session, but would not necessarily be noticed by present day listeners trying to figure out what all the fuss was about. The session was reportedly held at Lansdowne (perhaps before Joe was fired?).

The most successful artist on the Triumph roster was Michael Cox, a protégé of British music and television mogul Jack Good. In May of 1960 Cox's cover of "Angela Jones," which had been a hit in America for Johnny Ferguson, began climbing the charts. The song, an extremely catchy bit of pop pap, features the up-front snare brushwork of "Bad Penny Blues," a voice recorded mere microns away from the microphone, Glockenspiel, "heavenly choir," and amazing echo effects. It is artfully compressed and practically leaps out of the speaker. The flip, "Don't Want To Know," is similar in style, but considerably less memorable.

When the orders for "Angela Jones" began pouring in, Triumph Records hit the largest of the rocks that had been looming just below the surface all along: insufficient cash flow to supply the demand. [1] The problem was exacerbated by the fact that Joe had gone hog-wild booking time in expensive recording studios, bringing his productions in considerably over budget. In fact, some of the most expensive projects, such as a Charles Blackwell Orchestra pizzicato string album, never panned out. [2] To make matters worse, the Mechanical Copyright Protection Society discriminated against the label by forcing it to pay royalties in advance, rather than later like the major labels, and then added insult to injury by insisting that individual proof-of-payment stamps be placed (by hand) on every disc. Besides the financial burden of the up-front payments, there was the impossibly ridiculous task of affixing the stamps to tens of thousands of records.

These problems and their attendant difficulties cast the company into financial chaos, possibly resulting in the loss of millions of dollars. Meek had already been finding it increasingly difficult to work with Coupe, and suspected him of everything from financial improprieties to stealing his songs. By the end of July Joe Meek had had enough, and he pulled out of Triumph in a move that took many people by surprise, including William Barrington-Coupe, who had apparently somehow missed the fact that Triumph's artists were in fact signed directly to Meek rather than the label. When Joe left Triumph, he took most of the artists and a large quantity of master tapes with him. [3]

Upon Meek's departure, music publishers Southern Music approached him with an offer to head their new pop label. Meek had done some independent production work for Southern while he was still at Lansdowne, and one of the songs he'd recorded, "Be Mine" by Lance Fortune, had been successful enough to warrant starting the label. Meek considered the deal, but he was less than enthusiastic about getting involved with another indie, even one with Southern Music's clout. Instead, Joe signed an independent production deal with Top Rank, which immediately licensed and re-released "Green Jeans," which was still in the charts, and "Chick A'Roo." Top Rank also agreed to license John Leyton's cover of "Tell Laura I Love Her," which had originally been slated for release on Triumph.

When American vocalist Ray Peterson had a runaway hit with "Tell Laura I Love Her" (written by Jeff Barry, who would go on to pen "Sugar Sugar" for The Archies, and "Rock Me Gently" for Andy Kim), it must have been too much for Joe to resist. The song—banned by numerous radio stations and labeled a "Death Disc"—told the story of a young man who so wanted to buy a wedding ring for his sweetie that he entered a car race with a cash prize. His car spins out of control for some reason and he is killed, but not before he can utter the words—you guessed it—"Tell Laura I love her." The Peterson version's fairly banal arrangement consists mostly of nylon-string guitar, shaker, and upright bass, with low "bum, bum, bum, bum" backing vocals, cheesy organ (for the "In the chapel…" verse), and Peterson's quivering, whiny vocals. But the record also has *lots* of echo on the voice and some interesting stereo delay effects—both of which likely caught Meek's attention.

Meek and Blackwell's version, by comparison, employs a much more sophisticated arrangement and choice of instruments. It opens almost comically with Lissa Gray's angelic reverb-drenched soprano voice, followed by a strummed steel-string guitar chord with a buzzy clam note at the end. The acoustic bass and shaker in the original are replaced by electric bass (playing the "bum, bum, bum, bum" bits as well), and hi-hat and bongos, respectively. The almost Calypso string arrangement and soaring soprano voices place the disc squarely in Meeksville. John Leyton's voice cannot rival Peterson's four-and-a-half-octave pipes, but at least he sings the word "love" in a normal voice, rather than Peterson's excruciatingly nasal whine. Oddly enough, Meek uses a lot less echo on Leyton's voice than was used on the original vocal.

Meeksville or not, the record got lost in the shuffle when Top Rank was unexpectedly purchased by EMI, who were already backing a cover of the song by someone called "Ricky Valance"—a cover that went to the top of the charts. [4] "Along Came Caroline," Michael Cox's follow-up to "Angela Jones," met with the same fate. Much more significantly, Meek's production deal with Top Rank got lost in the same shuffle as the two records, and he was once again on his own—but not for long.

Some time back William Barrington-Coupe had split Triumph off from Saga Films, and opened a second division, the purpose of which was to manufacture shoddy tape recorders and phonographs. Now the owner of Saga Films, one Major Wilfred Alonzo Banks, approached Joe with a proposition. The deal called for Banks to bankroll Meek's creative efforts, with the funding conditional on Joe's adhering to some specific restrictions, primarily financial. Banks had seen what happened when Joe was left to his own devices writing checks for studio time, and they agreed that instead of handing money to other studios, Joe would build his own. Money would be tight in the beginning, so Banks offered to give Joe some recording equipment that had been warehoused when Saga Films had ceased production, and enough money to buy some other essentials. The Major would pay all of the operating costs, including the rent on the studio, and a small salary for Joe.

The new company would still be faced with the problem of establishing and maintaining credibility within the British record industry. Meek and the Major were now competing with all of the staff A&R men at the major labels, most of which openly ridiculed Joe's records. The A&R men's views were, of course, self-serving, but they also may have sincerely believed that the recordings did not meet professional standards—and in a sense they were correct. For example, at the time distortion on a track, let alone on all the tracks, was not a desirable characteristic. Nor was the presence of quantities of echo so great as to make a voice or instrument sound as if it had been recorded underwater, or in a large sewer pipe. And when multiple compressors were simultaneously pumping and breathing all over everything, it was clearly and unequivocally *wrong*.

The executives at the major labels were no doubt concerned about such things. There were professional standards in place, and it was important to maintain them if a company was going to compete in the commercial marketplace. That is, unless a "flawed" recording happened to become a major hit. In the same way that Triumph's distribution situation was reversed once they had some records that were being demanded by the public, RGM Sound would find it considerably easier to license its discs after one or two of them—licensed by some *other* label, naturally—had topped the charts. Fortunately, Meek was able to find homes for quite a few of his Triumph-era recordings: HMV took some sides by Michael Cox and John Leyton, while Pye opted for recordings by the Flee-Rakkers, Ricky Wayne and the Off Beats, Chick With Ted Cameron and the DJs (actually the Flee-Rakkers with Joy, Dave, and Brian Adams), Ian Gregory, and Peter Jay. He was also able to place some of his songs with publishers, primarily Campbell Connelly/Ivy Music—which had a sweetheart deal with Radio Luxembourg—and his old friends at Southern Music.

Ian Gregory was a handsome young actor who is widely regarded as the least talented singer ever recorded by Joe Meek. Legend has it that Gregory had so much difficulty singing "Time Will Tell" that Meek had Dave Adams sing a "guide vocal" for him to follow. The results were still so poor that Meek resorted to mixing a large percentage of Adams' voice in with Gregory's; not a bad idea, as the song spent eight weeks on the charts, topping out at #17. The flip, "The Night You Told a Lie," is considerably more interesting from a production standpoint. It opens and closes with a clap of what sounds like actual thunder, mixed with rolling tympani drums, or some passable substitution. The extremely quirky arrangement is full of choppy bursts of drums, guitar, and cheesy organ, with comic trombone (?) lines and snippets of backing vocals floating in and out of the mix unpredictably. (It makes you wonder what Captain Beefheart's first album might have sounded like if it had been produced by Meek. *Safe As Meek*?) Peter Jay's version of "Paradise Garden" takes what is basically a Wall Of Sound approach, and is as overblown and bombastic as anything Phil Spector ever turned out. It features the works: tympani, harp, brass, strings, heavenly choir, straight female backup singers, and orchestral snare rolls; all there to frame Jay's dramatic voice uttering the words of Robert Duke, and all completely drenched in heavenly echo. You can bet that it wasn't recorded at Joe's flat. The flip-side, an upbeat ditty called "Who's the Girl," makes excellent use of tape delay on both the vocal and what sounds like muted strings and Glockenspiel playing in unison.

Major Banks had offices alongside a toy warehouse (Banks was involved in several different lines of business) located on Holloway Road in North London. When Joe began looking for a suitable home for his new studio he did not have far to go. Just a few blocks down the street from the Major's office he found a three-floor unit for rent. It was located above a leather goods shop, in a dirty and depressing area of London, with a major thoroughfare passing by just outside. As Joe put it: "In the end I found this building in Holloway Road. This gave me three floors…I decided this was the place for me."

Figure 5.2:
Joe in front of 304 Holloway Road.

Photo: Clive Bubley

[1] The situation was comparable to that of Sam Phillips at Sun Records when he was forced to sell Elvis's contract to RCA because he didn't have sufficient cash flow to press enough records to meet the demand.

[2] Joe had held some very large sessions, occasionally with as many as twenty musicians on the payroll, attempting to find

the sounds he was after. If any of those recordings have survived, a comparison with Phil Spector's Wrecking Crew might prove interesting and instructive.

[3] Coupe was, however, eventually compensated for his loss when RGM Sound was funded. Also, Triumph continued on for a while after Meek's departure, releasing several records produced by Johnny Keating. As a result, accounting for non-Meek-produced Triumph releases proved to be a problem for some early Meek collectors and discographers.

[4] Marilyn Michaels released a follow-up entitled "Tell Tommy I Miss Him." Another version of "Tell Tommy I Miss Him" was recorded by someone named Laura Lee, and released on Triumph Records during its post-Meek period!

CHAPTER 6

304 Holloway Road

When Joe Meek moved into 304 Holloway Road he was on his own. There, finally, he had found a really big shed to work in. He was in complete control, and could establish his audio empire without having to answer to anyone. But the space was less than ideal for his purposes, and would need a lot of work before he would be able to begin recording there. He immediately set about making things happen.

Dave Adams was a skilled carpenter in addition to being a skilled musician, and over a period of three months he transformed the two bedrooms on the second floor into the control room and the main studio area. While the rooms were not very large, they were a definite step up from the Arundel Gardens studio, where the control room was not only located in a bedroom, it *was* the bedroom. And speaking of steps up, the only way to reach the second floor studio—which would be considered the third floor in America—was by climbing up several steep flights of long and narrow stairs. The stairs became nearly as much a part of the 304 Holloway Road mythology as the studio itself, especially to the many musicians who carried heavy equipment up them, or had that same equipment tossed down after them as they were being thrown out—a frequent occurrence. The musicians and their equipment would pass the first floor on the way, which housed Joe's living room and kitchenette, as well as a small office, and an even smaller waiting room. Only the most elite of Joe's friends and visitors were allowed access to the third floor, where Joe's bedroom—his spiritual sanctorum—and his tape storage room, later called the tea chest room, were located.

Figure 6.1:
The first floor was at the top of the first flight of stairs.

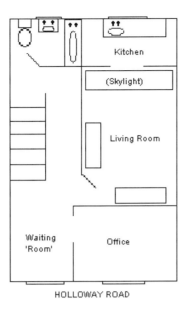

Figure 6.2:
The two-room recording studio was located on the second floor of the apartment, along with the legendary bathroom.

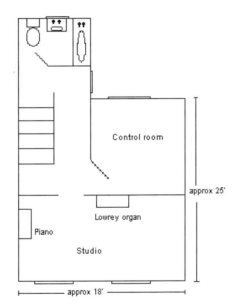

Figure 6.3:
The third floor was off limits to most visitors. Could the second small room have been used as an echo chamber?

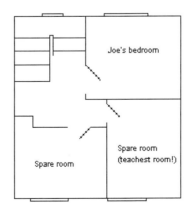

The main recording area measured slightly less than 18 x 14 feet, with a substantial portion of one corner taken up by a stairwell. The control room measured almost exactly 11 x 12 feet, with a door opening from the corner closest to the entrance of the main room, but not affording a direct view of it. There was no window between the control room and the recording area, and Joe chose not to add one. The bigger room was at the front of the building, and had two large windows overlooking the busy street below. Dave Adams recalls: "The studio windows were insulated, and then boards were nailed over them and acoustic tile and drapes [were placed] over the boards. We heard very little outside sound." Meek himself described the studio this way: "It's the size of an average bedroom, no larger. I've covered the walls with acoustic tiles…all the walls except one, which is covered with a thick curtain. This has very good absorbing power, and the studio is extremely dead. The floor is carpeted, and the ceiling is completely covered in tiles. One wall has some tiles missing, and this gives me a certain amount of brightness. But basically it's completely dead."

Figure 6.4:
Newspaper clipping from 1961 showing Meek in his minimalist control room—the Quad preamp is near his knee—and a shot of the recording area.

Over the years the "acoustic tiles" referred to have been at the center of what might be called the Egg Box Controversy. Several people—including several interviewed for this book—have said they clearly recall there being "egg boxes" on the walls while they were at 304. Adams is adamant about there being no egg boxes, and Joe's assistant Tony Kent concurred: "I never knew egg boxes. I've heard that story before—Chas Hodges come out with that one, didn't he? Strange: that used to be one of the big stories about Joe, recording in his bathroom, and egg boxes." The memories of the other observers notwithstanding, standard acoustic tiles, not egg boxes, are clearly visible in the few available photos of the studio—at least on the walls.

Courtesy of John Repsch and the JMAS Archive

Figure 6.5:
Detail of the recording area showing the edge of the piano, the Clavioline keyboard, and Neumann, Reslo, and AKG microphones.

And what of the other "big story," recording people in the bathroom? "I don't think he ever recorded anybody in the bathroom except for effects," says Kent. "I mean he used to go everywhere to get effects, (but) I don't think he ever put anybody in the bathroom."

Presumably Joe would have put a singer or instrumentalist in the bathroom in order to take advantage of the bathroom's acoustic reflectivity. Bathroom tiles, unlike acoustic tiles, reflect sound rather than absorbing it. A tiled bathroom is by definition a reverberant space, and one the size of Joe's would almost certainly have produced a distinctive sound with lots of quick reflections. At least one of Joe's artists, Screaming Lord Sutch, has confessed to being sent to "the loo" in order to echo-up his voice, and it is quite likely that he was not the only one to suffer that indignity.

But that is not the only issue involving echo and the bathroom—Joe may also have used it as an echo chamber. The question of whether there was or was not an actual echo chamber at 304 Holloway Road is not easily answered, as there are numerous contradictory accounts, including Joe's:

"Above my control room I have a room that I've made into an echo chamber. It's quite remarkable for the size of it; it gives me a great echo sound, which is on all my records." Peter Miller, the guitarist for Peter Jay and the Jaywalkers, elaborates: "He had a room upstairs that he turned into an ambient acoustic echo chamber. From time to time the vocalist would get sent up there—certain vocalists that couldn't sing in tune too well; I'm not going to mention any names—to sing from within the echo chamber, to try and help them. He had a speaker and a mic up there. It was a live room with nothing in it. He would pump the sound up there, as I do here (in my studio) as a result of seeing him do it, and it's great; it's better than any electronic device."

Ted Fletcher, a vocalist who worked for Meek between 1963 and 1965, and Ritchie Blackmore, a guitarist who recorded for Meek between 1962 and 1965, both recall the room upstairs, though Fletcher added that he doesn't recall anyone ever being sent upstairs to sing in it. It is also worth noting that Ted Fletcher doesn't recall anyone ever singing in the bathroom either. Ted's brother Guy Fletcher, on the other hand, recalled, "Joe used the tiled bathroom in his flat as an echo chamber, with a speaker at one end and a mic at the other. Although it never seemed to bother him, the yip yip of the neighbor's dog could often be heard on the echo return of the vocal channel. It was certainly audible on tracks by Heinz and Gene Vincent." Inexplicably, Dave Adams—who ought to know if anyone does—says he's absolutely certain there was no echo chamber at 304 Holloway Road. Dave's sister Joy, however, has said that she remembers a room painted completely black, which would indicate the presence of a chamber. There has even been speculation about a mysterious formerly existing room behind the control room at the *rear* of the flat, which if correct, would have the room suspended in mid-air and blocking two windows.

Joe may have been bluffing about the room upstairs to save face, just as he publicly denied having ever recorded anyone in his bathroom, but if so why do several others remember the room as well? I will have to leave it for greater minds than mine to sort all this out, but the fact remains that there is definitely an acoustic echo chamber sound on many if not all of Meek's 304 Holloway Road recordings, so he had to have rigged one up *someplace.* Any bets on the bathroom? [1]

Joe Meek also claims to have invented and patented an "electronic echo" but he doesn't describe it or give any details. [2] He may have been referring to his black box spring reverb, but it is also possible that he made some sort of tape-delay device, as one or two people vaguely recall seeing one. It would have been easy enough for him to make, but if it ever existed there is no trace of it now, and there is no way to know what it sounded like. We *do* know what his black box spring reverb sounded like, though, as it can clearly be heard on recordings he made in 1959—shortly after Adrian Kerridge says Joe constructed it— particularly the demos recorded at his Arundel Gardens flat. Though not all spring reverbs sound alike, they share some common characteristics, and anyone that has heard a few can easily recognize the "spring" sound. Ted Fletcher says he also remembers what may have been a second spring reverb, a modified Grampian (model 636?) that was, "a sort of semi-pro thing, not terribly good." Around 1966 Joe also acquired a Fairchild 658 professional spring reverb, which can be seen in photographs of his control room from that period.

Figure 6.6:
A letter addressed to R.G. Meek from T.E.S. Shanks inquiring about Meek's plan to purchase and install an extremely heavy disc-cutter. Shanks is not only concerned with Joe's potential liability for manslaughter, he's concerned with capital expenditures as well. Of course, Meek had already installed an EMI BTR2, which weighed nearly as much as the disc-cutter, and there was a heavy Ampex Model 300 sitting right next to it.

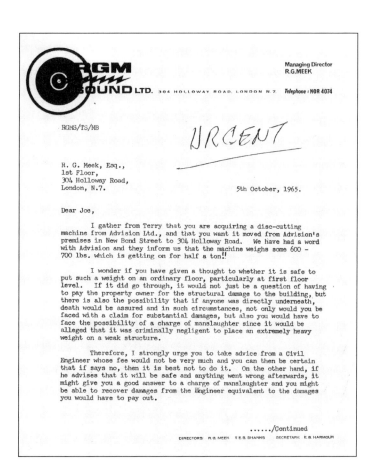

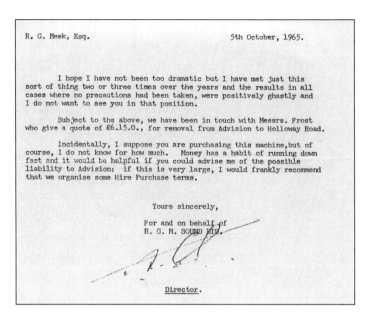

R. G. Meek, Esq.   5th October, 1965.

        I hope I have not been too dramatic but I have met just this
sort of thing two or three times over the years and the results in all
cases where no precautions had been taken, were positively ghastly and
I do not want to see you in that position.

        Subject to the above, we have been in touch with Messrs. Frost
who give a quote of £6.15.0., for removal from Advision to Holloway Road.

        Incidentally, I suppose you are purchasing this machine, but of
course, I do not know for how much. Money has a habit of running down
fast and it would be helpful if you could advise me of the possible
liability to Advision: if this is very large, I would frankly recommend
that we organise some Hire Purchase terms.

                        Yours sincerely,

                        For and on behalf of
                        R. G. M. SOUND LTD.

                            Director.

By September of 1960 RGM Sound was a registered business, and the studio at 304 Holloway Road was ready to begin operations. Reportedly, the first official recording session to be scheduled into the new studio was with Kenny Lord and the Statesmen, whose demo had caught Joe's ear because it included a Buddy Holly cover. Meek thought that the singer sounded a lot like Holly, and therefore might be useful. But the band didn't meet Meek's muster, and were quickly jettisoned (quite possibly down the stairs, followed by their gear). Kenny Lord's manager, who had originally sent Joe the demo, had also managed a recently disbanded group called the Stormers. [3] Guitarists Billy Kuy and Reg Hawkins, bassist Chas Hodges, and drummer Bobby Graham were pressed back into service for the gig, and Joe christened them the Outlaws. Joe changed Kenny's name too; Michael Bourne became Mike Berry, as in *holly* berry.

In November the group ran through some Buddy Holly numbers—the tape of which survives—and then recorded "Set Me Free," which Meek shopped to Decca. Decca rejected the song, but had them record a cover of the Shirelle's "Will You Love Me Tomorrow," surely a marvel of A&R genius if there ever was one. Joe was told that the original version would not be released in England, practically assuring that the Mike Berry cover would be a hit. They were mistaken, and when the original *was* released Meek was livid, even going so far as to suspect Decca of deliberate sabotage. Predictably, Berry's version stiffed, though its flipside had lots of merit. "My Baby Doll" captured the most obvious aspects of the Buddy Holly and the Crickets sound, including a very American-sounding production job. Billy Kuy's (slightly out of tune) guitar solo is tastefully executed, as is Meek's subtle addition of delay to the guitar for a few bars afterwards.

At that point the Outlaws more or less became the 304 Holloway house band. But they not only backed Joe's artists; they recorded quite a bit of material under their own name (including *Dream of the West,* one of only a handful of Meek-produced LPs). Joe Meek employed a different production style when recording the Outlaws, as evidenced on their first single, "Swingin' Low," a pseudo-country reworking of "Swing Low Sweet Chariot." The lead guitar has reverb (and maybe echo) on it, but the other tracks are dry, as can be heard at the beginning of the song when they play separately and then suddenly stop. The drumming and drum sounds were also unusual, as Bobby Graham explains: [4] "Joe was always dabbling with effects. We replaced the snare drum skins with thick, heavy taut cloth to give a tom tom effect. I also had a cowbell, and a clamped hi-hat. It was all used in those little percussion fills."

The flipside, "Spring Is Near," is a clever adaptation of "The Valley of the Saroos" [5], and forces the 6/8 meter of the original into a 4/4 framework by counting two quarter notes for every measure of six beats. The bass sound on both cuts has a sort of click to the attack, which is probably the EQ/choke effect Meek spoke of while describing his recording techniques. Regardless of how it was made, the record made it to #45 on the charts. The follow-up, "Ambush," backed with "Indian Brave," featured whooping Indian and gunfight sound effects on one side, and some nice slap-echo guitar work on the other. It did even better, reaching #43 in May.

Meek also had a minor hit with "Can't You Hear My Heart"/"I'm Waiting for Tomorrow" by Cliff Richard sound-alike Danny Rivers (David Lee Baker), backed by the Hunters, which made it to #36. Rivers was formerly the vocalist for the Stormers, and had a decent voice. From a recording perspective the most notable thing about both sides is the extremely big bass sound, which pushes the envelope a little bit even for Meek. The ineptly performed handclaps on the topside, however, sound ridiculous. The Hunters also backed Gerry Temple (Keith De Groot), another Triumph holdover, on "No More Tomorrows," which has a similar sound but didn't sell.

The Hunters' bassist may have been booming, but business wasn't. For every record that made it to market there were several more that were rejected, and all the recordings had to be paid for whether they sold or not. Meek was generating some on-the-spot income by recording jingles and a few songs for non-RGM artists, but with Major Banks looking ever more narrowly over his shoulder, Joe was feeling lots of pressure to produce a real hit. Fortunately, the forces that would bring him what he wished for were already in motion.

One fateful consequence of Joe's association with Southern Music was his being introduced to a gifted young pianist and songwriter named Geoff Goddard. After hearing Geoff run through some of his piano numbers Joe proclaimed that he would call him "Hollywood." Geoff was amenable to the name, and said that he had always liked the first name "Anton," so then and there he became Anton Hollywood. The idea was for him to be a singing piano player in the tradition of British star Russ Conway, but with a touch of Liberace, the sequin-encrusted and extremely popular American performer. But as they soon discovered, there was a hitch: Geoff could not perform without stomping his foot and making groaning noises when he wasn't singing. That proved enough to extinguish plans for him to become a solo performer, but he still had lots of potential as a songwriter, and certainly as a pianist. He had been classically trained at the Royal Academy of Music, and was probably talented enough to have made a name for himself in "serious" music circles, but he was not up to the intensely competitive lifestyle that would have been required to do so.

Geoff Goddard was a lot like Joe. They were both talented upstart country boys who were trying to make it in the big city, and shared an interest in the occult—spiritualism and séances in particular—as well as a fascination with Buddy Holly. The two would become good friends over the next four years before becoming involved in an acrimonious lawsuit that would permanently poison the relationship. Since their initial meeting Geoff had written some instrumentals, including one recorded by the Flee-Rekkers (who had changed the spelling of their name) called "Lone Rider," but he had yet to pen any lyrics.

It just so happened that floundering former Triumph artist John Leyton's manager, Robert Stigwood, had booked his boy on a major television program, where he would be given the opportunity to sing a song on the air. The problem was that Stigwood had no song, so he and Joe began shaking the bushes at the publishing houses along Denmark Street, but to little avail. Coincidentally, Goddard phoned Meek at the time, on a Friday evening, and Joe suggested that Geoff take a stab at writing something. The only catch was that he had to come up with it over the weekend. He struggled hard, but it wasn't until Sunday morning that Geoff sat down at the piano and, in ten minutes, wrote "Johnny Remember Me," a psychic Death Disc about a poor fellow whose recently deceased lover calls to him from beyond the grave. Later Goddard would say that the song came to him in an altered state, presumably due to the influence of the spirit world, and even suggested that Buddy Holly may have had a hand (or its ghostly equivalent) in the matter. Whatever the source of its inspiration, the song impressed both Meek and Stigwood, and on Monday the latter settled on it as the best of the bunch he had been considering. Joe brought the Outlaws in as the backing band, and hired Charles Blackwell to do the arrangement, which according to Leyton included brass and string sections, and several backing singers.

When interviewed for the BBC's *Arena* Meek documentary, John Leyton remembered the session this way: "When I recorded 'Johnny Remember Me,' I was in the sitting room behind a little screen, and the rhythm section was in the room with me. The violin section was on the stairs, the backing singers were practically in the loo, and the brass section was underneath, on another floor altogether. And there was Joe next door, playing his machine like another musical instrument. It was quite bizarre." In an earlier interview [6], Leyton recalled that: "We did it over and over. Joe wanted plenty of exciting atmosphere in it, and it was a really exhilarating sound with the galloping, driving beat. He (Joe) was getting all excited, slapping his leg and combing his quiff."

Leyton had recorded scratch vocals during the main session. When he returned later to record the final vocal track, operatic soprano Lissa Gray was also recorded, adding the crowning touch to the song. As the better part of the "heavenly choir," Gray had been a major contributor to many previous RGM productions; on "Johnny Remember Me" she ascended to a primary role.

There may be brass and strings on "Johnny Remember Me," but it is hard to tell by listening to it. The predominant instruments are the acoustic and electric guitars [7], bass, tat-a'-tat-tat hi-hat-driven drums, and what is either harp or (sped-up?) piano. Clusters of other sounds *do* emerge in some places—washes of sustained tones with only the slightest harmonic definition, yet somehow perfectly appropriate. But all of the instruments contributing to that cluster, whatever they might actually be, are smeared together into a dense sonic blur. They are combined in the same way that patches from several synthesizers are "stacked" via MIDI, and treated as one sound. Meek even works with the sound like it was a keyboard pad, bringing it in and out as it suits him. Meek also briefly adds fairly long delays on a few key words here and there, which these days is a cliché, but in those days was quite clever. The only really obvious unintentional recording flaw is the sibilant mouth noise on Leyton's track in some spots. Joe had his singers work the mic very closely, and those with limited microphone experience—particularly with an ultra-sensitive condenser such as his Telefunken/Neumann U47, as opposed to a dynamic stage mic—must have found it difficult. [8]

"Johnny Remember Me" is considered by many to be Joe Meek's finest recording. Listening to it today it is still quite impressive and captivating, with its sweeping energy and otherworldly ambience, but in mid-1961 it was absolutely revolutionary. That such a bizarre and yet compelling recording should have been made at all was strange enough, but the fact that it had been made in Joe's home studio was evidently difficult for some to swallow. According to British record producer Mickie Most:

"The record industry probably thought it was a prank. At the time, record companies were very, very disciplined. Studio engineers used to wear white jackets like doctors. I remember a sign at EMI Studios in Abbey Road, where it said, 'Sports trousers and jackets may be worn on Saturdays.' That's how disciplined recording was, and they took it all rather seriously. And here's this guy making these records—and selling millions—in his kitchen." [9]

Even Geoff Goddard felt that, "It wasn't really a studio. [10] It was some rooms above a shop. The studio was a double bedroom and the control room was the bedroom across the landing. The wires ran over the floor so you had to be careful where you walked and there was always the danger of electric shocks there. It was all very primitive, bits of old wires stuck together and old tape machines." [11] In the case of "Johnny Remember Me": "The recording would be played back onto another tape and the recording would be fed through his system. The indicator was often right in the red indicating that the level was too high, but he would be deliberately over-recording it to get a partic-ular sound. Nothing like that would have happened in a respectable recording studio. When the master tape for 'Johnny Remember Me' was sent to EMI (for cutting) they said that the sound quality was so bad that it would have to go back for re-dubbing. It was returned seven times." [12] Another sort of re-dubbing had been done at the last minute as well: Joe, fearing that BBC censors might object to the words, "…the girl I loved who *died* a year ago," changed them to, "…loved and lost." [13] Given the frequency of the BBC's banning songs only slightly transgressing its rigidly conservative standards, this bit of good judgment may have saved the song itself from an early death.

As planned, John Leyton performed "Johnny Remember Me" on *Harper's West One* in front of twelve million viewers. Within four weeks the record had shot to the top of the charts, where it sat for six weeks or more (depending on which chart you read), ultimately selling well over a half-million units, and receiving the honor of Disc Of The Year. Despite the song's widespread pop appeal, it had its critics. The A&R staff at the major labels, who were by default Meek's competitors, soundly renounced his amateur—and more than a little threatening—efforts. They complained about everything: the over-the-top compression, the out-of-control echo, the indistinct wall of sound (though they probably didn't call it that), and distortion, distortion, distortion! And, though the song has since come to be considered a classic, at the time many music critics echoed the A&R men's sentiments. [14]

With the excitement surrounding "Johnny Remember Me" still tangible, Joe Meek and Geoff Goddard felt the time was right for another go at musical necromancy. The two had been indulging their common interests in Buddy Holly and the supernatural by holding regular séances with the aim of contacting their deceased benefactor, and they were happy to report that they had been successful. But Buddy's benevolence extended beyond merely helping them to write songs: he also obliged them by predicting how well they would do in the charts. The next channeled work would be a song about—what else?—Buddy Holly!

Figure 6.12:
"Tribute to Buddy Holly."

Courtesy Kim Lowden

As Goddard put it [15]: "When I wrote 'Tribute to Buddy Holly' I had Mike Berry in mind. He too is an avid fan of Buddy's and wanted to do something to retain his memory. When I had written the song I asked Buddy what he thought of it. He thanked me for the honor and said, 'See you in the charts.' He seems to have an amazing foresight as far as my career is concerned." Buddy may have been behind the song, but Joe wanted to run it by Buddy's earthly representatives before releasing it, so he wrote to the London branch of the Buddy

Holly Fan Club and invited them over to his studio to check it out. The fans, many of them sporting thick black Buddy specs, took him up on his offer and not only approved of the song, they stayed to party while Mike Berry and the Outlaws ran through the Holly songbook. (Later, when Geoff Goddard went public about his psychic Buddy connection in a front-page story for the *Psychic News,* the club members were considerably less happy, and Joe had to write them an apology, denying that he believed in such nonsense to get them off his back.) Buddy Holly's parents were no doubt unaware of Geoff and Joe's dealings with their dead son when they sent a letter thanking them for the wonderful tribute. Norman Petty, who had produced all of Buddy's early hits, must have been equally uninformed when he too praised the disc.

Musically, the song is a buoyant little number, nicely executed by the Outlaws, with a nod to Holly's "Peggy Sue" during the instrumental break. Lyrically it is simply bizarre, employing a narrative style to recount the circumstances of Holly's death, and inform us that Buddy sings "up in heaven," before switching to what sounds like a news bulletin from beyond the grave: "Buddy Holly died in a plane crash in 1959," etc. The song was controversial and offensive to many, and was even banned by the BBC for its "morbid concern over the death of a teen idol." It was also a major hit.

In the meantime, so as not to lose any of the momentum they had built with John Leyton, Joe and Geoff knocked out a near carbon copy of "Johnny Remember Me" called "Wild Wind." It entered the charts at #8, while the former was still there and ultimately sold over a quarter-million copies. For a while "Johnny Remember Me," "Wild Wind," and "Tribute to Buddy Holly" were all in the Top 20 at the same time. Leyton's follow-up, however, while it stands as one of Meek's more interesting productions, signaled what was to come when it stalled in the charts at #15. Ironically, "Son This Is She," another Goddard composition with a Blackwell orchestration, is a much better recorded and mixed work than any of Leyton's previous efforts. It is built upon a basic martial rhythmic figure practically identical to the one used by Holst in "Mars: Bringer of War," with beautifully layered strings, and an easily identifiable

French horn part. Echo, reverb, and delay are used relatively conservatively—at least by Joe's standards—leaving room for the individual sounds to cut through. The effects are *there,* but there is less of them all around, perhaps in response to the accusations then being leveled at Joe regarding his over-use of echo to "fix" Leyton's naturally poor voice. [16] Though Meek railed back at his detractors, they may have affected him more than he consciously realized, at least temporarily. On Leyton's next release, "Lone Rider," he pulled out all the stops and created a record so full of dynamic energy (and distortion) that it caused the needle to jump the grooves on many phonographs. It topped out at #40 on the charts.

Another Meek recording from the same period that is of historical interest is Michael Cox's cover of Chuck Berry's "Sweet Little Sixteen." Cox was recording with several master session musicians: guitarists Big Jim Sullivan and Tony Belcher, bassist Brian Bennett, and drummer Brian "Liquorice" Locking—who had been Eddie Cochran's British back-up band while he was touring there before his death. Sullivan was demonstrating Cochran's arrangement of "Sweet Little Sixteen" when he got Joe's attention, and they decided to record the song. When you consider that in mid-1961 the pre-Ringo Beatles were still playing at the Star Club in Germany, this is a remarkable rendering of an American classic by a British band. It is also likely the first recording of a wah-wah pedal, which Sullivan uses in a very unique and musical way, long before any standardized techniques had evolved. [17] The record went nowhere in England, but topped the charts in Sweden—where Cox would be a major star for many years—and also sold well throughout Europe. Cox is usually associated with "Angela Jones," and not thought of as a rock and roll singer, but he does a good job with "Sweet Little Sixteen."

Building on his many recent successes, Meek decided to raise the stakes by recording two full-length LPs—*Dream of the West* by the Outlaws, and John Leyton's *The Two Sides of John Leyton*—in time to have them in the stores before Christmas. The Outlaws record was a "concept" album—if you can call a collection of songs about cowboys and Indians a concept—in much the same mold as *I Hear a New World,* and even

Creative Music Production: Joe Meek's Bold Techniques

included re-tooled versions of four songs that had originally appeared on it. [18] The songs were all written by Joe, as on the previous LP, and his intentions are made clear in his liner notes: "I guess the closest we will get to the West is to see the horses that ride through Hyde Park and the West End of London. But no one can stop us sharing a *Dream of the West*." A nice record overall, produced "Outlaws" style, with strong Shadows influences. The Outlaws were also given a fifteen-minute radio show on Radio Luxembourg called *It's the Outlaws,* which was produced by Joe at the same time that he was recording the two LPs. (There must have been *lots* of coffee made during that short period!)

The Two Sides of John Leyton also had a concept, at least of sorts. The original idea was to appeal to both the beat and ballad markets by having a side devoted to each, but in the end the major difference between the two sides is that there are more strings on the "ballad" side. Another thing that both sides have in common is an overall sonic fuzziness, which is explained as the result of Joe's having had to master the record at his studio rather than at IBC (or another more professional studio), presumably to meet the Christmas rush deadline. Then, as now, mastering studios and disc manufacturers become especially busy just before the holidays.

The album opens with Geoff Goddard's "Voodoo Woman," the best song on the album. Pounding "voodoo" drums (reminiscent of "Wipeout") lead the charge throughout the entire piece, with "Johnny"-esque guitar strumming, and buckets of echo-reverb-delay-madness all over everything, particularly the voice. There are some really obvious edits, however, and Leyton sings one note so consistently flat that you have to wonder if it was done intentionally. Other highlights include two more Goddard compositions: "Oh Lover," another galloping drum and guitar number in the now all too familiar Leyton mold, and "It's Goodbye Then," basically a slowed-down version of the same formula.

Covers include Charlie Gracie's "Fabulous," "(I Love You) For Sentimental Reasons," a hit for Nat King Cole, and a truly strange version of "I Don't Care If the Sun Don't Shine." The latter features a brilliant piano solo by Goddard, and a very peculiar sound effect. Leyton explains: "Joe was very adventurous in his recording—he'd try anything that appealed to him, and if anything odd happened during a session, he'd invariably try to work it in somewhere. I can remember, in between takes, the drummer—it might have been Bobby Graham or Clem Cattini—had taken his shoe off and was banging his heel against the stair, probably trying to bang a nail back in or something. Quick as a flash Joe picked up on it, jumped up, asked him to do it again, and taped it. He was delighted with it…he liked the sound so much he kept playing it back to us throughout the session, just like a big kid. He drove us mad with it!" [19] The sound was somewhat clumsily inserted into the song in several places, and later explained officially as a "handclap."

The cover of John Leyton's LP featured two images of him dressed to match the theme: on the left, a "gentleman" smartly attired in a dark suit and holding a rose; and on the right, a "cool" young pop star in a striped shirt. But at the same time that Leyton's LP was hitting the stores another one of Joe's artists had also released a record, and he not only bore no likeness to Leyton, he originated from an entirely different musical universe. David Sutch, who modeled his persona on Screamin' Jay Hawkins rather than the current crop of American soft-pop crooners, called himself Screaming Lord Sutch—and man could he scream. Not only that, he dressed like a total ghoul, and had "two feet of hair" that he combed straight up. He opened his shows by climbing out of a coffin. Onstage he was backed by a great band that at various times included some of the best musicians in the country, and his show—which utilized blood, skulls, and other horror-inducing props along with the coffin—would have given Alice Cooper and Ozzie Osbourne the creeps. Joe loved the guy and signed him immediately.

"'Til the Following Night" was Screaming Lord Sutch and the Savages' disc debut, and on it Joe and the Lord pull out all the stops. There are no traces of teen pop lightheartedness here, much less romantic string orchestrations. The Savages kick butt, plain and simple. The song opens with one of Joe's signature tape collages: howling wind, heavy rain, thunder, the creak of a coffin lid, rattling chains, and a blood-curdling scream—all accompanied by an out-of-tune piano dirge. No matter that the "wind" isn't entirely convincing, and the "rain" sounds more like someone splashing water around in a bathtub than a genuine downpour, the startlingly effective coffin lid sound is sufficient to insure Meek's place in the Sound Effects Hall Of Fame. And on the topic of intros, an entire minute passes before the vocal even begins, which must have seemed entirely absurd at the time, as the average total time for a record was just over two minutes. The monster—who speaks in the first person—has two horns, a twinkle in his eye, and a great big club; that's not to mention his "big black coffin," which was the original title of the piece until HMV changed it. The title change didn't help, though, as the record was still banned by the BBC. The flipside, a high-speed cover of "Good Golly Miss Molly," is equally rocking, with the same aggressive rhythm section, nasty sax, and driving electric guitar (Bernie Watkins?).

But "'Til the Following Night" wasn't Meek's first stab at horror rock. Just a few months earlier he had recorded a group calling themselves the Raiders, and after a series of fits and starts they turned out an instrumental called "Night of the Vampire." It featured opening sound effects almost identical to those used later on Sutch's record—almost certainly pieced together from many of the same bits of tape—but with an even more impressive coffin sound. The record, released under the name of the Moontrekkers, was promptly banned by the BBC as being "unsuitable for people of a nervous disposition," but played to death on Radio Luxembourg. Unfortunately, Parlophone had only pressed 5,000 copies, and the record sold out just as it charted. The Raiders cut a few more sides with Joe in the coming months, but they too were instrumentals, as he had auditioned their singer and found him not up to RGM standards. Rod Stewart would have to wait a little longer before getting his big break!

By the end of 1961 things were looking good for Joe Meek. He had recorded lots of records in his studio at 304 Holloway Road, many of which had been successfully licensed to major labels, with a few becoming major hits. He had managed to prove to the A&R men and other Studio Bigwigs that it was not necessary to have millions of dollars worth of recording equipment and huge studio spaces to get a good sound, or to make records that the public would enjoy. One of Joe's favorite expressions was, "It's not what you have, it's how you use it."

1 Peter Miller has since the time of the interview said that there may not have been an actual room, and that Joe may have used the bathroom for echo. It was, after all, a long time ago.

2 Dave Adams recalls that Joe was experimenting with something he called an "endless loop" echo while he was at Lansdowne—without the knowledge of Denis Preston or Adrian Kerridge.

3 The Stormers had worked previously with Danny Rivers, another Meek artist. Also, the Stormers' former singer, Billy Gray, had left the group to get married, but later recorded for Meek as both Mark Douglas and Billy Dean.

4 Rob Bradford, liner notes for *The Outlaws Ride Again* CD, See For Miles Records, 1990.

5 From *I Hear a New World*.

6 *Legendary* pg. 114

7 In *Play Like Elvis*, legendary session musician Eric Ford contends that he was the electric guitarist on "Johnny Remember Me" and that he played with John Leyton regularly, both live and in the studio. In the same quote Ford refers to Joe's studio as "a mess," but says that Joe a nice guy who always treated him well. Outlaw Reg Hawkins relates how they had to play the track repeatedly for an hour, after which his hand was bleeding.

8 Dave Adams recalls something else that Joe had his singers do: "One memorable technique Joe had for eliciting a good performance from an artist was to insist that they smile while singing. It didn't matter if the song was the most miserable you ever heard, the smile had to be there. Joe would know from the control room, without seeing the singer, whether they were in fact

smiling or not. In retrospect I see that it was a way of getting the singer to articulate. Try mumbling with a smile on your face."

[9] *Arena*

[10] *Halfway #520*

[11] Dave Adams recalls that sometimes Joe would just pick up wires from the floor and splice them together to see what would happen. If he was pleased with the "electronic scream of pain," he would record it onto his sound-effects tape. "That would be a gem to listen to now," muses Adams.

[12] *Halfway #528*

[13] Another account of this story has the BBC actually hearing and banning the original record before it was re-dubbed in response.

[14] Nigel Fountain, in the February 3, 1991 *Weekend Guardian*, describes "Johnny Remember Me" as, "Frankie Laine meets Emily Brontë in a drainpipe."

[15] *Legendary* pg. 124

[16] Echo wasn't the only thing Joe used to fix Leyton's voice. According to Outlaw bassist Chas Hodges there are over thirty hard tape splices on "Johnny Remember Me." Unless they were of the rhythm tracks, Joe probably just kept bouncing vocal overdubs to blank tape (along with the backing track) until he had enough usable bits to work with. Then when he edited the best parts together, the rhythm tracks would already be in sync, making it more difficult to detect the splices.

[17] The first wah-wah pedal using an active circuit was designed by Brad Plunkett of Thomas Organ Co. in 1966, but Ampeg had reportedly been experimenting with a passive circuit in 1961. Where Sullivan got a wah-wah is anyone's guess.

[18] "Orbit Around The Moon" became "Husky Team," "Entry of the Globbots" became "Tune for Short Cowboys," "The

Bublight" became "The Outlaws," and "Valley of the Saroos" became "Spring Is Near."

[19] From the liner notes to the West Side CD version.

CHAPTER 7

Joe's Equipment

We must first know what equipment Joe Meek had before we can know how he used it.

In trying to determine what technology Meek might have been working with at any given time it is important to bear in mind that his professional recording career spanned twelve years—from the time he began working at IBC in 1955 until his death in early 1967. During those years dramatic changes took place within the recording industry, and equipment evolved along with everything else. Although there were some lifelong constants in Joe's sonic vision, how he worked in 1956 was not the same as how he worked in 1960, or 1962, or 1966. One useful way of dividing Meek's studio setup into more manageable chunks is according to the tape recorders he was using at a given time. If we know the limitations of the technology he was using we can make some assumptions based on that information.

The first four years or so are fairly well documented. We can be almost certain that while Joe was at IBC he was using EMI BTR1 and BTR2 full-track (mono) recorders. There was even a "portable" version of the BTR2 that he used for recording road shows. According to Adrian Kerridge EMI TR50 (2-head) and TR51 (3-head) recorders, full-track and twin-track, were the first machines used at Lansdowne. Presumably the studio upgraded to EMI TR90 recorders shortly thereafter, as photos of the original Lansdowne control room contain what look like the electronics units for those machines. As for how Joe used these various mono recorders, Denis Preston recalled that Meek was already "overdubbing" by bouncing tracks between two machines while he was at Lansdowne, and possibly as far back as 1957 at IBC.

We have already dealt with the mysteries surrounding the recorders Meek used at his Arundel Gardens flat in 1959. It is a fact that Joe recorded lots of demos and a handful of masters there, even while he was still working at Lansdowne, and it is likely that among his recorders were at least one EMI TR50 and one EMI TR51.

When Joe arrived at 304 Holloway Road he brought some equipment that he already possessed, and some that Major Banks gave him as part of their arrangement. Fortunately, we have a few clues as to which was which, and the document that provides the clues also provides purchase dates for many pieces of Joe's other main gear as well.

An internal RGM document *[see RGM Sound Equipment List]* showing capital expenditures for recording equipment during the period from September 19, 1960 to May 12, 1964, lists seventy-seven pieces of equipment in order of purchase date. Costs are recorded in two columns: one labeled "actual cost," and the other "cost to company." The dates in the "date purchased" column were obviously assigned for accounting convenience and not historical accuracy, so they appear to be of limited use when trying to determine when Joe actually acquired a given piece of gear.

Figure 7.1:

The first section of the RGM Equipment List—dated September 19, 1960—with different figures in the Actual Cost and Cost to Company columns. Note that the Lyrec twin-track and its amplifier units account for 1,800 pounds, or well over half of the total amount.

R. G. M. SOUND LIMITED
SOUND RECORDING EQUIPMENT

Date Purchased		Number of Articles	Actual Cost	Cost to Company
19. 9.60	Advance signed generators (J1 and E2)	2		
"	Range Trecoscope serial No.5265 (oscilloscope)	1	75. 0. 0	
"	Lyrec tape recorder TR 16	1	1,800. 0. 0	
"	Lyrec Amplifiers AR 2	2		
"	Tape recorder EMI TR 51	1	324. 0. 0	
"	" " EMI TR 50	1		
"	Valve power packs	2	30. 0. 0	
"	Sagatone stereo Amplifier	1	20. 0. 0	
"	New Orthophonic R.C.A. Hi-fi amplifier filter and pre-amplifier	1	50. 0. 0	
"	Quad stereo pre-amplifier and pair of matched amplifiers	1	50. 0. 0	
"	Pre amplifiers for condenser microphones	3	22.10. 0	
"	Grashaw valve milli volt meter VV 60	1	15. 0. 0	
"	Lockwood 15" speakers	2	160. 0. 0	
"	Tannery speaker	1	20. 0. 0	
"	Microphone stands	2	15. 0. 0	
"	Piano microphone stand	1	2. 0. 0	
"	Telefunken condenser microphones S.	3	280. 0. 0	
"	S M 2.	1		
"	Conniseur Hi-fi gramafone	1	75. 0. 0	
"	Music stands	9	36. 0. 0	
"	Sundry Jackplugs etc.		50. 0. 0	
			3,024.10. 0	1,940. 0. 0

Courtesy of John Repsch and the JMAS Archive

Creative Music Production: Joe Meek's Bold Techniques

Figure 7.2:

The second and third sections of the RGM Equipment List, listing purchases in September 1962, and on various dates throughout 1963. Note that the Vortexian tape recorder and 4/15/M mixer are included in the 1962 group, and the EMI BTR2 and Ampex Model 300 are listed as being purchased on February 25 and March 27 respectively. The 301 pound price tag of the BTR2 suggests the possibility that it was a second-hand unit, whereas the Ampex machine cost the princely sum of 1,140 pounds.

				3,024.10. 0	1,940. 0. 0
In year to	D. 19/60 O. H. M. microphones	3	18. 0. 0		
30. 9.62	Reslosound Ribbon microphones	2	16. 0. 0		
"	Stands for Reslosound microphones etc.	5	15. 0. 0		
"	Disc cutter Ferranti	1	75. 0. 0		
"	Western Electric microphone	1	10. 0. 0		
"	Vortexion tape recorder	1	90. 0. 0		
"	" " " 4/15/m.	1	26. 0. 0		
			250. 0. 0	250. 0. 0	
25. 2.63	B.T.R.2.	1	301.10. 0		
15. 3.63	Tone Control Unit	1	40. 0. 0		
21. 3.63	Altec Compressor 436 B.	1	75. 0. 0		
21. 3.63	" " 438 A.	1	89. 0. 0		
21. 3.63	Stepdown 240/115 v Transformer	2	5.18. 0		
27. 3.63	300 - c Console 50 c/s	1	1,140. 0. 0		
27. 3.63	Stepdown 230/115 v Transformer	1	5. 3. 3		
7. 5.63	Top and Base Control	1	44. 0. 0		
	Carried forward		1,700.11. 3	2,190. 0. 0	

Figure 7.3:

The final two groups of purchases on the RGM Equipment List. Note the four models of Fairchild dynamics processors, including the very expensive Model 660. The "stereo recorder" listed in the 1964 group is almost certainly the Ampex PR99, but the "6 Channel Mixer" is a mystery, and is apparently not shown in any existing studio photographs. The charge of 65 pounds for "wiring control room" indicates that it required considerable work.

R. G. M. SOUND LIMITED

SOUND RECORDING EQUIPMENT (Continued)

Date Purchased		Number of Articles	Actual Cost	Cost to Company
	Brought forward		1,700.11. 3	2,190. 0. 0
7. 5.63	Mid lift control	1	40. 0. 0	
17. 5.63	Panels	2	2.10. 0	
11. 7.63	Correction Unit	1	140.14. 0	
27. 9.63	Fairchild Dynalizer Mod 673	1	89.10. 5	
27. 9.63	" Limiting Amplifier Mod 660	1	435.12. 0	
27. 9.63	" Auto ten Mod 661	1	56. 0.10	
27. 9.63	" Compact Compressor Mod 663	1	70. 8. 9	
			2,535. 7. 3	2,535. 7. 3
3. 1.64	Dynalizer	1	73. 6. 0	
31. 1.64	Stereo Recorder	1	545. 0. 0	
31. 1.64	Mixer Unit	1	176. 0. 0	
31. 1.64	Portable Case	1	56. 0. 0	
31. 1.64	Auto Transformer	1	15. 0. 0	
11. 5.64	Wiring Control Room		65. 0. 0	
7. 7.64	6 Channel Mixer	1	145. 0. 0	
11. 6.64	B.U. Conversion Unit	1	21. 1. 0	
11. 3.64	Beyer Microphone M 61	1	16.10. 0	
11. 3.64	" " M 23	1	18.15. 0	
12. 5.64	Recording Heads Metro Sound		51.10. 0	
			1,183. 2. 0	1,183. 2. 0

But the numbers are by no means meaningless. A careful examination reveals that the amounts recorded in the "actual cost" and the "cost to company" columns are identical for all of the groups except the first, and that the difference between the two in that case is 1,084.10 pounds. Apparently some of this equipment was assigned a value—perhaps for tax or insurance purposes—but not charged to the company. There are thirty-seven items listed in the first group. Using the sum of 1,084.10 pounds as our benchmark, it is possible by working backwards to divide the equipment list into two logical subgroups: a list of gear that Joe had prior to forming RGM Sound, and a list of gear purchased by the company. Here's how it breaks down:

EMI TR50 and TR51 Recorders	324
RCA Orthophonic Preamp/Amp/Filter	50
Quad Stereo Preamplifier and Matched Amplifiers	50
Preamplifier For Condenser Microphones (3)	22.10
Telefunken Condenser Microphones (3) + SM2	280
Tannoy/Lockwood Monitors (2)	160
Tannoy Speaker	20
Microphone Stands (2)	15
Piano Microphone Stand	2
Conniseur (sic) Hi-Fi Gramafone (sic)	75
Music Stands (9)	36
Sundry Jackplugs, etc.	50
TOTAL	1,084.10

Lyrec TR16 Recorder and (2) AR2 Amplifiers	1800
Valve Power Packs (2) [For the Lyrec Amps?]	30
Range Trecoscope (Oscilloscope)	75
Grayshaw Valve Milli Volt Meter	15
Sagatone Stereo Amplifier	20
TOTAL	1,940

(The gramafone and the oscilloscope could be swapped, but otherwise the groupings are entirely satisfactory.)

This list, however, is obviously incomplete. For example, Meek's homemade four-channel mixer, black box spring reverb, and disc-cutting lathe are not included. Also, if all of the equipment in the upper group already belonged to Meek in September of

1960, as it very likely did, the only gear that came from Saga was the Lyrec, some test equipment, the "Sagatone" amplifier, and possibly some miscellaneous equipment not worth listing.

As might be expected the remaining batches are much smaller, and their dates are also closer together, possibly indicating access to more detailed records. The second group, dated September 30, 1962, consists of a Vortexion recorder, a four-channel Vortexion 4/15/M mixer, a Ferranti disc cutter, and six microphones: three AKGs, two Reslosounds, and one Western Electric. (Five mic stands are also included.) Listings under 1963 indicate that Joe bought an EMI BTR2 in February and an Ampex Model 300 a month later. The list also includes a "stereo recorder" purchased in January of 1964 (possibly an Ampex PR10), and a "concert portable tape recorder," whatever they were. This latter item may have been the battery-powered portable recorder Joe used for field recordings in graveyards and other more savory spots.

Another useful document is the Auction List *[see Auction List]* of equipment compiled after Meek's death. As might be expected, it lists considerably more gear than the RGM Sound list, and the two lists taken together offer a fairly complete picture of Meek's gear—at least most of the major components. From the Auction List, and other sources, we know that by 1965 or so Joe had added an Ampex Model 351/2 twin-track, and an Ampex PR10 twin-track, to his collection of machines. There is also evidence indicating that Joe purchased another expensive Ampex machine in January 1966—possibly a multi-track—but there are many unanswered questions surrounding the issue, which we'll deal with later in this chapter.

Figure 7.4:
Page One of the auction manifest for the auction held April 4, 1968. Note that in addition to an overview of the most significant pieces of gear, there is also a huge supply of various fabrics, and slippers, frocks, gloves, hats, briefs, and 600 pairs of shoes. There also appears to be a quantity of cut glass, and 100 silver Churchill medals!

Re: R. G. Meek, deceased; Re: R.G.M. Sound Ltd. (in liquidation); Re: Meeksville Sound Ltd. (in liquidation)
By direction of the Official Receiver in Companies Liquidation, By Order of 4 Liquidators and others.

SALE ROOMS:

15 GREEK ST., SHAFTESBURY AVENUE
LONDON, W.1

Catalogue of

Recording and Other Equipment

Ampex portable Twin-track Recorder with Electronic Unit, Lyrec Twin-track Recorder with 2 Electronic Units, Oscillators, Stereo Pre-amp, Microphones, Clavioline, Tannoy, Dallas and other Speakers, Lowrey LSC Organ, Selmer and other Amplifiers, Honky Tonk Piano, Disc Cutter, Passive Equalisers and other Equipment

5,800 YARDS OF MATERIALS
including: Tweed, Serge, Coatings and Suitings, Cashmere, Worsted, Linens, Woollens, Suedette, Velvet, Melton, Taffeta, Tartan, Velour, etc., also Slippers, Frocks, Gloves, Hats, Briefs, 600 pairs of Shoes various

CUT GLASS
OFFICE FURNITURE AND EQUIPMENT, AN I.C.T. VERIFIER, 2 I.C.T. PUNCHES, 100 SILVER CHURCHILL MEDALS
A 1963 Ford Thames 7-cwt. Van

Five Scooters

FRANK G. BOWEN LTD.
(Established 1824)

will sell by Auction on the premises as above

On THURSDAY, APRIL 4th, 1968
at 11 a.m. precisely

On view day prior and morning of Sale

Catalogues (price 6d) of the Auctioneers

15 GREEK STREET, SHAFTESBURY AVENUE, W.1
Telephone: 01-437 3244/5

Figure 7.5:
Page Two lists the main recorders and some musical instruments. Note that there are no multi-track recorders listed.

RECORDING AND OTHER EQUIPMENT

re: R. G. Meek, deceased

re: R.G.M. Sound Limited (in liquidation)

re: Meeksville Sound Limited (in liquidation)

277 AN AMPEX PORTABLE TWIN-TRACK RECORDER, Model 351/2 P deck, complete with electronic unit

278 A LYREC TWIN-TRACK RECORDER, type TR16 deck, complete with 2 electronic units

279 An EMI BTR 2 Mono recorder, complete (requires re-assembly)

280 An Ampex Mono recorder console, type 300

Particular attention is drawn to Condition of Sale V which will be rigidly enforced

281 An Astronic response control unit

282 A Selmar amplifier and loudspeaker unit, and a Selmar pianotron

283 A clavioline and stand

284 An Ampex twin-track recorder, type PR10

285 A Trecoscope oscilloscope, an Advance oscillator, and an Advance oscillator

286 A WEM twin loudspeaker cabinet

287 A similar cabinet

288 A Cintel 117 volt. auto transformer

289 A WEM loudspeaker/amplifier, type GR 6QH

290 A WEM combined amplifier/twin loudspeakers AR coo16

291 A WEM Starfinder series loudspeaker cabinet

292 A WEM loudspeaker chrome stand

293 A WEM ditto

Figure 7.6:
Page Three lists some of the Fairchild dynamics processors, the WEM Fifth Man unit, a "6-channel stereo mixer," and other miscellaneous gear.

1209		1805
150	294 A LOWREY 2 MANUAL ELECTRIC ORGAN, with 13-note vamp board, and built-in speakers	1 15
	295	50
3 10	296 A Lee products amplifier, model AC 88	48
11	297 An RCA amplifier, model LM1/322 16 (incomplete), with an RCA Pre Amp. LM1/322 15A	74 18
32	298 A Dyna Stereo Pre-amp., model PAS/2 (U.S.A.), and 2 Dyna Power amps.	36
2	299 A Power amplifier	300
12	300 A Dyna limiter	76
11	301 An MSS disc cutter	74
4	302 An EMI degauzor tape head	5
20	303 A WEM Fifth Man unit	200
5	304 A G.E.C. 3-kw. fan heater	
7 10	305 A Grayshaw valve milli volt meter	
8 10	306 A Morcom combining unit, WQ 4572 EDA	
40	307 A Fairchild dynaliser, model 673	23
40	308 A ditto	9
53	309 A ditto limiter, model 663	15
12	310 A Univox (Jennings Organ Co.) amp./keyboard loudspeaker	36
26	311 A 6-channel stereo mixer	5
1 10	312 A Power amp.	5
10	313 A Simon sound services disc lathe (no lead)	50
66	314 2 Lockwood loudspeaker cabinets	110
8	315 A Hohner Granton glockenspiel	2
33	316 2 Tannoy corner loudspeakers	28
10	317 A corner loudspeaker	3
10	318 A BTH loudspeaker	11
18	319 2 Dallas column loudspeakers	5
6	320 A Lowther F/M tuner	1
5 10	321 A Shipton isolating transformer, 240/20/20/40, and an auto ditto	40
1805		3020 15

Courtesy of Kim Lowden

Courtesy of Kim Lowden

Figure 7.7:
Page Four lists Fairchild and Altec dynamics processors, Quad preamps and amplifiers, various equalizers, and lots of microphones.

322 A National loudspeaker for tape recorder
323 An IBC equaliser electronic CU-3H, and a ditto power unit
324 2 passive equalisers, EMI 843 and 844
325 An Altec compressor amp. 438A, and a ditto, 436B
326 A Vortexion 4 CH mixer, 4/15/M, and a ditto caso
327 2 quad pre-amps., and 2 ditto power amps
328 A Fairchild reverb system model 658 control, and a ditto spring
329 A Fairchild 655 compressor
330 A Fairchild 661 compressor
331 A 3x line amps., EMI 807, and a Power Pack EMI 807
332 A Fairchild limiter, model 660

Cheques cannot be accepted for goods purchased

333 6 microphone stands and booms, various
334 A 60-patch panel, EMI type 755/1
335 A quad power amp.
336 A quad pre-amp., and a quad power amplifier
337 A Consert portable tape recorder
338 A DC convertor 12v.-100v.-250v. out.
339 A Telefunken NSH condenser microphone and amplifier
340 2 Neumann U47 ditto
341 A Swell foot pedal
342 A Telefunken Elam 251 with amp.
343 An HMV ribbon microphone, 235CH
344 A Western Electric Cardiod ribbon microphone
345 A Reslo ribbon microphone
346 An RCF variable impedancemic
347 An RCA Dynamic microphone, 3 AKG headphones, a cord microphone amplifier, and an Elam 950 ditto

Courtesy of Kim Lowden

Figure 7.8:
Page Five lists mostly miscellaneous items and office furniture, but also the rack with a (EMI) patch panel and "mixer."

3030	15 ·	
9		348 Various amplifiers/components, and music stands (as lotted)
5		349 A Honky Tonk mini upright piano
2		350 A Ferrograph de fluxer
11		351 A 19in. rack unit with mixer and patch board panel, and a 19in. rack unit
52		352 AN OLIVETTI TEKNE 3 ELECTRIC TYPEWRITER
3		353 A typist's desk, and Dexion pieces (as lotted)
7		354 A plan chest of 6 drawers
7		355 A steel filing cabinet
2	10	356 2 Gardiner auto transformers
3129	5 ·	357
		358

Courtesy of Kim Lowden

Based on what we know for certain, these are the recorders Meek used:

Recorders Timeline
EMI TR50 (9/60)
EMI TR51 (9/60)
Lyrec TR16 twin-track, with two electronic units AR2 (9/60)
Vortexion WVB (9/62)
EMI BTR2 full-track (2/63)
Ampex Model 300 full-track console recorder (3/63)
Ampex Model 351/2 P portable twin-track (?)
Ampex PR10 twin-track (?)
"Concert portable tape recorder"
"Stereo recorder" (1/64)

In November of 1962 Joe Meek recorded himself walking around his studio describing his gear and how he used it. Here's an excerpt:

"The main machine is a Lyrec twin-track. I usually record the voice on one track, and the backing on the other. The other recorder is a TR51: this I use for dubbing. The artist [singer] has his microphone, a U47, in the corner of the studio, screened off from the rest of the musicians. He can sing his heart out, without anyone taking notice of him. He's going on a separate track [of the Lyrec]. The bass is fed in direct, the guitars have microphones in front of their amplifiers, and the drum kit has two or three microphones placed around it. Each musician has been given the chord sequence for a song, or has been listening to a record downstairs on my player, and dotted down the chords. Then we go ahead and we record until I have a very good track. I'm not worried if the artist [singer] is in tune, or phrasing properly, I want a good rhythm track for the A-side. We do the same for the B-side, and then it's all for the backing group. Off they go, and then I dub the artist's voice on again. I listen to the tracks we've already got…sometimes they're good enough, but as a rule, he wears headphones and the track's played back to him, and it's dubbed onto my TR51. So we have voice and rhythm tracks." Note that Meek does *not* record the voice onto the second track of the Lyrec, as he did the guide vocal cut at the same time as the rhythm track. Instead, he mixes it in real time with the rhythm track from track one of the Lyrec, straight to the EMI TR51, thus saving a generation of overdubbing on the main vocal track.

He continues: "When this is done I phone up Ivor Raymonde, who's a brilliant arranger that I use on most of my recordings. I tell him I'd like him to come and listen to some tracks I've got. Sometimes (we) use four strings, never any more, four violins, say, a French horn and a harp. Sometimes (also) a choir, say three girls. After I've finished I've ended up dubbing from my TR51 onto [one track on] the Lyrec. [And after recording the orchestra on the second track of the Lyrec] I have the extra orchestra on one side, and the voice and the [rhythm] track on the other. And that's all I do at my premises. I then edit out the best takes, and go along to IBC and mould them together." From this last statement it appears that at the time—late 1962—he did *not* mix the two tracks on the Lyrec down to mono at his studio, probably because the recording quality of the EMI TR51 was not up to a high enough standard. "Through the process of dubbing it three times onto a machine that I don't really think is quite up to standard you tend to add a little fuzziness, and a certain amount of loss each time. As a matter of fact, with my dubbing it seems to add top and lose the bass register."

Sidebar 7-1: "Walk with Me My Angel"

Don Charles's version of "Walk with Me My Angel" was released in January of 1962. A twin-track work tape from the session has the rhythm track and the lead vocal on one side, and strings and soprano voice on the other. The rhythm track combines acoustic guitar, bass, and drums. The lead vocal sounds like the one on the final version, so it has already been edited and assembled. On the overdubbed track you can hear bleed-through from either the player's headphones, or the control room monitors, or both. The musicians are obviously playing along to the previously recorded rhythm track. The lead vocal that bleeds in is identical to the one on the other track, so it was obviously recorded before the overdubs were added.

This situation changed in February 1963 when he acquired the EMI BTR2 professional full-track recorder—which is almost certainly the same type of machine that he had been paying to use at IBC. As he no longer had to worry about sound degradation resulting from using the TR51, he could modify his technique. Here's how guitarist and recording engineer Peter Miller recalls Joe's recording process at the time: "He only had two machines.

All he could do was ping-pong between the two machines, which he did a lot. He would very often get the band recorded onto the Lyrec, which was usually his first machine. He would put the band on one track, and put the vocal on the second track. The vocal track would also include maybe a guitar track or solo sax or something else—whatever lead instrument wasn't playing at the same time as the vocal. And then he would mix that onto his EMI BTR2, mono, one track. And at the time that he'd do the mix he would add on anything else that he wanted, either another track, or effects processing."

Ted Fletcher, who began working with Joe at around the same time or shortly thereafter, remembers a slightly modified version of the same technique. "The technique he used most of the time while I was there was to lay down the backing track on the full track of the BTR2 so that the recording occupied the full quarter-inch in mono. He would then remove the tape and put it on to the Lyrec machine where he would erase one half. There would still be the original backing track on the one half of the tape and he would add to that either the lead voice or backing vocal on the other half of the track. He would then mix the backing track and the vocal track together live while he was recording another part and send the three elements back to the BTR2, live in mono on full track. If he had everything he wanted by then, he would do a final mixdown with additional compression and EQ."

Note that in both descriptions Meek might add an additional track in real time as he was mixing down to mono, and that he might add processing at *any* point along the way. For example, if he had the lead vocal and a guitar solo on one track of the Lyrec, he could have added compression or some other effect to them individually at the time they were recorded or while they were being bounced. If he wanted to get really fancy he could even put one combination of effects on a sound at one point, stop the machine, change the effects, and start the machine again. Even if he got a glitch from stopping and starting the machines, he could razor edit differently processed sections together later, as he in fact often did. Viewed from this perspective, the total number of "tracks" that he recorded would not necessarily be the same as the total number of bounces.

Here's a hypothetical example: Joe records guitar, bass, and drums—each with their own individual compression, echo or other effects added—onto one track of the Lyrec. He then records a vocal track with its own effects processing onto the second track. Then he records a guitar solo with a different set of effects onto the same track as the vocal, in sections where no voice has been previously recorded. He now has the individually processed instruments comprising the rhythm section on one track and the individually processed vocal and guitar solo on the other. He likes the results, but wants to add some sound effects here and there, so he takes a third recorder (for example the EMI TR51) and records the sound effects onto it. Then, as he's mixing the two tracks on the Lyrec down to the BTR2— and remember, he can add even more effects to one or both of them as he's mixing—he mixes in the sound effects from the third tape machine. Now he's got the rhythm section, lead vocals, guitar solo, and special effects all mixed down to mono on the BTR2, and the only "generation loss" is the same as you get whenever you mix down. At this point he has six tracks recorded and he has done no bouncing at all.

He can now take the reel off the BTR2, as Ted Fletcher described, and place it on the Lyrec. He'll only get the benefit of half the tape width that way, but that's all he'd get by bouncing it over, and there's no generation loss. (Of course, if he wanted to add processing to all the tracks as a whole he could do that as he was bouncing them over to one channel of the Lyrec. But unless he wanted to use a single effect on two separate sounds he could do the same thing when he mixed everything back down to mono later, without the generation loss.) With his six previously recorded tracks now on one track of the Lyrec, he could record, say, a four-piece string section and three background singers— once again, all individually processed—on the second track, and then mix them all down to mono on the BTR2. He now has a mono master tape blending thirteen individually processed tracks, and he's only had to bounce once—twice if you count the mixdown. Obviously, if he wanted to add even more tracks, he could put the master reel back on the Lyrec and repeat the process.

A month or so after getting the BTR2 Meek also purchased an Ampex Model 300, which was another professional full-track mono machine. Why he chose to buy two of the same basic type of machine is unclear, though we know that he had always wanted an Ampex machine. Peter Miller recalls: "Then he got an Ampex 300, full track, 15/30 IPS, 3-head. [1] He always wanted American equipment; his desire was to get American equipment because he loved the way Americans made records. He found that he couldn't get that sound on British and European recorders. He couldn't afford the American machines until he'd had seven or eight hits, and then he started getting the American stuff in, and the first thing he had was the Ampex 300."

Ampex recorders such as the Model 300 were the American equivalents of the BTR2 in the sense that they were the staple machines found in almost all the professional studios. Sam Phillips recorded most of Elvis's Sun sides using two Ampex 350 recorders: he used a console model as his main recorder and a rack-mount model primarily for delay effects. [2] Norman Petty's main machine was an Ampex Model 600 portable, but he also had an Ampex 327 mono that he used for making copies, and for track bouncing to produce overdubs. Having two world-class mono full-tracks gave Joe even more recording options. For example, by bouncing between them he could build up a rhythm track using the full width of the tape, and only have to go to half width (on the Lyrec) once.

Sidebar 7-2: "Nobody Waved Goodbye"

In June 1966, the Cryin' Shames released "Nobody Waved Goodbye" on Decca. The instrumentation is acoustic guitar, upright bass, drums, brass, strings, and lead and backing vocals. The record opens with a brass and strings introduction, and then there's a hard tape splice into the actual song. A work tape from the session has the guitar, bass, and drums on one track; and strings, brass, and backing vocals on the other. You can hear a very faint bit of extraneous sound on the rhythm section track, but not enough to make it out. At one point it sounds like an organ, at another someone humming. Most likely this is the original track, with the three instruments playing together at once. It could have been recorded on a mono machine and then bounced to the Lyrec as the second track was being recorded, or it could have been recorded directly to one of the Lyrec's two tracks.

On the overdubbed track you can clearly hear bleed-through from either the player's headphones, or the control room monitors, or both. The musicians are obviously playing along to the previously recorded rhythm track. All of the instruments in the final mix seem to be on the work tape, so the two tracks were probably mixed together to mono later, at the same time that the lead vocal was added. If Meek had wanted to add even more parts he could have mixed the two tracks down to a mono machine, then transferred the reel to the Lyrec and overdubbed the additional part on one of its tracks. Then those two tracks would be mixed down to one of the mono machines.

It is unclear when Meek purchased the Ampex 351/2 twin-track, but after that point he would have been able to work in stereo if he chose to, and even to do two-track bounces between machines. He could also simply use the 351/2 in place of the Lyrec. At some point he even acquired a third Ampex machine—a small twin-track semi-pro model called a PR10.

One thing that is not clear is whether Joe ever got a multitrack recorder. There have been persistent rumors about his having had or leased a three-track, four-track, or even eight-track recorder in 1966, but no such machine was found in his studio at the time of his death. Meek did receive a letter from the credit department of Ampex Great Britain Limited dated May 24, 1966, *(see Fig. 7.9),* in which he is asked to pay an overdue balance of 938.29 pounds. Attached to the letter is a copy of a statement dated March 31, 1966, for the same amount, which references a sale date of January 10, 1966 *(see Fig. 7.9)*. Unfortunately there is no model number or equipment type listed; in the "details" column whatever it was that Joe owed money on is indicated only as "21842. 34349." If this was the mystery multitrack, he acquired it in January of 1966. The letter gives him seven days to settle the account, so if he was unable to do so the machine may have been repossessed, which would explain why it doesn't appear on the auction list.

Listening to Meek's recordings from the first half of 1966, there is no reason to believe that they were produced using a multitrack. Nothing is done which could not have been done using combinations of his other machines. Additionally, any of the Ampex multitracks would have used 1/2-inch tape, rather than the standard 1/4-inch, and there is no evidence that any of the

Figure 7.9:
A letter to Joe Meek from the Credit Controller at the UK division of Ampex, informing him that his account is overdue, and requesting payment within seven days. This may have been the elusive multi-track.

A Subsidiary of Ampex International S. A.

AMPEX GREAT BRITAIN LIMITED

ACRE ROAD · READING, BERKSHIRE, ENGLAND
TELEPHONE: READING 84411
CABLE: AMPEX READING · TELEX: 84345

Date: 24th May 1966

Meeksville Sound,
304, Holloway Road,
London. N.7.

Dear Sir,

OVERDUE ACCOUNT £938. 2. 9

Please accept this letter as a courteous reminder that your account as above stated, is now overdue. We shall be obliged if you would kindly arrange settlement within seven days.

If, however, settlement is delayed because of some query please let us have full details by return so that they can receive our immediate attention.

Yours faithfully,
for Ampex Great Britain Limited,

Credit Controller.

AMPEX

DIRECTORS: B. A. OLERICH, U. S. A. · P. E. AXON, O.B.E., PH.D., M.SC., M.I.E.E. · P. MARRIAGE

Courtesy of John Repsch and the JMAS Archive

Figure 7.10:
The statement attached to the previous letter. It lists two numbers—21842 and 34349—under "details," and a cost of 938 pounds, but no model number.

STATEMENT

AMPEX

AMPEX GREAT BRITAIN LIMITED
ACRE ROAD
READING

MEEKSVILLE SOUND L
304 HOLLOWAY ROAD.
LONDON. N.7.

Phone READING 84221
Cables AMPEX READING
Telex 84345

DATE 31st MARCH 1966.

DATE	DETAILS	DEBIT	CREDIT	BALANCE
1966 JAN 10	21842. 34349.	938. 2. 9.		£938. 2. 9
Cash since received				Last amount in the balance column is the amount due.

AG 35

Courtesy of John Repsch and the JMAS Archive

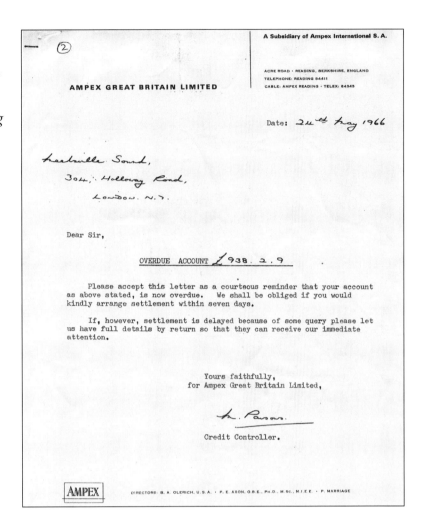

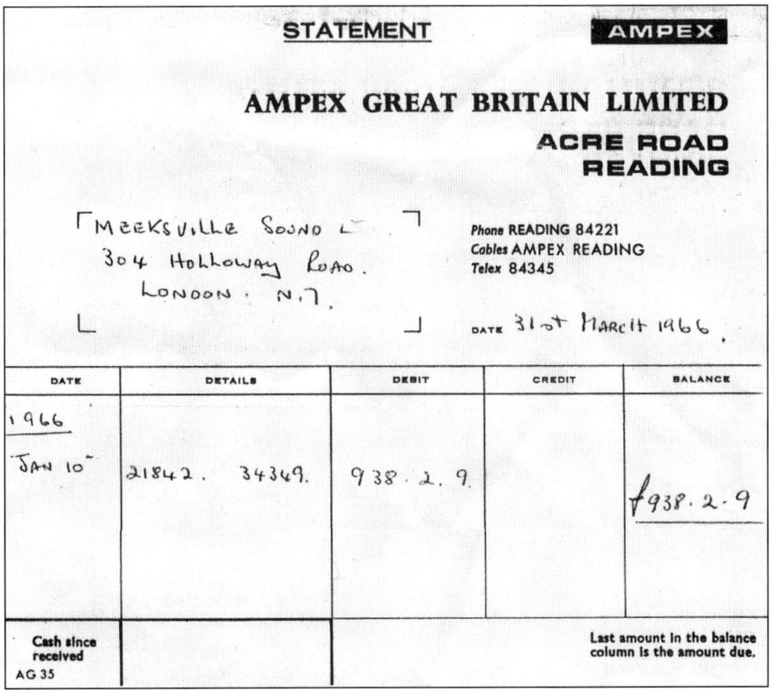

thousands of "Tea Chest" tapes Meek left behind were in that format. At the time of this writing, arrangements were being finalized for the Tea Chest tapes to be turned over to the Sound Archive at the British Library, and the curator there, who made an initial inspection of the tapes, does not recall seeing any 1/2-inch tapes among them.

SPOTLIGHT ON JOE'S RECORDERS . . . .

Lyrec TR16

The Lyrec TR16 was a fully professional recorder. Meek had the version with stereo heads, technically referred to as a TR16-S. It employed a heavy-duty synchronous main motor and individual high-speed motors for rewind and fast-forward; operated at 7.5, 15, or 30 ips; handled all reel sizes up to 11.5" including "cine spools"; and had a switch that allowed the right and left channels of the stereo head to be collapsed into mono and played back through a single amplifier (to check phase relationships). The stock TR16 did not have "sel-sync," the ability to monitor playback of one recorded track while recording a second track in sync with it, but Meek modified his machine for that purpose. The recorder was available in a chassis for rack mounting, in a carrying case, or on a rolling stand. Meek had the chassis version, which measured 25.5" (H) x 19" (W) x 10" (D), and weighed 85 lbs.

Figure 7.11:
Company photo of the Lyrec
TR16 tape transport

MAGNETIC TAPE TRANSPORT MECHANISM

MODEL TR 16 and TR 16-S

- THE LYREC STUDIO TAPE TRANSPORT MECHANISM TYPE TR 16 is a professional high quality recording and replaying instrument, and is able to meet the most exacting requirements of the broadcasting and the gramophone industry or other trades, where quality and reliability are of first importance.

- THE INSTRUMENT IS OF PLEASING APPEARANCE. Only the highest grade of materials is used in its construction, and all parts are manufactured to high efficiency and a long and troublefree operation. Extreme simplicity of operation is a valuable feature of this instrument.

- AN EXTRA HEAVY-DUTY SYNCHRONOUS MOTOR, a special drive and a heavy balanced flywheel ensure a constant speed and thus provide a constant tape speed with a minimum of wow and flutter.

- A SPECIAL FRICTION ARRANGEMENT ensures correct tension of the tape when passing across the heads, and prevents looping of the tape, whether in starting or stopping the recorder, or in rewinding or fast forward spooling. In Stop position the tape is automatically removed from the heads.

- THREE RECORDING AND REPLAYING SPEEDS, $7^1/_2$-15-30 inches per second are provided, and changing from one speed to another is accomplished by turning a knob, which at the same time automatically changes the equalizers in the amplifier.

- THE OPERATION OF START, STOP, RECORD AND PLAYBACK is easily activated by clearly labelled push buttons, and the functions are relay and solenoid operated. As erase is automatically on in Record position, the Record button is provided with a locking device to safeguard against unintentional operation of this button, and as a further precaution a red lamp is lit. Another push button switch ensures correct tension of the tape when changing from big to small reels. Fast forward and fast rewind, by means of two separate motors, are accomplished by a continuously variable rheostat.

- BY MEANS OF THREE DIFFERENT ADAPTORS, Cine European or NARTB reels can be used up to a diameter of $11^1/_2$ inches (295 mm). Two adaptors for Cine spools and two adaptors for either European or NARTB spools are included in the price for the tape transport mechanism, the third type of adaptors is available at extra cost.

- SEPARATE ERASE, RECORD AND PLAYBACK HEADS, each enclosed in protective housings, allow simultaneous recording and playback. The recording and the playback heads, potted and laminated for the longest possible life, are of the low impedance type, 7 mH and 70 mH respectively. The erase head is mounted in direct connection with the bias-and erase oscillator in one small unit. The coil and the core of the head are parts of the hf. circuit, whitch in connection with a double triode in push pull, at the same time provide the bias current and a very efficient erasing.

- AS A SUPPLEMENTARY EQUIPMENT the machine may be furnished with a tape cutting device, which is to be mounted in between the playback head and capstan, and which by depressing a button will cut the tape at an angle of 45°. This cutting device together with a splicing plate located conveniently on the front of the machine, will facilitate the editing work.

- FOR THE USE OF PLAYBACK OF TAPES, which are not recorded to standard alignment, a device with a thumb screw may be optionally supplied. This device should be fastened on the side of the mu-metal box of the playback head and by using it the head may be conveniently aligned. As the alignment screw and the tape cutting device have to be mounted on the same place, it is only possible to mount one of them.

- MODEL TR 16 is available either with full track heads or on request furnished with stereo heads (model TR 16-S).

- MODEL TR 16-S is furnished with a bias distributing unit that feeds the necessary current to each of the two halves of the recording heads. The two bias currents can be adjusted on the front plate by means of a screw driver. Further the TR 16-S is furnished with a push button by means of which the two halves of the playback head can be coupled in parallel on one of the two connected amplifiers, whereby a monaural playback is obtained and whereby it is possible to check if the two stereo signals are in phase.

THE LYREC TAPE TRANSPORT MECHANISN, model TR 16 or TR 16-S, is available either as a chassis for mounting in rack or console, or mounted in a carrying case with lid for portable use as shown below. It is also available mounted on a trolley with a receptacle underneath for an amplifier type AR 4 that contains a recording and a playback amplifier as illustrated overleaf.

MODEL TR 16 or TR 16-S in carrying case (lid removed)

$^A/_s$ LYREC . ELECTRO-ACOUSTIC EQUIPMENT

Hollandsvej 12 - Kgs. Lyngby - Denmark

Figure 7.12: Front side of a brochure describing the Lyrec TR16

SPECIFICATION AND DATA

TAPE SPEED: 7¹/₂-15-30 inches per second, selected by turning a knob.

REELS: Standard Cine, European or NARTB reels up to 11¹/₂ inches (295 mm) diameter by using exchangeable adaptors corresponding to the various types of reels. One set of adaptors for Cine reels and one set of adaptors for either European- or NARTB reels will be supplied together with the machine.

REWIND TIME: Minimum 2 minutes for a full 11¹/₂ inches (295 mm) reel, continuously variable by turning a knob.

CONTROLS:

1. Playback-Record-Stop push buttons with a locking device for the record knob. Red light indicates record position. In stop position the tape automatically is removed from the heads.
2. Big Reels-Small Reels push buttons changes the tape tension to a suitable value.
3. Rewind-Stop-Fastforward potentiometer. To be turned left for rewinding and right for forward winding. Stop in the middle position.
4. 7¹/₂-15-30 inches per second tape speed rotary change-over switch. This switch also governs relays in the amplifier for changing the correction filters.

MOTORS: One 2-speed 220 volts 50 c/s synchronous motor provides constant speed drive for recording and playback.
Two 220 volts 50 c/s split-capacitor motors provide high speed rewind and high speed forward spooling.

BEARINGS: All ball bearings or self-lubricating bearings, no lubrication required.

WOW AND FLUTTER: 7¹/₂ inches tape speed: well under .25% rms in the range of .5 to 100 c/s (.5% peak-to-peak including all flutter components from o to 300 cycles using a tone of 3000 cycles). 15 inches tape speed: well under .1% rms (.4% peak-to-peak). 30 inches tape speed: well under .08% rms (.3% peak-to-peak).

PLAYBACK TIME ACCURACY: .5%

MAGNETIC HEADS: The erase, record and playback heads are individually mounted, and each enclosed in protective housings. The record and playback heads are provided with alignment screws.
Recording head: airgap .0008 inch (20 micron) L = 7 mH
Playback head : airgap .0002 inch (5 micron) L = 70 mH

ERASING HEAD and hf. oscillator in one unit. Erase and bias frequency 75 kc/s approx Erasing attenuation more than 85 db. Bias current adjustable within 10-25 mA. Potentiometer for adjusting to symmetrical wave shape. Oscillator valve E C C 85.

INDICATOR LIGHT: Green light indicates that the machine is ready for use.
Red light indicates recording operation.

POWER CONSUMPTION: 220 volts a. c. 50 c/s single phase 150 watts

DIMENSIONS: Chassis (for mounting in rack or console):
24¹/₂'' × 19'', depth 10''. (622 × 462 mm, depth 250 mm)
In carrying case, including lid :
25¹/₂'' × 20'', depth 13''. (645 × 505 mm, depth 330 mm)

WEIGHT: Chassis 85 lbs (40 kilos).
In carrying case, including lid : 110 lbs (50 kilos).

MODEL TR 16 or TR 16-S in trolley 2569.
Underneath an amplifier model A R 4.
Dimensions: 25¹/₂'' × 20'' (650 × 510 mm),
height: 32'' (810 mm).
Weight: 140 lbs (65 kgs).

ᴬ/s LYREC . ELECTRO-ACOUSTIC EQUIPMENT

Hollandsvej 12 - Kgs. Lyngby - Denmark

O.C. OLSEN & CO. A/s
KØBENHAVN

Figure 7.13: Rear side of the brochure listing specifications for the TR16, and showing the optional roll-around stand.

EMI TR50/51

According to audio historian John O'Kill: "These single motor juniors in the EMI range were primarily designed to be portable for location use. Correctly set up they made a fine recording. Many fifties hits were mastered on these machines, but they were fiddly, needing constant tweaking to keep them on spec. The eight-inch spool capacity was only good for twenty minutes or so, running standard play tape at 15 IPS. The TR50 was only a two-head machine. The TR51 was a three-head machine, mechanically similar to TR50."

Figure 7.14:
Joe Meek's EMI TR51, now in the possession of John Repsch.

A press blurb for the TR50 in the July 1951 *Wireless World* read: "The new EMI portable magnetic recorder, Type TR50, which weighs 59 lbs. and measures 17 1/2 x 16 x 12 3/4 in, is available for tape speeds of either 15 and 7 1/2 in/sec or 7 1/2 and 3 3/4 sec. The frequency response is 50 c/s to 12,000 c/s within ±2 dB of the response at 1 kc/s at 15 in/sec, 8,000 c/s at 7 1/2 in/sec and 4,000 c/s at 3 3/4 in/sec. It is claimed that speed variations are less than 0.2 per cent at 15 and 7 (1/2) in/sec and less than 0.3 per cent at 3 3/4 in/sec. Equalizer networks appropriate to the conditions are automatically brought into circuit by the speed selector control."

Joe Meek on the TR51: "I must say it's turned out to be a marvelous little machine. I would prefer to change it soon for something like an Ampex, which would possibly be a little more reliable. This machine tends to 'pop' just a little bit. Sometimes you get a little bumping in the background—I think it's to do with the bias."

Figure 7.15:
Another shot of Joe Meek's
EMI TR51.

An advertisement for the TR51 offered this description and these specifications: "The design incorporates 3 heads (record/playback/erase); uses up to 8.25" reels; has an internal 3-watt amplifier with 6.5" speaker and an asynchronous, switched pole, 2-speed motor. The tape indicator is a triple drum numerical counter. The entire unit weighs about 60 lbs.

"Controls consist of Mains on/off; meter switch for Line In/Record Level/Line Out" and valve checking; Record Gain; Replay Gain; Bass Cut; Line Out/Speaker On-Off switch; Replay/Monitor/Record switch; Spool Left/Right switch; Cueing control and Tape speed select.

SPECIFICATIONS

Track configuration: Full track mono

Tape Speeds: 15 & 7.5 ips (TR51A) and 7.5 & 3.75 ips (TR51B)

Wow or flutter: Better than 0.2% @ 15 and 7.5 ips, better than 0.3% @ 3.75 ips

Rewind time: Approximately 2 1/2 minutes for standard 7" reel

Valve complement: Not known

Frequency response: 50-15 kHz at 15 ips, 50-10 kHz @ 7.5 ips and 50-7 kHz @ 3.75 ips

Recording inputs: 1 balanced for 20-30 ohm microphone, Standard 600 ohm unbalanced line input @ 1 mw level

Recording level meter: VU meter with 3-position switch, Line in, Line out

Signal-to-noise ratio: 46 dB, unweighted

Outputs: 600 ohm balanced line out

Output Power: 3 watts into an internal 6.5" High Flux speaker

Erase and Bias: Push-Pull circuit operating at 100 kHz

Dimensions: 13.25" (H) x 18" (W) x 17" (D)

Weight: 60lbs.

Figure 7.16:
A disassembled EMI TR52.
The TR52 was nearly
identical to the TR51.

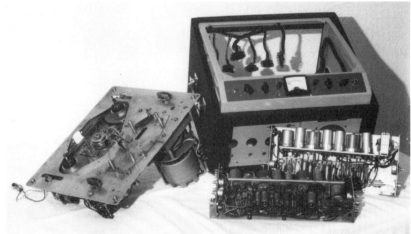

Photo by and courtesy of John O'Kill

Vortexion WVB

Vortexion tape machines were built around the Wearite (Wright & Weaire) tape deck transport developed for Ferrograph, but they used their own preamplifiers. Unlike the Ferrographs, they had low impedance mic inputs (30Ω), which could be used with long cable runs. They also featured a rheostat on the rear panel for adjusting the erase bias, and had wildly erratic meters that were difficult to use with any precision.

Figure 7.17:
Two Vortexion recorders. The model on the left is the type used by Joe Meek for tape-echo effects. The model on the right is basically the same machine, but with a more "modern" design.

Photo by and courtesy of John O'Kill

Ampex model 300

The Model 300 was introduced in 1949. It replaced the Model 200 and was quickly adopted as the standard mastering recorder by all the major studios in America, a status it maintained for nearly twenty years. Ampex produced over 20,000 Model 300s during that time, including solid-state versions, and the "bathtub" version that lacked built-in microphone preamps.

According to available documentation Meek's machine was mono, but most Model 300s were twin-track, and in 1957 a three-track model (recording on 1/2-inch tape) became available. The Model 300 transport was also the basis for the eight-track recorder designed by and custom built for Les Paul in 1958. Two of these machines were produced, the second one going to Tom Dowd at Atlantic Records. By the mid-sixties a four-track model was commercially available.

The standard machine ran at 7.5/15 ips, but a high-speed version called the Model 301 ran at 15/30 ips. The Model 300 employed an indirect capstan drive, which did not age gracefully. Absolute speed accuracy was difficult to attain and flutter increased with wear. The Model 300 transport was also the basis for the 3200 duplicator and various instrumentation decks.

Ampex Model 350 and Model 351

In April of 1953 the Model 350 replaced the Model 400. It had a direct capstan drive, simpler controls, and overall better electronics. At first it was only available in full-track format, but soon twin-track versions became available, and by the mid-sixties four-track Model 350s were being produced. The Model 350's electronics section featured point-to-point wiring and octal tubes, and had an outboard power supply. The electronics section was separate from the transport and was connected to it via a four-pin Jones plug.

Figure 7.18:
The transport unit of an
Ampex 351 tape recorder.

Introduced in 1958, the Model 351 was the first Ampex to be designed as either a twin-track or full-track machine from the beginning. The 351's electronics section employed printed circuit boards instead of point-to-point wiring, used miniature tubes, and had an internal power supply. The front panel of the electronics, of which there are several versions, is distinguishable from 350 electronics only by the black dot under the "input transfer" switch. The Model 351's electronics were connected to the transport via a six-pin Jones plug.

Ampex Model PR10:
A small, portable machine that used seven-inch reels and Model 354 electronics with a different faceplate.

Mixers
It appears likely that in the early days Meek had only his four-channel homemade mixer, and a small line mixer or two [3] that he used to sum line level feeds from various sources. The homemade mixer, shown in nearly all photographs of his studio, was a large black rack-mountable job with variable "top lift" on each of the four channels. (Top lift is the British term for high-frequency equalization, with boost but not cut capabilities.) By September of 1962 Meek had also acquired a Vortexion 4/15/M four-channel mixer, usually pictured with the other mixer sitting on top of it. Vortexion mixers were widely used in the recording and broadcast industries, as well as the military, and were known for their audiophile sound quality and reliability. Meek: "With the mixers, there's a varied selection. I have a homemade mixer that has four channels with top lift on each. Then I use a Vortexion mixer, which does a pretty good, solid job." Using these two units together gave him a total of eight high-quality mixer channels, four with EQ, which could be combined in various ways.

The Auction List includes a "6-channel stereo mixer," but there is no indication of when it was purchased or just what exactly it was. Usually when an item is listed without a brand name it indicates a homemade unit, but not always. How Meek may have used this unit, and when, is unclear. Its presence on the list, and his recent acquisition of several stereo recorders, does raise the issue of whether he was transitioning to stereo recording.

An advertisement for the Vortexion 4/15/M read: "This unit provides for four independent channels electronically mixed without spurious break through. Microphony, hum, and background noise have been reduced to a minimum by careful selection of components. The standard 15-50 ohm shielded transformers on each input are arranged for balanced line, and have screened primaries to prevent H.F. transfer when used on long lines. The standard five-valve unit only consumes 18.5 watts, H.T. is provided by a rectifier fed by a low loss, low field transformer in screening box. The ventilated case gives negligible temperature rise with this low consumption assuring continuance of low noise figures. 20,000 ohms is the standard output impedance, but the noise pick-up on the output lines is equivalent to approximately 2,000 ohms due to the large amount of negative feedback used. For any output impedance between 20,000 ohms and infinity half a volt output is available. Special models can be supplied for 600 ohms to equivalent voltage by an additional transformer, or 1 milliwatt 600 ohms by additional transformer and valve. The white engraved front panel permits of temporary pencil notes being made, and these may be easily erased when required. The standard input is balanced line by means of three point jack sockets at the front, but alternative connectors may be obtained to order at the rear. Size 18 1/8 inches wide x 11 1/8 inches front to back (excluding plugs) x 6 1/4 inches high. Weight 22 lbs."

Figure 7.21:
Vortexion 4/15/M and
3/PPM mixers.

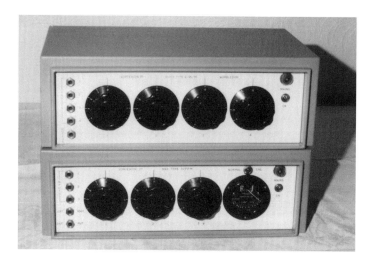

Meek also had several preamplifiers with multiple inputs that he could use to combine several signals before they ever reached a mixer. The most important of these was an RCA "Orthophonic" hi-fi preamplifier/filter unit that he referred to as his "cooker." It provided up to three inputs, had simple tone controls, and could be easily overdriven into a smooth and very musical distortion. Peter Miller described it this way: "Essentially it was something like you'd use on a fancy home stereo system. It was a mono unit, with volume, middle, treble, bass, slope, and a couple of filters. For its day it was quite a comprehensive little equalization device. It had five or six tubes in it, and you could overload the crap out of it to get some really cool sounds." One of the most common applications was to process the vocal mic, as Joe explains: "The vocal mic goes through a little cooker I've made, that has got bass, top, and middle lift in it. It was originally a small amplifier. It has three channels, so I can mix in a vocal group with it, and possibly a front-line instrument. It's quite handy; I can mix without having to walk around the control room too much." Other preamplifiers, acquired at various points, included an RCA LM1/322 15A, and an American Dyna PAS/2 stereo model. Any of these units could have been pressed into service to add additional inputs, or tone coloration, when needed.

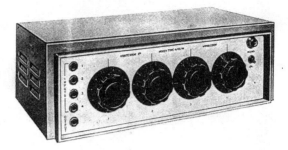

FOUR-WAY
ELECTRONIC MIXER

This unit provides for 4 independent channels electronically mixed without "spurious break through," microphony hum and background noise have been reduced to a minimum by careful selection of components. The standard 15-50 ohm shielded transformers on each input are arranged for balanced line. and have screened primaries to prevent H.F. transfer when used on long lines.

The standard 5 valve unit only consumes 18.5 watts, H.T. is provided by a rectifier fed by low loss, low field, transformer in screening box. The ventilated case gives negligible temperature rise with this low consumption assuring continuance of low noise figures.

20.000 ohms is the standard output impedance, but the noise pick-up on the output lines is equivalent to approximately 2,000 ohms due to the large amount of negative feedback used.

For any output impedance between 20.000 ohms and infinity half a volt output is available. Special models can be supplied for 600 ohms at equivalent voltage by an additional transformer or 1 milliwatt 600 ohms by additional transformer and valve.

The white engraved front panel permits of temporary pencil notes being made. and these may be easily erased when required. The standard input is balanced line by means of 3 point jack sockets at the front, but alternative connectors may be obtained to order at the rear.

Mixer with ½volt - 20,000Ω to infinity output **£50.0.0d.**

Mixer with 600Ω 1 milliwatt output **£55.0.0d.**

Size 18 1/8in. wide x 11 1/8in. front to back (excluding plugs) x 6¼in. high. Weight 22 lbs.

VORTEXION LIMITED, 257-263 THE BROADWAY, WIMBLEDON, LONDON, S.W.19

Telephones: 01-542 2814 01-542 6242-3-4   Telegrams: Vortexion, London, S.W.19

Courtesy George West

For his monitoring and playback system, Meek had several Quad preamplifiers and Quad power amplifiers that he used to drive Tannoy "Red" monitors (one located in the control room and the other downstairs in his lounge). The original Quad 22 preamplifier had three EQ switches that configured its equalization curve to match the response of various record manufacturer's discs produced before 1954. After 1954 there are standard settings for both 45 and 78 rpm records. The Tannoy speakers were 15-inch dual concentric models, which is to say that they had a high frequency driver mounted at the center of the speaker, with the main speaker cone handling the low frequencies. They had an amazing frequency response (for the time) of 23 Hz to

20 kHz, with an active crossover fixed at 1 kHz. The speaker had a 13-pound magnet assembly, and weighed nearly 21 pounds not counting the crossover, which was an additional 3 pounds. The Tannoy Red was built into a Lockwood enclosure (developed by the BBC) measuring 44" (H) x 24" (W) x 17.5" (D), and weighing 83 pounds without the speaker. It came with "concealed castors fitted as standard," which is not surprising! It was renamed the "Monitor" because during its first few years of production the Red speaker had been installed in major recording and broadcast studios throughout Britain and Europe, and become the de facto reference standard. Peter Miller, looking at a photo of the control room, said, "Those are Lockwoods, Tannoy Reds, which are 15-inch speakers, and they sound *killer;* they still sound killer. They were the best speakers I ever heard—so sweet." Meek also had another Tannoy that he used to solo the vocal channel (in 1962): "I've also got in my control room, for the vocal channel, I've got another Tannoy speaker cabinet—the smaller type that fits in a corner—I don't know the model. This I find rather metallic, and I only use it at low levels. I can't really balance (read 'mix') on it, although I've tried. It seems to have an artificial top lift that rather misleads you."

Figure 7.23:
Quad II power amplifier. Joe Meek had several of these.

Figure 7.24:
Quad 22 pre-amplifier.

LOCKWOOD *Acoustically Designed Enclosures*

MODEL L.E.1. Height 44" Width 24" Depth 17½"
Weight 83 lb. Acoustic capacity 9 cu. ft.
Concealed castors fitted as standard. **£38 10s. 0d.**

MODEL L.E.2. Height 37½" Width 22" Depth 16"
Weight 70 lb. Acoustic capacity 6½ cu. ft.
Concealed castors fitted as standard. **£30 0s. 0d.**

MODEL L.E.3. Height 32½" Width 20" Depth 12¾"
Weight 40 lb. Acoustic capacity 4 cu. ft.
Castors not fitted to this model. **£20 0s. 0d.**

MODEL L.E.4. Height 27½" Width 17½" Depth 12¼"
Weight 31 lb. Acoustic capacity 3 cu. ft.
Castors not fitted to this model. **£15 15s. 0d.**

Finishes

Oak, Mahogany or Walnut veneer. Teak and other veneers to
requirements. Highly polished to almost any shade. Coloured and
Hammered finishes.

All the above model L.E. Enclosures have the same outward appearance and design, the difference between each type being
overall dimensions. All types can be 'tuned' to suit almost any Loudspeaker unit or combination of units. Provision is made
in all types for vertically mounting the 'tweeter' unit, if desired. We suggest the following size of Loudspeaker Units, for use
with these enclosures.

Model L.E.1. 15" Dual Concentric unit, or a three
speaker combination.

Model L.E.2. 12" Dual Concentric unit, or a three
speaker combination.

Model L.E.3. 12" Dual Concentric unit, or 'full range'
single unit. There is ample accomodation for a 'tweeter'
if desired.

Model L.E.4. As type L.E.3 or single 10" and 8" units
can be used with excellent results.

Please apply for separate lists of recommended Loudspeaker Units.
All enclosures can be supplied complete with any unit or combination
of units.

Baffle. Holes cut as required, at
no extra charge.

Packing. Felt lined packing case
extra. Credited in full, if returned
carriage paid.

Carriage. Paid, per British Road
Transport or Goods Train. England,
Wales, Scotland or N. Ireland.

LOCKWOOD LOUDSPEAKER ENCLOSURES, are of vented design developed from the B.B.C. monitoring Loudspeaker
Cabinet, as used by the B.B.C. *B.B.C. Patent No. 696/671*

LOCKWOOD
BROCHURE E.2.

HARROW

MIDDLESEX

Figure 7.25: Information sheet describing various models of Lockwood speaker enclosures.

TECHNICAL SPECIFICATION	"FIFTEEN"	"TWELVE"	"IIILZ"†
Frequency response	23—20,000 c.p.s.	25—20,000 c.p.s.	27—20,000 c.p.s.
Polar Distribution for 60° inc. Angle	−4dB at 10,000 c.p.s.	−3dB at 10,000 c.p.s.	−2dB at 10,000 c.p.s.
Power Handling Capacity	50 watts°	30 watts°	15 watts°
Impedance Via Crossover Network	16 ohms	16 ohms	16 ohms
Flux Density L.F. Gap	13,500 gauss	11,500 gauss	10,000 gauss
Flux Density H.F. Gap	18,000 gauss	15,000 gauss	15,000 gauss
H.F. Voice Coil Diameter	2″	2″	2″
L.F. Voice Coil Diameter	2″	2″	2½″
Intermodulation Products	less than 2%	less than 2%	less than 2%
Bass Resonance	32 c.p.s.	35 c.p.s.	27 c.p.s.
Magnet Assembly Weight	13 lb.	7½ lb.	6¼ lb.
Magnet Material	Ticonal G	Ticonal G	Ticonal G
Crossover Frequency	1,000 c.p.s.	1,700 c.p.s.	1,700 c.p.s.
Overall Diameter of Frame	15¼″	12⅜″	12½″
Overall Depth	9″	7½″	6½″
Fixing Holes P.C.D.	14½″	11¾″	11⅝″
Weight: (Crossover network in separate unit)	20 lb. 13 ozs. (crossover 3 lb.)	10 lb. (crossover 2 lb.)	9 lb. (crossover 2¼ lb.)
Finish: Cover and Frame	Stove enamel	Stove enamel	Stove enamel
Magnet Assembly Parts	Cadmium plate	Cadmium plate	Cadmium plate

* Depending on type of enclosure
† The III L Z unit is fitted with a treble control

TANNOY (AMERICA) LTD.
BOX 177, EAST NORWICH,
LONG ISLAND, N.Y., U.S.A.

TANNOY (CANADA) LTD.
36 WELLINGTON STREET EAST,
TORONTO, I, ONTARIO, CANADA.

TANNOY PRODUCTS LTD., WEST NORWOOD, LONDON, S.E.27

Printed by W. H. & A. Nutting Ltd., Morden, Surrey, England.   *Tannoy is the Registered Trademark and property of Tannoy Limited, London, England.*

Figure 7.26: Tannoy brochure listing specifications for three models of dual-concentric speakers.

At some point Joe added an EMI 755/1 60-point patch bay, which must have made life considerably easier for him. On the RGM Sound equipment list there is a listing for "panels" dated May 17, 1963, but the cost is given as just a little over two pounds, suggesting that they were small. (Perhaps rack panels for the Quad preamplifiers?) A more significant listing is a charge of sixty-five pounds for "wiring control room" dated May 11, 1964. By then Joe had *lots* of new outboard gear, and that seems like a logical time to have connected the patch bay.

Figure 7.27:
Photo of a Tannoy speaker in a Lockwood cabinet, very similar to the ones used by Joe Meek.

Courtesy of Barry Fox and Tannoy

Compressors

The outboard gear that he connected to the patch bay no doubt included the highly coveted (as a result of their being used by the Beatles) Fairchild compressors and limiters that he had purchased in September of 1963. They included a Model 660 limiting amplifier, a Model 663 compact compressor, a Model 661 "Auto Ten," and a Model 673 Dynalizer. (He got a second Model 673 four months later, and a Model 655 after that.) Six months earlier he had bought two American Altec compressors, a Model 436B and a Model 438A. He had wanted to upgrade his compressor collection for many years, as before 1963 he was limited to a BBC limiter and some homemade units. "These include an old BBC limiter, which I use on the voice track. It is very ancient, as it has the old large pin type valves. It must be at least thirty years old. This is very efficient and isn't all that noticeable in its operation. Then I have a compressor that I built myself. I found the design in one of the magazines."

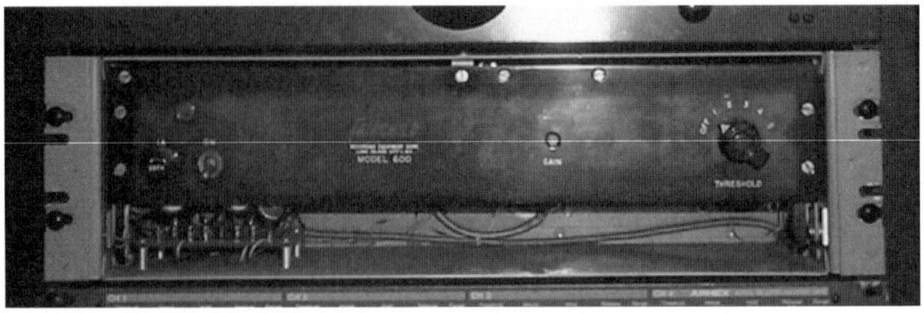

Figure 7.28: Fairchild Model 600 compressor.

Peter Miller was there at the time that Meek switched over to the newer compressors, and he sought to determine just how much difference they made to the sound of Meek's recordings. "After I found out about the compression and I'd analyzed the techniques he was using, I decided to pinpoint where he changed over from his BBC and homemade ones to the Fairchilds that he got. I determined the actual date they came in, and then I listened to the recordings he'd made prior to and after that date to see if I could hear any difference, and I couldn't. And I was listening with a very focused 'compression' kind of ear." That was a rather enterprising endeavor for a young lad, but quite instructive.

The explanation may have been that it was the *way* that Joe used the gear rather than the gear itself (which gives rise to the question of why Joe bought new gear at all), but there is another possibility. According to Ted Fletcher: "His compressors at the time were American tube leveling amplifiers modified by Joe to decrease the attack and release times to get the heavy 'pumping' effects. He often spoke of the earlier Langevin' unit that Adrian Kerridge claims to still have, but the serious compression effects were achieved using various modified bits of Fairchild photoelectric compressors often fixed in tobacco tins with Selotape." Perhaps Joe's modifications resulted in the various compressors behaving very similarly, and it was merely the overall audio quality that improved rather than the actual sound of the units? [4]

Equalizers

Joe Meek's selection of outboard equalizers was also a combination of professional and homemade units. Dates of purchase are unclear, as they are only assigned to what are probably the homemade units. On the RGM Sound List a "tone control unit" is dated March 1963, and a "mid lift control" is dated to May of the same year. The auction list contains two EMI passive equalizers, models

843 and 844. Also listed is an IBC CU-3H (with power unit), which almost has to be an in-house engineered item, possibly dating from Meek's IBC days. The auction list also includes an Astrosonic response control unit *(see Fig. 7.29)*. This may be the "tone control unit" listed on the RGM Sound list. According to Ted Fletcher some of Joe's other EQs were "things in tobacco tins, with little inductors and capacitors soldered together."

Figure 7.29:
The Astronic Response Control Unit was a 9-band graphic equalizer with 13 dB of boost or cut at 40; 80; 160; 320; 640; 1,280; 2,560; 5,120; and 10,240 Hz. There is also a master gain reduction control with a range of 0 dB to off.

Delays and Modifications

We know that Joe used a three-head Vortexion recorder to produce tape delay. That's not to say that he didn't use any of his other three-head machines for that purpose when it suited his needs, but the Vortexion was dedicated exclusively to that application. There are also reports of his having used a Binson echo device (which records to a metal disc rather than tape), and even a Watkins Copicat, but neither appear on any equipment lists, or in any photographs. On this last point, however, keep in mind that in all likelihood there was a constant flow of equipment coming into and out of the studio. A piece of gear might be used once or twice, or for a week or a month, before being replaced by something else. There are only a few photographs of the control room at 304 Holloway, taken years apart, and three equipment lists—all of which offer no more than clues as to what was actually being used at the time. Real estate in the control room was clearly limited, and you can bet that Meek had *lots* more gear that he kept in other places, any piece of which might have been brought in briefly for some special purpose. Gear was also probably loaned to him, and he may even have received demos from manufacturers from time to time. [5]

Sidebar 7.3: The WEM Fifth Man

The WEM Fifth Man Unit was a collaboration between Charlie Watkins and Joe Meek, and it may have been the earliest attempt at creating a guitar synthesizer. It did not perform well, and never went into production. The controls on the unit are divided into two groups of eight pushbuttons, which are further divided into eight sub-groups. The row of labels along the top reads: On, Treble, Flute, FF, Bass Sax, Flute, FF, Treble Cut, Clarinet, Reed, Flute, FF, Horn, Trumpet, Salicet, and On. The group labels below the buttons are mostly "foot" markings (4', 12', 14', etc.) like those found on organs, possibly indicating that this was a guitar/organ device of some sort. The three non-foot groups are labeled Guitar, Effects, and Reverb.

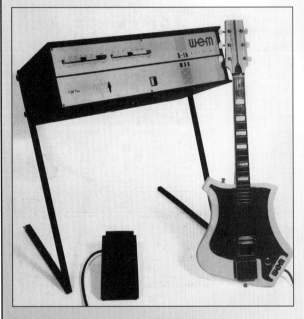

Figure 7.30: Product photo for the WEM Fifth Man Unit.

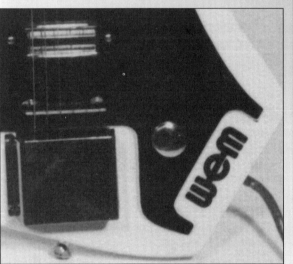

Figure 7.31: Detail of the guitar controller's bridge and pickups.

But even if it were possible to document Meek's gear, the information would be of no practical use in terms of recreating his "sound," because nearly everything had been modified to some extent, often drastically. "Three of his main pieces of equipment were his sine wave generator, his oscilloscope, and his soldering iron," proclaims Peter Miller. "Without those three Joe would never have been the man he was. He used them for adjusting and modifying his equipment, because he messed with everything. As soon as he got it, it came out of the box—he wanted to see what was in there and how he could make it different." "It literally looked like a workshop because nothing had its cover on," corroborates Ted Fletcher. "He never had the tops screwed on to anything; absolutely nothing. Everything was in chassis form, with the sides off or the top off; even the old EMI BTR2 machine was always operating with the amplifiers half pulled out, and the doors always open on the front. Always it looked like a collection of skeletons."

Meek's Mics and How He Used Them

When it comes to Meek's microphones we are on firmer ground. "The main microphones are two (Telefunken/Neumann) U47s. [6] I think this is a marvelous microphone, and I use it for all my vocalists. It has a very good characteristic for close work; that is for vocalists and instruments you need a lot of presence on. To help this I use a small piece of foam plastic; this stops pops and bangs when a vocalist is working close to it. I did have a stereo condenser mic, the Neumann SM2, but this has broken down on me. I believe it has a habit of doing this. First one side went, and then the other, and to be quite truthful I haven't mended it recently because it didn't stand out more than the other microphones I use. The others are AKG mics, the small microphones—dynamic types that are very popular today—I have about six of those. I have also a couple of Reslos: I use one on the bass drum, and one, sometimes for a vocal group, working on both sides of it. Really the microphones aren't all that expensive, but they're very efficient. Being such a small studio they're used very close to the instruments."

SM 2: The First Neumann Stereo Microphone. In the mid 1950's, the recording and broadcasting industries made major breakthroughs in the development of stereophonic sound recording and transmission. Neumann has supplied technical equipment to the recording industry since 1928, and in 1955 introduced a novel editing device for their industry standard disc cutters. In 1956, a cooperative venture with the record label TELDEC resulted in the first stereo disk cutter head ZS90/45. Although stereo records could not be made with two monaural disk cutter heads, the stereo program material, however, could be captured with two monaural microphones.

Figure 7.32:
Neumann SM2.

For example, for A-B stereo recordings two cardioid microphones can be set up at some distance from one another to record the left and right channels. When "Sender Freies Berlin" (Radio Free Berlin) conducted their first stereo test broadcast on December 26, 1958, the right and left channels were transmitted on two different FM frequencies, which could then be heard on two separate monaural FM receivers. Mono compatibility with stereo broadcasting was not achieved until 1963 with the introduction of the multiplex pilot tone system.

Full mono compatibility of recordings is only possible with intensity stereophony, where identical microphones are placed at virtually the same location, thus avoiding phase differences caused by different distances to the sound sources. In some of these coincident techniques the microphones may have different directional patterns. In other cases they have the same pattern, but are set up along the main axis pointing in different directions. To simplify this recording process, Neumann developed a single appropriate microphone.

Their latest miniature microphone at that time, the KM 56, possessed many features readily adaptable for use in the first Neumann stereo microphone. It has a small dual-diaphragm capsule, switchable to any of the three main directional patterns: omnidirectional, cardioid, or figure-8. In a stereo microphone two capsules of this type are mounted one above the other in a single head. Combined with two microphone amplifiers, placed alongside one another in a tube measuring only 30 mm in diameter, the SM 2 was created.

The power supply for the SM 2 features two rotary switches for adjusting the directional patterns of both channels independently to any of the three main patterns: omnidirectional, cardioid or figure-8. A further three intermediate settings can be selected, for a total of nine different patterns per element. In addition, the upper transducer can be rotated over a range of 270 degrees referenced against the lower capsule. The resulting microphone is ideal for the various types of intensity stereophony. For use as an X-Y microphone, identical (unidirectional) patterns are selected for both channels, and the recording "aperture" is controlled by the angle between upper and lower capsules against the main axis.

In M-S technology, the capsules are positioned with the patterns for the M-channel set to cardioid and on axis, while the S-channel is set to figure-8 and offset by 90 degrees. The cardioid microphone thus picks up the complete sound event exactly like the principal microphone for a monaural recording. All directional information is captured by the figure-8 pickup. In M-S stereo recording technology the two microphone outputs are combined in a matrix to form the sum and difference signals, which become the left and right channels.

True to its pedigree, the sound quality of the SM 2 is very similar to that of the KM56. It was produced between 1957 and 1966.

Even today, audio professionals consider it a "secret weapon" for piano recordings. *From the Georg Neumann Historical Archives (**www.neumann.com**). Reprinted by permission.*

U47: The Legend. For approximately 20 years Neumann had manufactured and sold throughout the world the condenser microphone CMV3, also known as the "Neumann-Bottle." Building on its success it became time to start something new. The cardioid M7 microphone capsule had been manufactured for many years with two equal diaphragms fixed on both sides of a perforated center electrode which is also provided with a number of cavities on both sides. One of the membranes is gold coated and thus electrically active. This membrane is directed towards the sound source.

The sound coming from the front causes movement of the front membrane and reaches the inner side of the rear membrane through the perforations in the electrode. The sound also reaches the outside of the rear membrane. The acoustic properties of the center electrode cause the forces acting on the rear membrane to be equal in size, but opposite in direction. Therefore, the rear membrane does not move and does not produce any electrical signal. For sound arriving from behind, the rear membrane moves and the front membrane does not. As a consequence, the microphone does not respond to rear sound, and the directional characteristic is cardioid. Both capsule halves thus act as a cardioid capsule and led Neumann to make the rear membrane electrically active by coating it with gold too. When connecting both cardioid halves in parallel, the capsule produces an omni directional pattern. If only one membrane is connected, the microphone works as described above as a cardioid.

The prerequisites for an easily switchable microphone with two directional characteristics were now fulfilled. A steel vacuum tube VF 14 M was selected for the impedance converter/amplifier, a pentode being operated as triode. The microphone was fed with one supply voltage only, from which the filament voltage was derived by means of a wire wound resistor inside the amplifier housing.

Figure 7:34:
The AKG D19E cardioid microphone was designed for semi-pro use. Joe's were designated D19/60, indicating that they were the 60 ohms impedance models.

Consequently the microphone itself produced a fair amount of heat, which may be partially responsible for its legendary longevity by providing a low humidity environment for the capsule. This was certainly not responsible for the "full, rich and warm sound" the U47 is famous for, a sound quality still highly regarded in our days. Many recording studios are proud to claim ownership of a working U47.

During the 1950's Neumann microphones also were sold through Telefunken, and carried the Telefunken logo. Thus the U47 was also known as the "Telly." It was reported about "The Voice," Frank Sinatra, that he wouldn't sing without his "Telly", the Neumann U47. From the Barclay Studios in Paris, which were technically supervised by Gerhard Lehner, we learned of people admiringly claiming: That's a microphone to drive nails into walls with. Whether this is understood literally or figuratively, it is a compliment for the U47 either way! *From the Georg Neumann Historical Archives (**www.neumann.com**). Reprinted by permission.*

Figure 7.35: AKG D19C microphone. Another example from the D19 series.

AKG ELAM 250: The AKG ELAM 250 microphone was introduced in 1959. When Neumann withdrew the distribution of its U47 microphone from Telefunken, the company commissioned AKG to develop a large-diaphragm tube condenser microphone. The design incorporated the capsule from AKG's CK-12 microphone, and featured a two-pattern selector switch (cardioid and omnidirectional). The ELAM model 251 added a third (bidirectional) pattern. The "E" designation indicates export, and the export models utilized a different amplifier type than the domestic German models. Joe owned the domestic versions of both the 250 (mistakenly listed as "950" on the Auction List) and the 251. Both models are among the most sought after and expensive vintage tube microphones on the market today.

Figure 7.36: The AKG ELAM 250.

Regarding the vocal mic and the "small piece of foam plastic," Ted Fletcher recalls: "The vocal mic, which was stuck in one place always—it was fixed in the same place—was suspended on a huge, great industrial mic stand. And the U47 was swathed in foam rubber, until the head of the mic was actually as big as a football. It was swathed in pop shields, and the approved method was to sing so that your nose was just about touching the pop shield. You get a very close, present sound, and that's how he did it."

Figure 7.37:
Reslo VR microphone.

When it came to miking other instruments Joe's aim was to maintain as much isolation as possible, which meant putting the mics in close, and blocking extraneous sounds. (Besides blocking out the sounds of other instruments, he also had to block less musical sounds, like large trucks going by outside, the phone ringing, and neighbors banging on the wall!) "He was fanatical about separation," says Fletcher. "Although he couldn't get good separation really, he was pretty fanatical about it." When recording electric bass guitar he didn't use any microphones at all, making him one of the earliest—perhaps *the* earliest— engineers to "direct inject" the bass. "I feed the electric bass through an equalizer unit. On this unit I experimented and I feed the output back. It's possible to get feedback this way, but when put through a choke it gives you the effect of a string being plucked. This sounds effective on recordings. I don't always use it, but on the Outlaws records for instance, I have used it."

Figure 7.38:
Reslo VTL microphone.

Meek's drum miking technique was also quite unusual for the time. According to Peter Miller: "He'd often use a Reslo on the bass drum, which now I realize…how did he get away with that; a ribbon mic? Maybe he just put new ribbons in every morning when he had his coffee *(laughs)*. He always used that Reslo on the bass drum, and he used an AKG on the snare, and an AKG on the overhead. Or occasionally maybe a U47 on the overs. But he never used more than three mics on the drums. And this was new—I'd never seen any other engineer do this: he would put a big blanket right across the front of the drums, draped actually on the drums, and tape it to the tom toms, with the mic between the blanket and the drum. I told you he was goofy! But he got great drum sounds." When asked if he too remembered miking the bass drum with a Reslo, Ted Fletcher replied: "Yes, but not the normal Reslo. There was a Reslo type that was used for PA— like for factory announcements—and he had one of those. It was so heavily padded that there was no way that you could have damaged the ribbon by putting it in front of a bass drum. It was a type of Reslo that was almost indestructible." Close miking the bass drum, and even covering it with a blanket, became common several years later—but both men believe that the technique originated with Joe Meek. Meek also close-miked and put blankets over guitar amps. "Usually a Vox AC-30, recorded with an AKG D19 rammed up against the front, and a large blanket thrown over the whole thing," says Fletcher.

Other microphones that Joe had collected by 1967 included a Western Electric cardioid; an RCF (sic) variable impedance; an

RCA dynamic; an HMV 235CH ribbon; and Telefunken NSH, ELAM 251, and ELAM 950 models. Fletcher also recalls there being a pair of Grampian ribbon mics, but he doesn't recall Joe actually using them on anything.

Figure 7.39:
An array of vintage Reslo, AKG, and STC microphones, with five brands of recording tape: Scotch Dynarange 202, Agfa Magnetonband PER 525, Ampex Mastering, Scotch 206, and Racal-Zonal RZ.

Photo by and courtesy of John O'Kill

Besides recording the usual rhythm section and lead vocals, Meek routinely worked with string sections, brass, and vocal "choirs" consisting of two to four vocalists. "The method I use for recording strings is to have a microphone pretty close to them. The four of them sit two opposite each other, and then I delay the signal with the (third) head of the Vortexion. I feed this back in again which adds a reflection that gives you eight strings. On this, I put my echo-chamber sound and also some of my electronic echo: this way I seem to get a very big string sound. The other instruments are recorded pretty ordinarily. I do add quite a lot of top (high frequencies) to the harp, and a lot of echo on the French horn.

"When I first started recording here, I used to get a lot of leg-pulls from the musicians, who are top musicians, often playing in, say, Mantovani's orchestra, and classical orchestras—really the cream of the musicians. They used to come in, look around, and say, 'Where do you want me? Am I supposed to be in the bathroom?' But after they've heard a playback, I don't usually get any more criticism. They realize what presence there is on their instruments, and that they've really got to be on form or it'll show up in the recording."

Sidebar 7-4: Joe Meek's Main Equipment

The following list is a composite of items found on the Auction List (set in regular type) and the RGM Sound List (set in italics).

AUCTION LIST/*RGM Sound List with purchase dates*

Recorders

EMI TR50 (9/60)

EMI TR51 (9/60)

Lyrec TR16 twin-track, with two electronic units *AR2 (9/60)*

Vortexion (9/62)

EMI BTR 2 *(2/63)*

Ampex Model 300 *50 c/s (3/63)*

Ampex Model 351/2 P portable twin-track, with electronic unit

Ampex PR10 twin-track

Concert portable tape recorder

"Stereo recorder" (1/64)

Mixers

"Mixer unit" Meek's homemade 4-Channel

Vortexion WVB 4/15/M 4-Channel *(9/62)*

"6-Channel Stereo Mixer" *(7/64)*

FM Tuners

Lowther

Preamplifiers

RCA LM1/322 15A

RCA Orthophonic Hi-fi amp/filter/pre-amp

Dyna PAS/2 (USA) stereo

(3) Quad

Power Amplifiers

(4) Quad

Lee Products AC88 amplifier

RCA Model LM1/322 16 (incomplete)

(2) Dyna

(2) "A power amplifier"

Sagatone stereo

Monitor Speakers

(2) Tannoy Lockwoods

(2) Tannoy corner speakers

"A corner loudspeaker"

BTH loudspeaker

(2) Dallas column speakers

National loudspeaker for tape recorder

Compressors

Altec 438A compressor amp *(3/63)*

Altec 436B compressor amp (3/63)

Fairchild 661 auto ten (9/63)

(2) Fairchild 673 Dynalisers *(9/63) (1/64)*

Fairchild 655

Limiters

Dyna

Fairchild 663 compact compressor (9/63)

Fairchild 660 (9/63)

Reverb

Fairchild 658 Spring Reverb (control unit and spring unit)

EQ

"Tone control unit" (3/63)

"Mid lift control" (5/63)

IBC CU-3H, with power unit

EMI 843 passive

EMI 844 passive

Astrosonic response control unit

Patchbay

EMI 755/1 60-Patch Panel

Microphones

Telefunken NSH condenser and amp

Telefunken ELAM 251 with amp

Telefunken ELAM 950 with amp [sic; a type for 250]

Telefunken SM2

(2) Neumann U47s and amps

HMV 235CH ribbon

AKG D19/60 (9/62)

Western Electric cardiod (sic) ribbon (9/62)

(2) Reslosound ribbon (9/62)

RCF variable impedance

RCA dynamic

Beyer M61 (3/64)

Beyer M23 (3/64)

Keyboards

Selmar (sic) Pianotron

Clavioline w/stand

Lowrey 2-Manual electronic organ, with 13-note vamp board

Honky Tonk mini upright piano

Musical Instruments

Hohner Granton Glockenspeil

WEM Fifth Man unit

Instrument Amplifiers/Speakers

Selmar (sic) amp/spkr.

WEM twin loudspeaker cab

A similar spkr. cabinet

WEM GR 6QH amp/spkr.

WEM AR cool6 amp/twin spkr.

WEM Starfinder Series spkr.

(2) WEM chrome spkr stands

Univox (Jennings Organ Co.) amp/keyboard loudspeaker

Test/Maintenance Equipment

Range Trecoscope oscilloscope

(2) Advance oscillators J1 and E2

EMI tape head degauzor

Grayshaw valve milli volt meter

Ferrograph De-fluxer

Disc Cutters

MSS disc cutter

Simon Sound Services disc lathe

Ferranti disc cutter (9/62)

Power Equipment

Cintel 117-volt auto transformer

(2) Shipton isolating transformers 240/20/20/40 (1 auto/1 man)

12v-100v-250v out DC Converter

Gardino auto transformers

Misc.

G.E.C. 3-kw fan heater

(6) microphone stands (booms)

Swell foot pedal

(3) AKG headphones

(2) 19" rack units, one with "mixer and patch board panel"

Conniseur Hi-fi gramafone

Metro Sound recording heads (5/64)

Mystery

Morcom WQ 4572 EDA combining unit

EMI 807 and EMI Power Pack 807 3x line amps

"Correction unit" (7/63)

Tape Editing

One of the most important editing and compositional tools in Meek's production arsenal was the razor blade. He did an exceptional amount of tape editing to come up with final versions of many of his songs. Besides simply trying to patch together an acceptable version of a song, he might want to employ hard tape editing for other reasons. For example, he might splice if he wanted to use a lot of overdubs in one or two short sections such as an intro or a bridge, without reducing the overall sonic quality of the recording. He might also want to use dramatically different sounds in two sections, using different processing, in which case he would record the parts separately and edit them together later. Ted Fletcher says that he, his brother, and his brother's wife often worked that way.

Another thing Joe used his razor blade for—besides shaving, which he is said to have done up to six times a day—was making tape loops. Fletcher recalls: "Yes, there were 30 or 40 (tape loops) hung on nails on the wall, five or six loops per nail. They weren't labeled." The loops contained short bits of sound, or musical phrases, which would be added to recordings wherever appropriate. This reinforces Meek's connection with the French tape composers; links him to Brian Eno, Robert Fripp, and other seventies tape loopers; and makes him the Great-Grandfather of the loop-based musics of today, including electronica, rap, and hip-hop.

[1] **The high-speed Model 300 was technically referred to as a Model 301.**

[2] **Phillips acquired the Ampex machines in 1954. Tape recordings made previous to that were made on a Presto 900-P recorder made in New Jersey. He also originally used a Presto five-input mixer, replaced in 1955 with an RCA 76-D broadcast console.**

[3] **Included on the auction list are "Morcom WQ 4572 EDA combining unit," and "EMI 807 3x line amps," but there is no indication as to when they were in use.**

[4] **Kerridge does indeed have Joe's original modified compressor/limiter, and he was good enough to provide a photograph of it.**

[5] **For example, the Tornados endorsed WEM amplifiers and were provided with free units.**

[6] **The same microphone used by Norman Petty to record Buddy Holly's vocals. Petty also sometimes used it to record guitar and as a drum overhead. Petty used a Stevens "tie" microphone, placed inside the f-hole, to record the upright bass; RCA 77s and 44s on the kick drum; and an Electro-Voice RE15 on the snare drum.**

CHAPTER 8

Telstar

The first day of 1962 did not go well for the Beatles. When John Lennon told Dick Rowe at Decca Records that on behalf of himself and the band he hoped they'd passed the audition, he was no doubt disappointed to find that they had not. Legend has it that the group was turned down by nearly everyone in London, and another legend has it that Joe Meek was one of those who turned them down. Whether the story is true or not, trying to imagine what a Meek/Beatles collaboration would have sounded like is an enjoyable exercise. To begin with, Joe probably would have tried to change their name to something he considered more "commercial."

After sending the Beatles packing Joe got back to recording artists like Don Charles, Danny Rivers and the Rivermen, Tony Victor, Alan Klein, and Andy Cavell. By this time the Outlaws had developed a following and were touring a lot, which made them increasingly unavailable to serve as Joe's studio band. In their place Meek hired guitarist Alan Caddy and drummer Clem Cattini (from Johnny Kidd and the Pirates), along with rhythm guitarist George Bellamy, and bassist Heinz Burt. Organist Norm Hale joined the team just long enough to cut one side, and was then replaced by Roger LaVern. Besides backing Meek's artists, the band became pop star Billy Fury's backing band, and also made records under their own name, the Tornados. [1] "Love And Fury," the Tornados' first record, featured some super-compressed tracks and a great over-the-top solo guitar sound using heavy delay and reverb. It bombed, but the band would have considerably better luck next time.

Meek's recordings from the first half of 1962 fall roughly into three categories: full-blown productions, usually ballads, with orchestration, heavenly choir, and sometimes brass; straight rock and roll songs; and strange hybrids of the two. Don Charles's "Walk with Me My Angel" (which charted at #39),"It's My Way of Loving You," and "Moonlight Rendezvous" fall easily into the first category; while his "Lucky Star" and "The Hermit of Misty Mountain" fall into the third. Danny Rivers and the Rivermen's "Movin' In" (written by Dave Adams) falls squarely into the second category, as do unreleased tracks by the Scorpions.

On the rock and roll records, Joe seemed to be going for an American sound, and Tony Victor's cover of the American hit "Dear One" nearly pegs it. The song features an uncharacteristically rocking rhythm track by the Tornados, with "girl" backing vocals, strings, and jaw harp(!). Though bassist Heinz was to be Meek's "answer" to Eddie Cochran, Tony Victor captures Cochran's spirit and energy in a way that Heinz, as he later came to be known, seldom if ever would. Altogether different were the Dowlands and the Soundtracks, who played rock and roll with country touches, particularly on their cover of "I Walk the Line." Meek would venture further down country lane later in the year with a *real* country singer—from England via Canada. During this period Meek also continued to release records by the Outlaws, Ian Gregory, John Leyton, and Mike Berry. Gregory's "Can't You Hear the Beat of a Broken Heart" went to #39 with more than a little help from Dave Adams, who actually sang the song—Gregory's voice is mixed in with Adams'. Leyton had two chart entries, "Lone Rider" at #40, and "Lonely City" at #14.

Outside the confines of 304 Holloway Road things were definitely up in the air. In February of 1962 John Glenn became the first American astronaut to orbit the Earth, three months later a laser beam was successfully bounced off the Moon, and two weeks after that Scott Carpenter orbited the Earth three times. In September ABC Television would debut its first color television series: an animated spoof on the Space Age called *The Jetsons*— but some truly spacey television had already taken place just two months earlier.

On the tenth of July in 1962 an event took place that for many signaled the beginning of the Telecommunications Age. The

American Telephone & Telegraph Company—using communications technology developed at Bell Labs, and a NASA Delta launch vehicle—placed the Telstar 1 satellite into orbit. Telstar 1 was only one of dozens of satellites that had been developed and launched since the Russians began the Space Race with Sputnik 1 in 1957, but it had a special destiny: it was to facilitate the first transatlantic television transmission via satellite. [2]

Figure 8.1:
The Telstar satellite before launch.

The transmission took place on Wednesday, July 11. Signals were bounced between stations in France and England on one side of the Atlantic, and America on the other. Viewers in North America and Europe watched spellbound as first AT&T Chairman Fred Kappel spoke to American Vice President Lyndon Johnson, and then a television image appeared out of a cloud of static. American president John F. Kennedy, foreseeing the event's implications, issued the following statement: "The successful firing and subsequent operation of the Telstar communications satellite is an outstanding example of the way in which government and business can cooperate in a most important field of human endeavor. The achievement of the communications satellite, while only a prelude, already throws open to us the vision of an era of international communications. There is no more important field at the present time than communications and we must grasp the advantages presented to us by the communications satellite to use this medium wisely and effectively to insure greater understanding among the peoples of the world." [3]

Kennedy admirer and former television technician and RAF radar man Joe Meek was also excited by what he had seen. He decided that he would compose a song in honor of the occasion and call it "The Theme of Telstar." Joe could hear the melody for the main theme in his head, but as usual he employed his typical method of composing: "singing" over a pre-existing backing track—often in an entirely unrelated key—with no apparent awareness of, or at least regard for, harmonic relationships. At least one of Joe's first Telstar demos is extant—over the backing track for "Try Once More"—and though it is obvious why people laughed at Joe's singing, it is also obvious that he knew exactly what he wanted to sing, but was simply unable to produce the pitches.

In Meek biographer John Repsch's account of the story [4] Joe worked on the song to no avail until he went to bed, where after sleeping for a short time he awakened and lay thinking about the satellite. Suddenly a tune came to him and he got back up and recorded a demo of it—perhaps the very demo previously referred to. The next day he got Dave Adams to help him work out the melody on a keyboard, again playing over a pre-recorded backing track. Once the song had taken shape sufficiently Joe booked the Tornados, who came into the studio on the following Sunday morning and recorded the basic rhythm tracks for both "Telstar" and the flipside, "Jungle Fever."

Repsch interviewed Tornados drummer Clem Cattini, who had this to say: "Joe played the demo a few times and then Alan [Caddy] worked out the chord sequences. Joe wanted a moving rhythm; he sang the beat—like dum-diddy-dum—and imitated the guitar sound and bass, and then we just kicked it about and he'd direct each individual into the shape he wanted it to go. He knew what he was after but if someone did something he liked he'd say, 'Keep that, I like it.' Then he'd say, 'Right, that's it up to there,' and it went on like that until it was more or less ready. Then he'd record it and change a few things here and there. I played the basic beat with brushes on the cymbals and it was almost exactly the same as 'Johnny Remember Me' and 'Wild Wind.'" The Sunday session lasted twelve hours, and the group returned for a few additional hours the following morning, before having to leave for a gig. On Monday morning they recorded some guitar overdubs on "Telstar," but they didn't have a chance to record the main melody.

That's when Geoff Goddard arrived. "I got there just as the Tornados were finishing off the backing track and they were going to a booking in Great Yarmouth. I then spent about five hours working on 'Telstar' for him. I played a little organ that was fixed to the side of the piano [the Clavioline]. It was triple-tracked in the end, with harp-like chords on the piano to go over the guitar break. I also added a vocal sound at the end to give it more body. In a big studio, an engineer would be restricted in what he did: a piano would have to sound like a piano and a guitar like a guitar. The sound would be spaced out and you would get a good, clean recorded sound. Meek wanted none of that. He would go over the top and mix all the sounds up, pumping them through different amps and coming up with a mushy sound that would lead to hands being raised in horror in a major studio." [5]

Dave Adams relates the story slightly differently: "'Telstar' was born at a late night demo session with just Joe and myself. In his inimitable way he sang the melody in the usual, atrociously out-of-tune caterwaul into my right ear while I tried for a very long time to get what he heard into the keys, without it sounding like the second line in Rule Britannia. I heard 'No No Noooo' many times that night, almost as many times as I heard different mixes and arrangements of the original 'Telstar.' The following weekend the Tornados came up from Yarmouth and laid down a rhythm track and established the chords with a basic melody played by Roger on his Vox (or was it a Farfisa?). They left to go back to their gig feeling they had just recorded a piece of shit, which was the general consensus of most of us. Following that Geoff played the Clavioline and piano, then I the Lowrey and piano. Various other musicians came in and did little things on it in the next few days and finally Joe took it and worked his sound effects and mixing magic and we heard what you hear now."

Adams says that the demo was in the key of G, but that after attempting to fit it onto various backing tracks, it wound up in A. Joe sped up the recording just slightly, so that on the record it is pitched just below B-flat. Sheet music for the song has it in B-flat, because it was transcribed from the record.

There are several drum tracks: fast brushed hi-hats, medium hi-hats, and probably a kit drum set with kick and snare, but they are buried so far back in the layers of overdubs as to be almost indistinguishable from all of the other low mid-frequency sounds. The occasional cymbal crash suggests their presence. The hat tracks were probably overdubbed, or recorded loud so that they would still cut several more dubs in. There seem to be two bass tracks, one playing half as fast as the other, but once again it is hard to distinguish what's going on in the low mid-range, as there also seem to be some low piano notes. The bass line itself is a variation on a standard country and western line.

Geoff Goddard's piano playing follows the chords, but with romantic flourishes characteristic of his style. During the B section he provides harmonic support for Alan Caddy's guitar line by playing harp-like arpeggios in the higher registers, and once the tape was sped up the resulting sound was reminiscent of an autoharp. The piano also plays the melody, but it is very faint. The guitars play simple chords throughout, strummed quickly, except for the lead guitar in the B sections. Caddy played a Gibson ES 335 TD Blonde through a Vox AC30 amplifier.

The Clavioline is obviously the primary lead instrument in the A section, and layering it three times created the same fat sound that a three-oscillator analog synthesizer gets with the oscillators tuned three octaves apart and tied together. One big difference, however, is that each Clavioline overdub was played with a slightly different articulation—not to mention the instrument's natural tendency to glissando into the initial attack of the note. It is these interesting ornaments that give the otherwise simplistic melody its charm and character, and the personality that comes through is largely Goddard's. The Lowrey organ is in there too, and only Joe knows what else. During the final A section Geoff Goddard sings along with the keyboards, adding a human touch to the electronic blend.

The sounds that open and close the record have been the source of much speculation, and Joe is said to have taunted people by daring them to guess how they were made. Several people have said they believe that the sound of a toilet being flushed and played backwards is part of the collage. Perhaps, but if you simply play the recording in reverse you will be hard pressed to identify a toilet sound. Almost all of the sounds were produced the same way as those found on *I Hear a New World,* and in fact some of the same tapes may have been used, as they are quite similar. Meek begins with different sound sources, none of which can be precisely identified by listening because he never presents them in their original forms. He feeds them into his spring reverb and his tape delay, with the regeneration on the delay up so high that it immediately goes into self-oscillation. Much of what you hear is the sound made by the recorder/delay unit itself, not the source sound used to trigger it. He also gets the "spring" sound—not the signal passing through the spring, the actual spring itself—by knocking against it. Joe's now-familiar electronic "tapping" sound, which may be the test oscillator, puts in a cameo appearance as well. These sounds were all edited together and then played in reverse. Anyone who has ever plugged a microphone into a tape delay set on high regeneration and played around with plosives and other vocal sounds will understand the basic principle. [6]

The song embodied the youthful and optimistic outlook that was the Gestalt of the time. "Telstar" (its shortened title) served as an archetypal anthem for a world poised on the brink of the Space Age—a time of miracles where anything might be possible. It also provided a respite from the ever-present horrors of the Atomic Age, and the apocalyptic destruction that might be released at any moment. Somehow Joe Meek managed to capture what people were feeling all over the world in a three minute and fifteen second song. By September "Telstar" had topped the charts in England, and would go on to become the best-selling instrumental in the country's history. Three months later it became the first record by a British group to top the American charts, beating the Beatles to that distinction by a year. [7] "Telstar" sailed into high positions on charts throughout the world, and dozens of cover versions were recorded.

Figure 8.2:
The U.S. release of "Telstar."

"Telstar" was backed with "Jungle Fever," a Geoff Goddard tune that is not as strong melodically as most of his compositions, but features some very interesting keyboard figures nearly buried in the mix, and some nice dampened drumming from Clem Cattini. The "jungle" noises are intriguing, and sound almost like slowed-down bird sounds. Joe supposedly kept a parakeet up in his bedroom, and it's not hard to imagine him recording it. There are also little bits of keyboard sounds tossed in, with delay, for spice.

Figure 8.3:
There were hundreds of cover versions of "Telstar" released worldwide. This one, by Bud Ashton (1962), is particularly obscure.

With "Telstar" topping the charts worldwide Joe laid plans for an EP, an LP, and a follow-up single. There were also offers for an American tour, including television appearances. But the

Tornados were locked into their deal as Billy Fury's backing band, and the only limelight they enjoyed onstage was a three-minute spot quickly performing their hit before falling back into the shadows behind Fury. There had already been a power struggle between Joe and Fury's manager when Joe (according to one version of the story) convinced the band's bassist to bleach his hair white, making him look like one of the children in the movie "Village of the Damned." The White Tornado, as Heinz was sometimes called, drew some of the attention of teenage girls away from Billy Fury, if but momentarily, and was therefore perceived as a threat.

Figure 8.4:
Another "Telstar" cover, this one by The Tides.

Joe Meek was clearly fascinated with Heinz, and shortly after their first meeting the lad moved into 304 Holloway Road, where he lived for several years. Heinz always denied that he and Joe had an intimate relationship, but few people were fooled. Joe was madly in love with him, and he had decided that the boy was a suitable candidate for "star" treatment. After all, most of the band's fan mail was for him, so there must be *something* about him other than his hair color that they liked. Whatever it was, it certainly wasn't his bass playing, which was marginal at best. Before long Joe would convince Heinz to break away from the Tornados and embark on a solo career— one that Joe felt sure would make him the next Cliff Richard, if not the next Elvis.

But in the meantime there were records to be made, and Joe made quite a few, many with the Tornados providing the backing tracks. "Three Coins in the Sewer," by songwriter/singer/comedian Alan Klein, opens with the sound of coins hitting a sidewalk and plopping into a sewer. Meek had Klein drop coins first into a bucket of water (from high enough up to get a good splash), and then onto the sidewalk outside the studio to get the basic sounds that were then combined to produce the effect. In a variation on the story it's marbles in the sink and coins in a bucket, but however it was accomplished the result is convincing.

Mike Berry's "Don't You Think It's Time" was more of the same for him (though it went to #6 in January of 1963), but the flipside, "Loneliness," is a moody masterpiece full of dark atmosphere. Joe wrote the lyrics, which are a far cry from his usual pop pap and arguably among his best. Another Holly-inspired disc was by Carter-Lewis and the Southerners, who emphasized the country elements of Holly's work.

Figure 8.5:
"Don't You Think It's Time"
by Mike Berry.

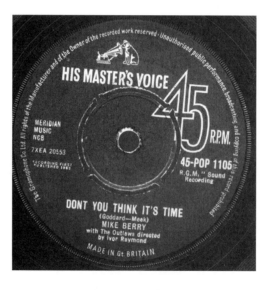

Joe had always been a country and western fan—he loved Hank Williams, Sr.—and though he had fooled around with some country-flavored ditties by the Outlaws, Silas Dooley (Dave Adams), and others, he got serious about it when he signed Houston Wells and the Marksmen. Wells (Andy Smith) was an Englishman, but had begun singing country and western while living in Canada. Meek recorded 29 songs by Houston Wells, most of them backed by the Marksmen, but several of the later ones backed by the Outlaws. There was an LP, an EP, and six or seven singles. A few of Houston's songs actually made the British pop charts, which was no mean feat in the early '60s.

Some Meek writers have said that the Houston Wells recordings are also remarkable for their lack of typical "RGM Sound" elements. I'm not sure what they mean, as the recordings feature the same up-front mic sound and use of compression, EQ, and ambient effects that characterize nearly all of Meek's recordings. In fact "North Wind," which Meek wrote, is really a country and western "Telstar." It has the same rolling hi-hats, bouncing bass line, ethereal atmosphere, and even a beautiful Alan Caddy-style guitar break in the middle.

Figure 8.6: "North Wind" by Houston Wells.

Wells and the Marksmen's first release, "Only the Heartaches," has a classic 3/4 country lope to it, and the vocal harmonies definitely convey an authentic "high and lonesome" sound, but the music combines staccato string-mute guitar lines (gurgling with slap-back delay), choppy acoustic rhythm guitar, and bouncy British Pop-style strings. The sound mixing job is simply breathtaking, particularly the handling of the voices. The harmony vocals are extraordinarily rich and warm sounding, surging forward and falling back at precisely the right moments. There is even a brief bit of Lissa Gray's soaring soprano. From a technical standpoint, this largely overlooked record is one of Meek's finest recordings. Also, no country and western band would be complete without a lap-steel guitar, and the Marksmen's Pete Willsher played with real feeling, and used either the volume knob on his instrument or a volume pedal to get some very smooth fade-in effects. "Only the Heartaches" opens with an unaccompanied voice, bathed in several types of echo, delay, and reverb—you can even hear the reverb springs twang a little at one point—affording a rare opportunity to hear a single sound source in what is effectively "solo" mode in mixing terms.

The second half of 1962 also saw more discs by Leyton, the Outlaws, and Mike Berry with the Outlaws, all in basically the same mold as previous releases. One record worth noting is Mark Douglas's "It Matters Not," a classic early 304 effort with all the trappings: Ivor Raymonde's strings, Lissa Gray and the heavenly choir, and a snappy rhythm track by the Tornados. Douglas (Billy Gray) actually sings pretty well, too. The song also features what sounds like a contrabass clarinet (or a large sax) playing tasty lines here and there, and some well-placed Glockenspiel notes. Ironically humorous lyrics by Mike Leander round out a nice package. On the other end of the scale was a pathetic vocal version of "Telstar" called "Magic Star," sung by a 15-year-old boy sporting the name Kenny Hollywood. Fortunately, it never got off the ground.

There were also a number of instrumentals: some garden-variety stuff by the Chaps, jazzy numbers by the Packabeats, and a surprise hit called "Can Can 62" by the highly underrated Peter Jay and the Jaywalkers. Jaywalkers guitarist Peter Miller recalls: "My band was signed to Decca records in 1962, and they appointed Joe as our producer. We cut our first record at Decca, not at Joe's place. Joe was so unhappy with the sound he got there with our first record—although it got into the charts and was a minor hit—he refused to work there anymore. He told Decca that he was going to do all the other work that he was appointed producer for at his place."

When asked what it was that Meek didn't like about the sound Miller clarified: "It wasn't so much the sound as the fact that he was working with engineers who, in those days, wore white uniforms like hospital overalls, right? They were scientists, essentially; they were boffins. And they had this boffiny attitude, and upstart Joe came in there and wanted to do all sorts of strange things by, you know, turning compressors upside down and putting them in the bath, and they totally freaked out and wouldn't let him do that. You'd see them flailing away at each other in the control room's glass window. He persevered with that first recording of ours, and did get it finished; but he told us afterwards that we were not doing any more at Decca, that we'd do the rest at his place. And from then on we worked at Holloway Road. We did about eight sides that were released, plus about ten or twelve that came out later on compilations. These were mostly instrumentals; we were an instrumental band at that time. We turned into a vocal band after a couple of years when the Beatles and Stones got famous and made more money than we did."

"Can Can 62" went to #31 in early November. Three weeks earlier a number called "Love Me Do" had made it to #17. There were still lots of songs on the charts by the likes of Cliff Richard, Billy Fury, and the Shadows. Records by Little Richard, Jerry Lee Lewis, the Four Seasons, and the Crystals were arriving from America—but the Beatles had fired the first serious shot in what would come to be called the British Invasion.

[1] **The name is also spelled *Tornadoes* on many recordings.**

[2] **Little Richard experienced a fiery dream about Sputnik 1, and when an airplane engine caught fire while he was flying over Australia in 1958—while on tour with Gene Vincent and Eddie Cochran—Richard prayed for his life, and upon touching down safely proceeded to renounce rock and roll and attend divinity school, where he remained until 1962.**

[3] **Three days before the launch of Telstar the American military had conducted a high-altitude nuclear test called Starfish, and the satellite's orbit took it through the radiation left behind by the test. Four months later the Russians increased the radiation levels with a test of their own, which caused some of Telstar 1's transistors to fail. A temporary workaround kept the unit operating for an additional two months.**

[4] *Legendary* pg. 152

[5] *Halfway #533*

[6] In fact, in an article in the *New Music Express* published in November 1962, Meek states that the "in orbit" sounds were created by blowing into a microphone connected to a tape delay.

[7] Four records by individual artists had topped the American charts previously, one in 1952, another in 1958, and two more before "Telstar" in 1962.

Beat by the Beat

As 1963 got underway, Joe Meek was at his peak. "Telstar" had sold its second million, and Joe was scanning the horizon for another chart-topper. In January the Tornados released their follow-up record, but "Globetrotter" met with more modest success, rising to #5 on the British charts. The song had a different melody than "Telstar," but was structured almost exactly the same way, and used basically the same combinations of instruments. Two months later, "Robot," which opened and closed with the sproing of a plucked reverb spring, reached #17. The Tornados would see their final chart action for 1963 in June, when "The Ice Cream Man" would go to #18 before melting down. There would be no more major hits for the Tornados once "Telstar" finally returned to earth. Nonetheless, the Tornados would continue to record for Joe Meek for three more years, though their lineup would change several times.

The first person to leave the group was Heinz. After grooming him for months, Joe felt that Heinz was ready to become the next Big Thing, and he arranged a coordinated media blitz coinciding with the release of Heinz's first disc, "Dreams Do Come True." Heinz was even booked on a tour opening for Gene Vincent and Jerry Lee Lewis, with the Outlaws as his backing band. (The Outlaws didn't care for Heinz, but they agreed to take the gig when Joe bought them a lot of new equipment.) Unfortunately, Joe had arranged it so that Heinz was filming during the days and performing the same evenings, which over-taxed him. Also, Heinz was at that time a very inexperienced performer with a less than fabulous voice, and his show was geared to teenage girls. The mostly male leather-clad Lewis and Vincent fans wanted no part of his teen idol performance, and let him know it. Heinz and Joe's worst nightmare came true instead of their dreams.

Meanwhile, "Please Please Me" by the Beatles had gone to #2 in January, and in mid-April "From Me to You" topped the charts, establishing the Fab Four as a power to be reckoned with. Gerry and the Pacemakers had also scored a #1 with "How Do You Do It," and were set to repeat that performance with "I Like It" in May. In June the Searchers would top the charts with "Sweets For My Sweet," and in July the Rolling Stones would get to #21 with "Come On." The Beat Boom Express was definitely steaming out of Liverpool Station and everyone in Britain was desperately trying to get onboard. Everyone, that is, except Joe Meek.

Joe was convinced that the trend wouldn't last, as he made clear in public statements. He even complained about there being a glut of Beat Boom records in the marketplace, most of which were not very good, making it hard for him and other purveyors of more substantial music to sell their products. He would damn well continue making records the way he always had until the whole thing blew over, which shouldn't take very long. And he made some *great* records in 1963; it was, in fact, his most prolific period.

He had made a tidy bundle on "Telstar" and his other hits so he was able to buy some important new equipment, including EMI BTR2 and Ampex 300 tape recorders. After the first quarter of the year his recordings took on a new clarity, and he was able to attempt even more ambitious recording tricks without the fear of ending up with a muffled mess. However, the "Telstar" money stopped flowing in May when the song became the subject of a bizarre lawsuit, wherein Meek was accused of plagiarizing a French film score written by composer Jean Ledrut. Once the suit began, all revenue from "Telstar" was held in reserve pending the outcome, and though the record had sold over three million copies by that time, Joe never saw more than a tiny fraction of what was owed him. The suit would eventually be resolved in his favor, but not until many months after his death.

As a quick glance at Meek's discography for 1963 will confirm, he released over seventy-five records that year—and he made many more recordings that were never released. Joe worked around the clock, day after day, week after week, month after month. The styles of music represented span a huge range, from the pure pop of Gerry Temple's snappy "Angel Face," to Screaming Lord Sutch's horror-infused "Jack the Ripper," and from the countryish "San Francisco Bay" by Burr Bailey (Dave Adams) and the Six Shooters to Pamela Blue's delightful version of Geoff Goddard's death disc "My Friend Bobby." An entire book could be written about Meek's output in 1963, but the following songs are some of the more interesting ones from an engineering and production viewpoint:

Figure 9.1:
"My Friend Bobby"

"I Lost My Heart at the Fairground" by Glenda Collins features location recorded "fairground" sounds (including what sounds a lot like an actual calliope), strings, backing vocals, and a masterful job of mixing them with the rhythm and vocal tracks into a seamless whole. Collins was a very good vocalist, and Joe recorded her many times. In fact, it is quite likely that he intended to release an entire album of her songs.

"The Spy" by the Original Checkmates features a very early use of what was to become a popular organ sound, and a *huge* bass sound. There is also what sounds like compressed echo added towards the end. This is a particularly full-sounding mix, and foreshadows Joe's later work.

"March of the Spacemen" by the Thunderbolts is one of Joe's many "Telstar" knockoffs, and is filled with interesting sounds and textures, including a rocket taking off at the beginning. It is done in the old style, but combines the pounding beat associated with Joe's later work, with the usual galloping hi-hats.

"Midgets" by the Saints is an instrumental that sounds a lot like Les Paul's "multiples" recordings, including the sped-up guitars. Even the guitar tone and arrangement are reminiscent of Paul's work. The song also has sped-up "midget" voices at the end, however, something Paul would *never* have done. Compare this to Paul's "Lover" and other early hits. The Saints also had a minor hit with a cover of "Wipeout."

"Order of the Keys" by Sounds Incorporated is a sax and twangy guitar number in the Jaywalkers/Flee-Rakkers mold. It is notable for the very odd delay and envelope filter effect used on the guitar.

"Powercut" by the Cameos is a perfect example of what happens when a song is sped-up more than a little bit too much. Speeding up entire songs was one of Joe's favorite tricks, but in this case he pushed it to the point of absurdity.

"Sky Men" by Geoff Goddard is his best-known solo recording, and features much of the same instrumentation as "Telstar." Goddard's vocals are sped-up, giving them a most peculiar edge, and there is another very interesting treatment on the "alien voice" sections. The raspier end of the Clavioline's sonic range is also used to good effect.

"Merry Go Round" and "Go On Then" by Gunilla Thorne are both amazing recordings with extremely interesting vocal treatments, and a very pronounced *flanging* effect, most noticeable on the drums. The former is a catchy Geoff Goddard tune with a sophisticated keyboard arrangement, and the latter features great guitar work by Ritchie Blackmore. The record was a stiff.

"The Theme of Freedom" by the Joe Meek Orchestra almost swings, and features a very American sound, with lushly layered strings, voices, and trumpet bits. This recording is atypical and demonstrates how Joe handled these instruments more conservatively than was usual for him.

Despite having made lots of great records, Joe had only a handful of hits in 1963: "Don't You Think It's Time" (#6) and "My Little Baby" (#34) by Mike Berry and the Outlaws; "Cupboard Love" (#22) and "I'll Cut Your Tail Off" (#36) by John Leyton; "Only the Heartaches" (#22) by Houston Wells; the three Tornados songs already mentioned; and "Just Like Eddy" (#5) by Heinz—a Geoff Goddard "tribute" to the deceased American rocker Eddie Cochran.

Figure 9.2: "Diggin' My Potatoes" by Heinz.

Courtesy Kim Lowden

Meanwhile, the Beat continued to grip the record industry, with "She Loves You" and "I Want to Hold Your Hand" by the Beatles as well as the Dave Clark Five's "Glad All Over" all going to #1. And as if that were not enough, American surf bands such as the Beach Boys, the Surfaris, and Jan and Dean were also making inroads into the British charts, and Phil Spector's Crystals and Ronettes were doing some of their most memorable work. All of this major talent meant trouble for Joe Meek, and he knew it.

Sidebar 9-1: Phil Spector and Joe Meek

Joe Meek has often been called England's Phil Spector, and there are some parallels between the two producers. Both men were extremely precocious as well as idiosyncratic, developing signature sounds early in their careers. Both acted as A&R men, selecting the artists and repertoire for their productions, and sometimes even writing the music and lyrics. Both mixed to mono and continued to do so after most other producers had switched to stereo. Both were early proponents of machine-to-machine "overdubbing," and used echo chambers to excess. Both were also quite charming and funny, while at the same time being secretive about their personal lives, and "difficult" to work with.

The differences between the men, however, are also striking. Spector was a skilled guitarist, vocalist, and arranger, whereas Meek was tone-deaf and incapable of playing any instruments. Meek was a skilled engineer, capable of modifying and building gear, whereas Spector had limited hard technical knowledge. Spector preferred to focus on one song at a time, with the specific aim of making it a hit (which it nearly always was), whereas Meek recorded large quantities of songs very quickly, presumably in the hope that a few of them would chart.

As for the two men's production styles, they are actually quite different. Spector achieved his Wall of Sound by recording large numbers of musicians in relatively large and reverberant spaces. He recorded the "room" sound mostly, blurring distinctions between individual instruments. Meek, in sharp contrast, recorded small ensembles and close-miked all of the instruments. He placed blankets over drums and guitar amps, and recording the bass direct, resulting in little or no room sound. Meek sought to get maximum separation between sounds, the direct opposite of Spector's sonic wash.

Perhaps the reason that the two men are so often compared is that they each were in a sense more important to the overall sound of their records than the actual recording artists.

And something else happened in 1963 that Joe felt would almost certainly destroy his career: He was arrested for "importuning" at a roadside gentleman's convenience at Madras Place. The bust was a setup, but he pled guilty, as to contest the charges would no doubt have led to public scandal. It was by no means the first time that Joe had gone out cruising, but it was the first time he had been picked up by the police, and he felt certain that the news would be splashed across the headlines of all the

Creative Music Production: Joe Meek's Bold Techniques

London papers. It wasn't. One paper ran a small notice below the fold, and lots of people did see it, but none of the major direct repercussions Joe feared ever took place. The fact is that Joe already had a reputation for having a high libido, and his advances towards many of the handsome young men that came through his studio were not exactly held in the strictest confidence. But this "official" notification opened the door to blackmailers and other schemers, eventually increasing Joe's woes exponentially.

By the start of 1964 Don Charles and Mike Berry had departed the RGM Sound stable, and Joe had begun adding some new artists, including some female vocalists. Flip and the Dateliners featured Vivienne Chering, and their version of Chip Taylor's "My Johnny Doesn't Come Around" is one of the best and most interesting sounding recordings from the period. It begins with a drum deeply submerged in spring reverb, and an almost gong-like cymbal wash on the first beat of each measure. The rest of the drums are heavily compressed and there is a great delay/doubling effect on the voice. "Dumb Head" by the Sharades (noted session singers Maggie Stredder and Gloria George, a.k.a. the Ladybirds) could have been a New Wave hit in 1980, and makes clever use of the lower register of the Clavioline, and levels of echo and reverb that are excessive even by Joe's standards. "Baby It Hurts" by Glenda Collins has big American-style pop production values, and really should have been a hit. Kim Roberts, too, did some nice work.

Meek's male artists didn't fare as well. De facto Elvis impersonator Davy Kaye was years out of date, and his inane tribute to the King, "In My Way," is an embarrassment at best. Tony Dangerfield and Thrills must have been less than thrilling to the Beat crowd. Even Andy Cavell tried to go "beat" with "Tell the Truth"—and almost pulled it off, thanks mostly to his energetic backing band. "Chahawki" by Burr Bailey (Dave Adams) is an unclassifiable piece of novelty work about an American Indian who dies of heartbreak when his dog is slain at the Battle of Wounded Knee. There were also new records by Michael Cox, Houston Wells, the Cameos, the Outlaws, Screaming Lord Sutch, Heinz, and the Tornados. The Outlaws, now with Ritchie Blackmore on guitar, produced consistently good work, though it wasn't keeping up with the times. Heinz had improved considerably by this point, and had adopted an almost punk stance on some of his records, as well as putting together a convincing live show. The Tornados sounded like, well, the Tornados. One notable exception is "Do You Come Here Often," which is a lounge-style number backing a comedic conversation between two gay men in a nightclub bathroom.

In addition to all of the work just listed, and despite his earlier resistance, Joe Meek was also moving towards the newer sound. The Puppets, the Syndicats, the Blue Rondos, and, most importantly, the Honeycombs were all groups that more or less qualified as Beat Boomers. The Puppets were from just outside Liverpool, and did directly incorporate some elements of the sound. One of their better recordings was a version of "Shake with Me," which was also covered by the Outlaws. The Outlaws version, however, featured a stunning guitar solo by Ritchie Blackmore that clearly distinguished it. The solo is one of the first of its kind, and marks something of a milestone in rock guitar playing. [1]

The Syndicats, featuring a young Steve Howe on guitar, recorded a cover of Chuck Berry's "Maybellene." They weren't exactly Mersey Beat, but they were certainly some sort of beat, and far removed from, say, Don Charles. The members of the group lived just down the street from 304 Holloway, and the bassist's mother had taken them to see Joe, insisting that he give them an audition.

The Blue Rondos were a very different story. In November they released "Little Baby" backed with "Baby I Go for You," both of which should have received greater recognition. The first is a moody Roy Orbison-style ballad, beautifully produced by Meek, with a crisp and punchy sound. The flipside is a real stomper with a nasty distorted guitar sound that is employed well in the manic solo played by Roger Hall (not Jimmy Page, as credited on some Page collections). The group released one more record a few months later before disbanding. "I Don't Want Your Lovin' No More" and "What Can I Do" were as good or better than the first record and feature the same rich and beautiful production work. All of these tracks were obviously recorded using Joe's vastly improved late 1964 setup.

The Honeycombs, named after and propelled by female drummer "Honey" Lantree, burst onto the scene in June and gave Joe his final #1 hit. "Have I the Right?" also went to #4 in America, and topped the charts in Australia, Japan, South Africa and Sweden. The song employed the now legendary gimmick of a "bass drum" sound created by several musicians stomping loudly on the studio stairs, with microphones placed just below. Less well known is an additional trick performed by Guy Fletcher. Guy's brother Ted recalls: "On the final mix of 'Have I the Right?' we were just sort of tickling it up and getting it ready, getting the master ready with Joe late one evening. And this thing was going to the record company the next day and he'd done all the jumping on the stairs and that stuff—which is true, he did all that—but the 'come right back' line still wasn't heavy enough for him. He tried all sorts of things to get this right: we kicked cardboard boxes, hit card-board boxes with sticks, and in the end he said, 'No, Guy, it's not loud enough; what you've got to do is this.' And he put an AKG D19 microphone on a little short stand on the floor, and gave a tambourine to my brother, and said, 'Hit the micro-phone with the tambourine.' So my brother gently tickled the microphone, and Joe said, 'No, no, hit it, hit it, hit it!' During the takes my brother was smashing this tambourine onto the top of the microphone so hard that he completely destroyed the microphone, and the tambourine. But that was the final recording. There's a horrible cracking noise on the record and if you listen carefully you can hear it."

Figure 9.3:
The Honeycombs' "Have I the Right?"

As the Honeycombs had scored a #1 with their first record, unless they did as well with future releases, they had no place to go but down. And on the topic of downers, Geoff Goddard brought a lawsuit against Joe's publishers claiming that he, Geoff, and Joe had written "Have I the Right?," or at least a song that it was based on, and demanding compensation. Goddard's lawyer eventually persuaded him to drop the suit, but not before irreparable damage had been done to Geoff and Joe's relationship. The two men never spoke again after that.

Unfortunately, the Honeycombs were on a long tour of Australia when the record hit, and were unable to promote it while it was still hot. The group tried to catch up by releasing an entire album in September, but none of their later material made the same impact. The group's songs all feature Honey's distinctive pounding drums, but there are *lots* of interesting production touches including a full string and brass arrangement on "Something Better Beginning." On "That's the Way" Honey's voice is out front, giving the song a softer feel than on their others. "I Can't Stop" has a thumping rhythm and a massive bass sound. "Colour Slide," and "Is It Because" (which nicked the British charts at #38) both utilize some nice production touches, including interesting distortion and modulation effects, and have a very full and clean overall sound.

At about the same time that the Honeycombs were recording "Have I the Right?," a singer named Tommy Scott and his band recorded a few sides at 304 Holloway. There was talk of him entering into a formal agreement with Joe and signing a contract with Decca, but the deal didn't pan out for various reasons. One reason was that Joe reportedly took an interest in Scott—particularly his tight trousers, according to some—and Scott was offended. There was also some behind-the-scenes political monkey business with Decca, or at least Joe thought that there might have been. One thing led to another, and in the end Joe is said to have sent Scott sailing down the stairs. A year later Scott had his first major hit, using his new name: Tom Jones. Joe wasted no time in releasing the recordings that he had been sitting on—much to Jones's chagrin and pubic denouncement—and they sold moderately well.

Tom Jones obviously had difficulties getting along with Joe Meek, and their relationship didn't survive long enough to get off the ground. But what was it like for other musicians who worked with Joe? The following are first-hand accounts from three guitarists who recorded at 304 Holloway Road: Peter Miller, Steve Howe, and Ritchie Blackmore.

Peter Miller: "You wouldn't bullshit with the guy after the session. He would focus in on what he was doing right now—whether it was a little unknown person or a big star. You'd do the job, finish the recording, and get out of there—because he'd have something else to do. He would allow me to stay around for a few hours if another session was coming in, after he realized that I was interested in the technical aspects of recording. I wouldn't be his assistant, but I would do bits and pieces, and watch what was going on, and move a mic around or even cut a piece of tape once in a while. He was very secretive about his ideas—he didn't want any of them to be stolen—as many engineers were for so many years. In the old days a lot of engineers had their secrets about how they did things and they wouldn't tell anybody, because if they gave them to everybody else then they'd get 'their' sound, and they wouldn't get the gig. Meek was particularly paranoid.

"People lived next door [to the studio] and we always had to stop recording at 6:00 because of the neighbors. He could not have a session after 6:00 at night. We'd have three hours to do two sides, and very often we'd do four or five sides in those three hours. And that was the same in Decca or anywhere else in those days. Whenever you went in there there was always a pile of masters all over the place—he was a messy bastard. You know half of these wires [points to a picture of the control room], right, didn't have plugs on them; they were twisted together. I swear to god. He wasn't big on plugs; he would twist all the wires together. And when you went into the room he'd say "Don't step there, don't step there." And I stood in this mess many times, doing a guitar overdub or something, because he didn't have speakers in the studio. He had headphones, but he never had any speakers out there."

When asked if Joe made elaborate preparations, or recorded multiple takes, Miller replied: "He would come in and adjust a microphone once in a while. He would get a sound, he would run through the sound two or three times, and he would be ready to cut it. If you'd done it right the first take that was it. You'd go to Joe and say, "But, but, that, that," and Joe would say, 'Shut up, that was it.' He went for feel; he didn't care about bum notes. As long as he had the sound that he liked, which normally he did—after two or three run-throughs he would have that sound—it was then up to you to get the feel, and that was it. Bad notes didn't worry him."

Steve Howe recorded at 304 Holloway Road while he was playing with the Syndicats. "I vaguely remember the first time I carried amps and guitars up three flights of stairs. One of the most memorable contents of his studio was that—usually people think of tape as being in reels, right? Well Joe had cut so much tape in his life, and yet he'd never picked any of it up, so the floor was a bed of broken bits of edited tape, and it was quite unreal. You did literally stumble over piles of tape that were all discarded, edited off. I remember an afternoon when I was looking towards the control room and Joe was standing there. And there was all this tape there, and he was playing the music back and he looked 'round at me and kind of smiled as if to, not to seek my approval, but I think almost to see if I was really listening—was I hearing what he was hearing. And I think that's something he passed on to musicians and producers—that ability to understand what they're trying to do.

"I know that the first record I made with him, called 'Maybellene,' written by Chuck Berry, was the backing track with us playing, and then the vocalist, and then I added a guitar solo. [2] And then the strange thing was—and this is the experience of most musicians there—when they actually heard it, it didn't sound anything like what they thought it was going to sound like (laughs). It had this huge thudding sound in the middle, this bass drum, doong, doong, doong, doong, but kind of a little bit sloppy. And Joe loved it; and a lot of his records have this thudding sort of sound. But the great thing he did with me was that he put delay repeats on the guitar solo and it made it sound pretty zany. After we recorded the song Joe looked unhappy and said, 'The vocal's not in tune.' So he sped it up and then said, 'Here, I like it, this sounds alright.' What he did was…it was the first time that I ever heard sound, my own sound, being changed. Also, the singer was singing in the bathroom, and he had reverb on his voice, and suddenly I thought, 'Anything's possible with this recording thing.'

"When we made the second record he threw a tantrum on us and screamed at us and stomped his feet, and said that we were playing terribly badly. And he gave us an hour to sort it out and he'd be back. Well in about three hours he came back and he was much calmer and he came in and said, 'Play it,' and we played it, and he said 'OK we'll record it.'

"When he pressed a button and something went 'round we didn't know what it was; we didn't know how to do what he was doing when he would fiddle and get irritated and say, you know, 'The bass drum's not sounding right,' and come running out and fuss with it. Because he felt so passionately about things, it was never just a cool person who walked into the studio and said, 'Oh, we'll just move the mic.' We didn't know how to act, after all; we might have been crashing and bashing and he had to come in and scream and tell us to shut up. It can be a little chaotic, but people respond to experience. I had to buy what he did because he knew what he was doing, and we didn't.

"The other side of it was a bit embarrassing really. Sometimes he'd come in—and this happened repeatedly—and he'd sit down, and he'd say, 'Steve, would you come into the office?' And he'd come to say, 'Well, um, I like your trousers.' And I'd say, 'Joe, you've got to get it. Look, I've got a girlfriend, her name's Brenda, alright; she's very cute.' And he'd say, 'But I do like those trousers though.' And he'd be, like, trying to get close to me. And, although I dealt with it quite well, underneath I was quite shocked, you know—I couldn't really connect the two things: that I was working with a producer that kept liking my trousers. I was stuck with it; I was the guy in the band that he fancied. And, of course, looking back I can see how I could have got my career to go a long way if I'd wanted to agree to being that way. I held onto this idea that I had my girlfriend and I didn't want this guy touching me, and that was all there was to it."

Ritchie Blackmore began working for Joe in 1962, while he was playing with Screaming Lord Sutch and the Savages. He played in the second lineup of the Outlaws, and later with Heinz and the Wild Boys, and worked as a session guitarist on many of Joe's recordings. "I could never quite understand Joe's … what he wanted. Because if the Outlaws would play something, and he would come in, and sometimes there'd be a big smile on his face, saying, 'That was wonderful,' and we had no idea of knowing…so we'd all be quite happy. Or sometimes he'd come in and throw the reel of tape at our rhythm guitarist, and tell us to get out, and that it was a waste of time; and usually we were playing exactly the same on each take. It depended a lot on his mood.

"I suppose he was looking for something that only he knew about. But it was quite nerve-racking; we never had a clue as to how the session went until he would come into the room. If he came into the room combing his hair and smiling, then we all knew that we were going to get paid. (But) he would come in sometimes and literally throw the reels at the rhythm guitarist—always at the rhythm guitarist because he never liked our rhythm guitarist—and then we'd have to run, and get all our instruments together and get the hell out of the house. Very, ah, temperamental. And he would think that there was a conspiracy against him if we weren't playing what it was he thought we should play; he thought that we were doing it on purpose. With him it was just that he was mad at the moment; he would always quiet down a couple of hours later. He was basically a nice guy, but his moods were quite extreme. You never knew what kind of mood he was in.

"Whenever we did the sessions they always started at ten in the morning. Chas would always be late, and Chas had a way with words. He's a very funny guy and he'd always turn up late. Joe would be so angry that he'd come late, until Chas talked him out of it by saying, 'Oh Joe, I was here on time, but I found this little bird in the street.' And he would always come out with these ridiculous stories, and Joe would just start laughing, and then everything was ok. But he was always an hour late, and Joe used to go berserk that we were all kept waiting, and Chas always knew how to gloss over it."

One reason that Joe was probably lenient with Chas Hodges is that he was one of the people who would routinely translate Joe's concepts into music. Blackmore continues, "Joe would come up to Chas the bass player and say, 'I have this tune,' and he would hum it to Chas. And it was quite funny because he wasn't that pitch-perfect and so some of the notes would be wrong, and Chas would basically have to make up a melody of his own sometimes to appease Joe. And then Joe would be very happy with what Chas put down, and that's how we followed it up. It was kind of a quite frightening situation for Chas to be in, because if he didn't pick up the melody, and come up with results, then we were all thrown out again. Chas did an amazing job because he's an incredible musician, with an incredible ear, and he knew how to bend the note, and change the note, without Joe thinking he was doing it purposely. He knew how to interpret, sometimes, bad ideas into good ideas."

When asked if he had ever experienced anything like Howe's "trousers" incident Blackmore replied: "Yeah, Joe was a little bit that way from what I gather. You'd hear very weird stories, and I tended to get a little nervous when I was there late at night doing overdubs. I did a solo once with Freddie Starr, and Freddie as you know is an extrovert, and he came down to a session when we were backing him and doing his record. It's quite funny actually—a strange story. When it came to my solo—I was trying to play a solo as we were going along, no overdubs—and Freddie Star started getting his private parts out, and he's trying to attack me, and he's trying to put it in my ear as I was playing. So with that, I couldn't concentrate and was kind of losing and things were crashing around us. And then Joe came flying in saying, 'What the bloody hell's going on in here?' And then he went 'Ooh,' and Freddie quickly put his private part away. I don't think Freddie was that way, but ah, it certainly changed Joe's mood. So things like that would go down, you know."

Blackmore also recalled the famous stairs: "You often heard bands coming down the stairs with their equipment behind them. We'd be arriving for a session and there'd be some band from Liverpool being kicked out. You never knew what was going to happen in that place."

As 1964 drew to a close Joe's star sat squarely on the ground. The "Telstar" case was devouring time and money with no end in sight, his partnership with Geoff Goddard had ended, and though he was still making lots of recordings fresh hits were not forthcoming and resources were running low. Even his relationship with Heinz was not working out since he had discovered that his boy was looking for a way out of their business arrangement. Once Joe got wind of that he had Heinz's boat and automobile—both of which had been lavished on him as part of the star treatment—repossessed.

The success of "Have I the Right?" put Joe in the position to buy out Major Banks, and to form a new company that he called Meeksville Sound. [3] From that point on all of the money he made would go into the new company rather than RGM Sound, just in case the "Telstar" lawsuit didn't go his way, and the Frenchman attempted to grab his assets. Joe also began to scale back on the quantity of his work, leaving more time for leisure activities such as painting, holding seances, and wandering around a graveyard attempting to record spirit voices with a portable tape recorder. The results of this latter activity, where a spirit spoke to him by possessing a cat, can be seen and heard on the BBC *Arena* documentary. A psychic also informed Joe that he had some famous spirit guides—one of which, the Egyptian Pharaoh Ramses The Great, was an even bigger celebrity than Buddy Holly and Al Jolson, who Joe was already on friendly terms with.

By 1965 the British Invasion was a fait accompli, and the original waves of sound-alike bands had receded, leaving some extraordinary artists firmly entrenched on the beachhead. Groups like the Dave Clark Five, Herman's Hermits, and even the Shadows were still on the scene, but by mid-year the Who's "Can't Explain," the Animals' "Please Don't Let Me Be Misunderstood," the Yardbirds's "For Your Love," and Bob Dylan's "The Times They Are A-Changin'" had raised the bar significantly. On April 29th the Honeycombs' "Something Better Beginning," a song written by the Kinks' Ray Davies, stalled at #39, while Dylan's "Subterranean Homesick Blues" towered above it at #9.

Joe Meek made some very interesting records in 1965 and 1966. "I Don't Love You No More" by the Hotrods uses a stomping sound practically identical to the one on "Have I the Right?," and sounds very similar to it generally. "Wishing Well" by the Millionaires is a great song as well as one of Meek's most beautiful and inspired productions. "Whatcha Gonna Do Baby" by Jason Eddy & the Centremen is a hooky number in 3/4 time, with a sound combining the sweeping organ washes of the Animals with touches of the quirky psychedelia of Syd Barrett-era Pink Floyd. The group also did a demented cover of "Singing the Blues," with a brilliant but whacky runaway guitar overdub (overdubbed after the original session, without the group's blessing). The drum sound on "Diggin' for Gold" by David John and the Mood is extremely compressed, even for Joe, resulting in an all-encompassing thumpiness. The guitar on "Fast Cars and Money" by the Four Matadors sounds like it's being played through a Leslie rotating speaker system—but not exactly. The same sound, more or less, appears on "I'm Not Sleeping Too Well Lately" by the Honeycombs. And speaking of Leslies, "September in the Rain" by Paul and Ritchie and the Cryin' Shames has what sounds an awful lot like a Hammond organ on it. (Pity the poor fools who had to carry *that* up the stairs!) "Bring It to Jerome" by David John and the Mood is a Yardbirds-style cover of the Bo Diddly classic, featuring a passable harmonica part, and singing with the right attitude if not authentic execution.

In addition to these more obscure artists Joe made a number of fabulous recordings by the Riot Squad, a group which at various times included Mitch Mitchell on drums. "I Take It That We're Through," "It's Never Too Late to Forgive," "Bittersweet Love," and "Gotta Be a First Time" are in some ways the high-water mark of this period. Besides having all of Meek's colorful production touches—present on recordings by even the lamest artists—the songwriting and musicianship are quite good, and occasionally outstanding.

On the other hand, if you view Meek's output within the context of the times, the music doesn't fare as well. For example, while David John and the Mood sound sort of like the Yardbirds, they sound like the Yardbirds did circa 1964, two years earlier—and even so, their guitarist is no Eric Clapton. By 1965 Clapton had left the Yardbirds and recorded the groundbreaking *John Mayall's Bluesbreakers with Eric Clapton* album, and by 1966 he had formed Cream, a group that simply cannot be compared to any that ever recorded at 304 Holloway Road. Similarly, by 1966 the Beatles had released *Revolver,* a record that is light years beyond anything recorded by the Riot Squad, both musically and sonically. On the album George Harrison's "Taxman" features a huge bass sound locked to a deep kick drum, edgy rhythm guitar, and beautifully blended harmony vocals—all presented in a highly imaginative and effective stereo mix. That said, the wild tape effects on "Tomorrow Never Knows," the backwards guitars on "I'm Only Sleeping," and the boat sound effects on "Yellow Submarine" resonate with Meek's more experimental work, going all the way back to *I Hear a New World* in 1959. And just in case these examples aren't sufficient to make the point, within weeks of Joe Meek's death, pop music was changed forever when the Jimi Hendrix Experience, featuring former Riot Squad drummer Mitch Mitchell, released "Purple Haze." [4]

Just why Joe Meek failed to flourish during the Beat Boom and the British Invasion years has been hotly debated. It is commonly held that he was simply out of touch with what was going on, and though he made some "Beat" records the artists and/or the material he chose were substandard. Meek's defenders point to excellent records by the Blue Rondos, the Riot Squad, and the Millionaires, which were in many cases brilliantly produced. They say that if Joe failed it was not because he was out of touch or didn't try, and therefore some other factors must have come into play—possibly even deliberate attempts by record companies to sabotage his success by delaying the release of his discs. These are the two extreme positions, but there are also other factors worth considering.

As good as some of Meek's artists were none of them were serious songwriters, and the emerging trend was for self-contained groups that wrote and played their own material. Joe Meek was a control freak, plain and simple, and one of the basic criteria for working with him was that he was the one calling the shots. He could change your name, tell you what to sing and play, and even dye your hair white if he thought that it would make you successful. Bands like the Who, the Animals, and the Beatles—particularly in 1966—would not have been amused. On the other hand, it is very possible that Meek would have evolved himself, and that if he had been stable enough to keep his business affairs in order he could have arranged to work with some truly world-class artists. In fact, the head of EMI/Abbey Road was courting him aggressively in late 1966, hoping that he would join them as a staff producer. If he had taken the job he would have been instantly connected with some of the leading groups, including the Beatles, though how he would have fared is anyone's guess.

Figure 9.6:
Joe Meek in his studio control room in 1966. The EMI BTR2 recorder is in the bottom left corner of the photo. Behind him are the Astrosonic graphic equalizer and the Ampex PR10 recorder. In the rack to his right are, from top to bottom, an unidentified (Fairchild?) unit, the Altec 438A compressor, the homemade 4-channel mixer with top-lift, the Vortexion 4/15/M 4-Channel mixer, two Quad 22 stereo preamplifiers, the Fairchild 658 spring reverb control unit, and two patch panels.

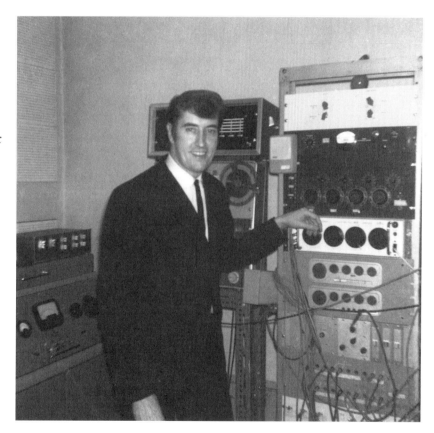

One problem that Joe would have faced is that he was not "hip" in the 1967 sense of the word. On the surface he might have appeared like the prototypical hippie, living the "sex, drugs, and rock & roll" lifestyle years before it had become popular; at heart, however, he was the product of another era. Meek was also mostly apolitical and apparently largely uninformed about the "issues" of the day, putting him farther out of step with the times. Rock songs were becoming increasingly infused with social and political commentary, and, by 1966, with expanded consciousness and "spiritual" matters. Pop entertainment, no matter how clever and well performed, took a back seat to more meaningful concerns. That said, Joe Meek was clearly a caring individual with a social conscience, as his semi-protest song "It's Hard to Believe It" demonstrates.

There's also the matter of Joe's mental instability. During the final years of his life he was a very sick man. By 1966 his paranoia had increased to the point where he was convinced that everyone was out to get him, and even those who loved and cared for him the most found it more and more difficult to communicate with him and to maintain his trust. Joe wasn't just "eccentric"" he was a textbook paranoid schizophrenic who was unfortunate enough to have lived at a time when his illness was highly stigmatized, and what medicines were available were inadequate. That Joe found it difficult to work with artists and carry on normal business relationships with record companies should not be surprising— the fact that he carried on for as long as he did is remarkable.

When asked if he thought Joe was out of touch towards the end of his life, Ted Fletcher, who spent hundreds of hours working with Joe, had this to say: "Yeah, that's true, though I wouldn't put it quite like that. He was always his own person, with his own ideas—it wouldn't have occurred to him that he was out of touch. He was never *in* touch. The world became in touch with him for a short time, and then it was the rest of the world that went out of touch, not him. He lost contact with reality—he was never really very in contact with reality anyway. But at the time that he fell out with me, he'd really lost contact with reality in a big way.

"Over the weeks and months of 1963 to 1965 we saw a change in Joe, the pressure of work was too much, his finances were not in good order, and his style of production was being copied by other producers, while other sounds (Phil Spector) were appearing from across the Atlantic. He became generally disliked in the business for his unpredictable rages and unconventional behavior, and his own paranoia became more and more obvious. He was convinced that the engineers at Decca had 'bugs' planted in the walls at Holloway Road and he started to live the life of a recluse. Late in 1965 after a period of about three weeks of having a backing vocal session delayed and postponed time after time, I received a four page hand-written letter from Joe. The letter accused me of setting up a studio to compete with him, stealing his ideas and techniques and telling stories about him behind his back!

"His temperament was the interesting thing. With everybody except musicians he was really quite awful and used to be very, very abrupt, or he would hide. You know he used to avoid talking to people. I suppose it's like schizophrenics are; on the one hand they seem very overt, and on another occasion they'll want to hide all the time. He was very much like this. That is my enduring memory of that time, of his unpleasantness really, with people around him, apart from musicians. He used to make a habit of throwing people down the stairs—he used to do that all the time."

Despite all of the obstacles to his success, there is evidence suggesting that during the final year of his life Joe Meek was hoping to expand his musical vision far beyond his work to date. In several letters written to a Mr. Ginnet, an attorney recommended to him by his banker, Meek spoke of how he had wasted a lot of time and energy fighting the "Telstar" case, and that if it could be resolved he would be able to regroup and move ahead. He gave Ginnet control over his failing finances with the hope that he could straighten out the almost inter-minable problems arising from his many debts and his less-than-substantial income. Meek said that he felt his career had only just begun, and should he be able to clear up his financial problems he could create musical works of a very high standard that would greatly exceed the limitations of the pop world.

On the other hand, by early 1967 Meek had burned lots of bridges to his past and he was becoming increasingly isolated. Also, the speed that he had been taking for years, partly to ward off depression, was finally catching up to him and he was suffering from mental exhaustion. Several of his former artists, including Heinz and Lord Sutch, were pushing him hard for payment of royalties, and they were prepared to ratchet up the pressure if he didn't pay. There was even a chance that his landlord would not allow him to renew his lease, and he would be forced to leave 304 Holloway Road.

Besides all that, Joe had been beaten up pretty badly, possibly by gangsters who hoped to muscle in on one of his groups, and his car had been stolen and trashed. Perhaps most importantly, the London police were preparing to interrogate all "known homosexuals" in connection with a bizarre murder and decapitation of a young boy, and there is a chance that Joe may have known something about it, and possibly even known the boy. There is absolutely no evidence that Joe was involved in any wrongdoing, but having already been framed by the police once, he was naturally apprehensive.

Figure 9.4:
Photo from a newspaper clipping in the Evening Standard, Feb 3, 1967. The newspaper article is about Meek's murder/suicide.

Just exactly what occurred on the evening of February 2nd is not entirely clear, but on the following morning Joe asked his office assistant Patrick Pink to let his landlady know that he would like to see her upstairs. Shortly afterwards an argument took place, or at least Joe was screaming at her, and a few moments later he murdered her with a shotgun before turning it on himself. Why he would want to kill her or commit suicide has never been satisfactorily explained. Some believe that at least his own death was premeditated, as it took place on the anniversary of Buddy Holly's death, but others feel strongly that it was a spontaneous act, and that the timing was coincidental. Perhaps someday new information will come to light, but for now Joe Meek's death remains as mysterious and enigmatic as his life.

Figure 9.5:
A letter to Joe Meek acknowledging receipt of payment in full for a Fairchild Model 655 "Bass X." Payment was apparently received January 31, 1967, and the letter is dated February 3, 1967, the day of Meek's death.

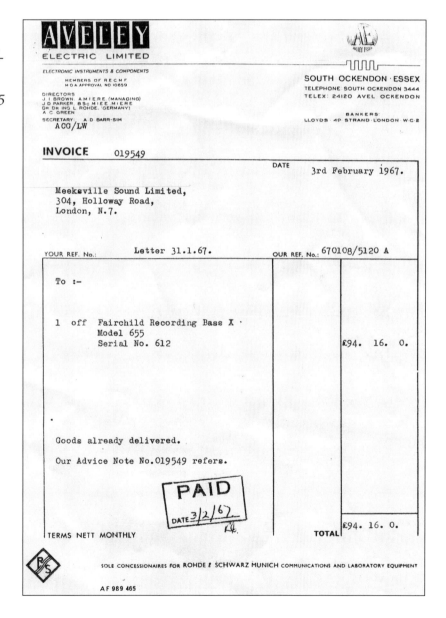

1 Blackmore had this to say about the solo: "Jeff Beck was telling me that in 1967 he played that solo for Jimi Hendrix, and Jimi Hendrix wanted to know who I was. That was 1963 I believe I did that one. It came out well because Joe said 'I want you to go crazy on this solo, with abandon,' so I just kind of played as many notes as possible that were vaguely relative, and it worked. It didn't come across like I'm playing a session; it sounded like we actually had more feeling than that."

2 Here he is describing one of Joe's typical recording arrangements: rhythm track to one track of the twin-track, vocal to the other track, with the guitar solo on the same track as the vocal in spots where there's no singing.

3 Likely a spoof on Hitsville USA.

4 In fact, Hendrix was overdubbing the final parts onto "Purple Haze" at Olympic Studios in London the very morning of Meek's death.

Appendix A

DISCOGRAPHY OF JOE MEEK PRODUCTIONS

By Shaun Brennan with thanks to Kim Lowden, Jim Blake, Roger Dopson, Steve Fay, Chris Davies, and Meek archivists everywhere.

NOTE: Unless noted, all records listed originate from the U.K.

ARTIST: HUMPHREY LYTTLETON BAND
TRACKS: 'Bad Penny Blues' b/w 'Open Your Eyes'
CAT #: Parlophone R4184
RELEASED: 6/1956
NOTE: The B-side is a Denis Preston production, engineered by Meek.

ARTIST: JIMMY MILLER AND THE BARBECUES
TRACKS: 'Sizzling Hot' b/w 'Freewheeling Baby'
CAT #: Columbia DB4006
RELEASED: 7/1957

ARTIST: JACKIE DAVIES WITH HIS QUARTET
TRACKS: 'The Land of Make Believe' b/w 'Over the Rainbow'
CAT #: Pye N15115
RELEASED: 11/1957

ARTIST: JIMMY MILLER AND THE BARBECUES
TRACKS: 'Jelly Baby' b/w 'Cry Baby Cry'
CAT #: Columbia DB4081
RELEASED: 2/1958

ARTIS: MIKE PRESTON
TRACKS: 'A House, a Car and a Wedding Ring' b/w 'My Lucky Love'
CAT #: Decca F11053
RELEASED: 8/1958

ARTIST: JOY AND DAVID
TRACKS: 'Whoopee' b/w 'My Oh My!'
CAT #: Parlophone R4477
RELEASED: 9/1958

ARTIST: MIKE PRESTON
TRACKS: 'Why, Why Why' b/w 'Whispering Grass'
CAT #: Decca F11087
RELEASED: 12/1958

ARTIST: MIKE PRESTON
TRACKS: 'Dirty Old Town' b/w 'In Surabaya'
CAT #: Decca F11120
RELEASED: 3/1959

ARTIST: JOY AND DAVID
TRACKS: 'Rockin' away the Blues' b/w 'If You Pass Me By'
CAT #: Decca F11123
RELEASED: 3/1959

ARTIST: TERRY WHITE AND THE TERRIERS
TRACKS: 'Rock around the Mailbags' b/w 'Blackout'
CAT #: Decca F11133
RELEASED: 5/1959

ARTIST: CHICO ARNEZ AND HIS LATIN-AMERICAN ORCHESTRA
TITLE: "THIS IS CHICO" (ALBUM)
TRACKS: 'This Is Chico'/'Heatwave'/'La Cucaracha Cha-Cha'/'Ole Mambo'/'Yashmak'/'Ain't
She Sweet'/'Para Cha-Cha'/'Havana 1850'/'Swing Low Sweet Cha-Cha'/'Harlem
Mambo'/'Malaguena'/'My Funny Valentine'/'Charmaine'/'This Is Chico (reprise)'
CAT #: Pye NPL18053
RELEASED: 5/1959
NOTE: Co-Produced with Denis Preston

ARTIST: CHICO ARNEZ AND HIS LATIN-AMERICAN ORCHESTRA
TITLE: 'Yashmak' b/w 'Ain't She Sweet'
CAT #: Pye 7N15196
RELEASED: 5/1959
NOTE: Co-produced with Denis Preston.

ARTIST: MIKE PRESTON
TRACKS: 'Mr. Blue' b/w 'Just Ask Your Heart'
CAT #: Decca F11167
RELEASED: 10/1959

ARTIST: EMILE FORD AND THE CHECKMATES
TRACKS: 'What Do You Want to Make Those Eyes at Me For' b/w 'Don't Tell Me Your Heartaches'
CAT #: Pye 7N15225
RELEASED: 10/1959
NOTE: Co-Produced with Michael Barclay

ARTIST: CHRIS WILLIAMS AND HIS MONSTERS
TRACKS: 'The Monster' b/w 'Eton Boating Song'
CAT #: Columbia DB4383
RELEASED: 12/1959

ARTIST: LANCE FORTUNE
TRACKS: 'Be Mine' b/w 'Action'
CAT #: Pye 7N15240
RELEASED: 1/1960

ARTIST: PETER JAY AND THE BLUE MEN
TRACKS: 'Just Too Late' b/w 'Friendship'
CAT #: Triumph RGM1000
RELEASED: 2/1960

ARTIST: RODD, KEN AND THE CAVALIERS
TRACKS: 'Magic Wheel' b/w 'Happy Valley'
CAT #: Triumph 1001
RELEASED: 2/1960

ARTIST: JOY AND DAVE
TRACKS: 'Let's Go See Granma' b/w 'Believe Me'
CAT #: Triumph 1002
RELEASED: 3/1960

ARTIST: YOLANDA
TRACKS: 'With This Kiss' b/w 'Don't Tell Me Not to Love You'
CAT #: Triumph 1007
RELEASED: 3/1960

ARTIST: THE BLUE MEN
TITLE: "I HEAR A NEW WORLD- PART 1" (E.P.)
TRACKS: 'Entry of the Globots'/'Valley of the Saroos'/'Magnetic Field'/'Orbit around the Moon'
CAT #: Triumph RGX ST5000
RELEASED: 3/1960

ARTIST: THE FABULOUS FLEE-RAKKERS
TRACKS: 'Green Jeans' b/w 'You Are My Sunshine'
CAT #: Triumph RGM1008
RELEASED: 4/1960

ARTIST: RICKY WAYNE AND THE FABULOUS FLEE-RAKKERS
TRACKS: 'Hot Chick'aroo' b/w 'Don't Pick on Me'
CAT #: Triumph RGM1009
RELEASED: 4/1960

ARTIST: GEORGE CHAKIRIS
TRACKS: 'I'm Always Chasing Rainbows' b/w 'Heart of a Teenage Girl'
CAT #: Triumph RGM1010
RELEASED: 4/1960

ARTIST: THE BLUE MEN
TITLE: "I HEAR A NEW WORLD- PART 2" (E.P.)
TRACKS: 'Glob Waterfall'/'The Dribcots' Space Boat'/'Love Dance of the Saroos'/'The Bublight'
CAT #: Triumph RGX ST5001
RELEASED: Not released, but scheduled for 5/1960.

ARTIST: THE BLUE MEN
TITLE: "I HEAR A NEW WORLD" (ALBUM)
TRACKS: 'I Hear a New World'/'Orbit around the Moon'/'Entry of the Globots'/'The Bublight'/'March of the Dribcots'/'Love Dance of the Saroos'/'Glob Waterfall'/'Magnetic Field'/'Valley of the Saroos'/'The Dribcots' Space Boat'/'Disc Dance of the Globots'/'Valley of No Return'
CAT #: Triumph RGX ST9000
RELEASED: Not released, but scheduled for 5/1960. Reached white label stage.

ARTIST: MICHAEL COX
TRACKS: 'Angela Jones' b/w 'Don't Want to Know'
CAT #: Triumph RGM1011
RELEASED: 5/1960

ARTIST: JOHN LEYTON
TRACKS: 'Tell Laura I Love Her' b/w 'Goodbye to Teenage Love'
CAT #: Top Rank JAR426
RELEASED: 8/1960
NOTE: Recorded for release on Triumph records, but leased to Top Rank when the label collapsed.

ARTIST: THE FABULOUS FLEE-RAKKERS
TRACKS: 'Green Jeans' b/w 'You Are My Sunshine'
CAT #: Top Rank JAR431
RELEASED: 8/1960
NOTE: Re-pressing of the Triumph single.

ARTIST: RICKY WAYNE AND THE FABULOUS FLEE-RAKKERS
TRACKS: 'Hot Chick'aroo' b/w 'Don't Pick on Me'
CAT #: Top Rank JAR432
RELEASED: 8/1960
NOTE: Re-pressing of the Triumph single.

ARTIST: THE FLEE-REKKERS
TRACKS: 'Sunday Date' b/w 'Shiftless Sam'
CAT #: Pye 7N15288
RELEASED: 9/1960
NOTE: Recorded for release on Triumph records, but leased to Pye when the label collapsed.

ARTIST: RICKY WAYNE AND THE OFF BEATS
TRACKS: 'Make Way Baby' b/w 'Goodness Knows'
CAT #: Pye 7N15289
RELEASED: 9/1960
NOTE: Recorded for release on Triumph records, but leased to Pye when the label collapsed.

ARTIST: PETER JAY
TRACKS: 'Paradise Garden' b/w 'Who's the Girl'
CAT #: Pye 7N15290
RELEASED: 9/1960
NOTE: Recorded for release on Triumph records, but leased to Pye when the label collapsed.

ARTIST: MICHAEL COX
TRACKS: 'Along Came Caroline' b/w 'Lonely Road'
CAT #: HMV POP789
RELEASED: 9/1960

ARTIST: EVE BOSWELL
TRACKS: 'Bridge of Avignon' b/w 'Hey Round the Corner'
CAT #: DURIUM
RELEASED: 9/1960
NOTE: Originally recorded for Triumph Records, but not released as the label collapsed.
Believed to have been an Italian only release on the Durium label.

ARTIST: CHICK WITH TED CAMERON AND THE DJS
TRACKS: 'Early in the Morning' b/w 'Cool Water'
CAT #: Pye 7N15292
RELEASED: 9/1960
NOTE: Recorded for release on Triumph records, but leased to Pye when the label collapsed.

ARTIST: JOHN LEYTON
TRACKS: 'The Girl on the Floor Above' b/w 'Terry Brown's in Love with Mary Dee'
CAT #: HMV POP798
RELEASED: 10/1960

ARTIST: JOHN LEYTON
TRACKS: 'The Girl on the Floor Above' (ITALIAN) b/w 'Terry Brown's in Love with Mary Dee' (ITALIAN)
CAT #:?????
RELEASED: c.10/1960
NOTE: Italian only release.

ARTIST: JOY AND DAVE
TRACKS: 'My Very Good Friend the Milkman' b/w 'Doopey Darling'
CAT #: Decca F11291
RELEASED: 10/1960
NOTE: Recorded for release on Triumph records, but leased to Decca when the label collapsed.

ARTIST: IAIN GREGORY
TRACKS: 'Time Will Tell' b/w 'The Night You Told a Lie'
CAT #: Pye 7N15295
RELEASED: 11/1960
NOTE: Recorded for release on Triumph records, but leased to Pye when the label collapsed.

ARTIST: DANNY RIVERS
TRACKS: 'Can't You Hear My Heart?' b/w 'I'm Waiting for Tomorrow'
CAT #: Decca F11294
RELEASED: 11/1960

JOE MEEK PRODUCTIONS (1960–1962)

ARTIST: GERRY TEMPLE
TRACKS: 'No More Tomorrows' b/w 'So Nice to Walk You Home'
CAT #: HMV POP823 RELEASED: 1/1961
NOTE: Recorded for release on Triumph records, but leased to HMV when the label collapsed.

ARTIST: MIKE BERRY
TRACKS: 'Will You Love Me Tomorrow?' b/w 'My Baby Doll'
CAT #: Decca F11314
RELEASED: 1/1961

ARTIST: MICHAEL COX AND THE HUNTERS
TRACKS: 'Teenage Love' b/w 'Linda'
CAT #: HMV POP830
RELEASED: 1/1961

ARTIST: THE FLEE-REKKERS
TRACKS: 'Blue Tango' b/w 'Bitter Rice'
CAT #: Pye 7N15326
RELEASED: 2/1961

ARTIST: THE OUTLAWS
TRACKS: 'Swingin' Low' b/w 'Spring Is Near' CAT #: HMV POP844
RELEASED: 3/1961

ARTIST: DANNY RIVERS AND THE ALEXANDER COMBO
TRACKS: 'Once Upon a Time' b/w 'My Baby's Gone Away'
CAT #: Decca F11357 RELEASED: 5/1961

ARTIST: THE OUTLAWS
TRACKS: 'Ambush' b/w 'Indian Brave'
CAT #: HMV POP877
RELEASED: 5/1961

ARTIST: THE FLEE REKKERS
TITLE: "THE FABULOUS FLEE-REKKERS" (E.P.)
TRACKS: 'Isle of Capri'/'Brer Robert'/'Hangover'/'P.F.B.'
CAT #: Pye NEP24141
RELEASED: 5/1961

ARTIST: CLIFF BENNETT AND THE REBEL ROUSERS
TRACKS: 'You Got What I Like' b/w 'I'm in Love with You'
CAT #: Parlophone R4793
RELEASED: 6/1961

ARTIST: THE FLEE REKKERS
TRACKS: 'Lone Rider' b/w 'Miller Like Wow'
CAT #: Pye-Piccadilly 7N35006
RELEASED: 6/1961

ARTIST: CHRIS AND THE STUDENTS
TRACKS: 'Lass of Richmond Hill' b/w 'Ducks away from My Fishin''
CAT #: Parlophone R4806
RELEASED: 7/1961

ARTIST: JOHN LEYTON
TRACKS: 'Johnny Remember Me' b/w 'There Must Be'
CAT #: Top Rank JAR577
RELEASED: 7/1961

ARTIST: MICHAEL COX
TRACKS: 'Sweet Little Sixteen' b/w 'Cover Girl'
CAT #: HMV POP905
RELEASED: 8/1961

ARTIST: MIKE BERRY AND THE OUTLAWS
TRACKS: 'Tribute to Buddy Holly' b/w 'What's the Matter'
CAT #: HMV POP912
RELEASED: 9/1961

ARTIST: THE MOONTREKKERS
TRACKS: 'Night of the Vampire' b/w 'Melodie D'amore'
CAT #: Parlophone R4814
RELEASED: 9/1961

ARTIST: JOHN LEYTON
TRACKS: 'Wild Wind' b/w 'You Took My Love for Granted'
CAT #: Top Rank JAR585
RELEASED: 9/1961

ARTIST: THE OUTLAWS
TRACKS: 'Valley of the Sioux' b/w 'Crazy Drums'
CAT #: HMV POP927
RELEASED: 9/1961

ARTIST: GEOFF GODDARD
TRACKS: 'Girl Bride' b/w 'For Eternity'
CAT #: HMV POP938
RELEASED: 10/1961

ARTIST: CLIFF BENNETT AND THE REBEL ROUSERS
TRACKS: 'When I Get Paid' b/w 'That's What I Said'
CAT #: Parlophone R4836
RELEASED: 10/1961

ARTIST: GERRY TEMPLE
TRACKS: 'Seventeen Come Sunday' b/w 'Tell You What I'll Do'
CAT #: HMV POP939
RELEASED: 10/1961

ARTIST: JOHN LEYTON
TITLE: "THE TWO SIDES OF JOHN LEYTON" (ALBUM)
TRACKS: 'Voodoo Woman'/'Can't You Hear the Beat of a Broken Heart'/'Fabulous'/'Thunder and Lightning'/'Oh Lover'/'I Don't Care If the Sun Don't Shine'/'(I Love You) For Sentimental Reasons'/'That's a Woman'/'Walk with Me My Angel'/'That's How to Make Love'/'The Magic of True Love'/'It's Goodbye Then'
CAT #: HMV CLP1497
RELEASED: 11/1961

ARTIST: JOHN LEYTON
TITLE: "JOHN LEYTON" (E.P.)
TRACKS: 'Wild Wind'/'You Took My Love for Granted'/'Johnny Remember Me'/'There Must Be'
CAT #: Top Rank JKP3016
RELEASED: 11/1961

ARTIST: THE BOWMAN HYDE SINGERS AND PLAYERS
TITLE: 'SING ME A SOUVENIR' (ALBUM)
TRACKS: 'Sing Me a Souvenir'/'The More We Are Together'/'The Old Kitchen Kettle'/'The Fleet's in Port Again'/'The Voice in the Old Village Choir'/'Wheezy Anna'/'Abie My Boy'/'Try a Little Tenderness'/'Anniversary Song'/'I Love You Truly'/'Just an Echo in the Valley'/'Ole Faithful'/'Leaning on a Lamp Post'/'The Lambeth Walk'/'Over My Shoulder'/'We'll All Go Riding on a Rainbow'/'Sing Me a Souvenir'/'Sing Me a Souvenir'/'Jolly Good Company'/'Let's All Sing Like the Birdies Sing'/'I'm Happy When I'm Hiking'/'Cruising down the River'/'Just a Wearyin' for You'/'Garden in the Rain'/'The Very Thought of You'/'In an Eighteenth Century Drawing Room'/'Dancing with my Shadow'/'I'm a Dreamer, Aren't We All?'/'The Girl in the Alice Blue Gown'/'Dreaming'/'The Wheel of the Wagon Is Broken'/'Goodnight

Sweetheart'/'Show Me the Way to Go Home'/'Sing Me a Souvenir'
CAT #: Parlophone PMC1155
RELEASED: 11/196

ARTIST: IAIN GREGORY
TRACKS: 'Can't You Hear the Beat of a Broken Heart?' b/w 'Because'
CAT #: PYE 7N15397 RELEASED: 11/1961

ARTIST: BRYAN TAYLOR
TRACKS: 'The Donkey Smile' b/w 'Let It Snow on Christmas Day'
CAT #: Pye-Piccadilly 7N35018
RELEASED: 11/1961

ARTIST: THE OUTLAWS
TITLE: 'DREAM OF THE WEST' (ALBUM)
TRACKS: 'Dream of the West'/'The Outlaws'/'Huskie Team'/'Rodeo'/'Smoke Signals'/
'Ambush'/'Barbecue'/'Spring Is Near'/'Indian Brave'/'Homeward Bound'/'Western Sunset'/'Tune
for Short Cowboys'
CAT #: HMV CLP1489
RELEASED: 12/1961

ARTIST: SCREAMING LORD SUTCH AND THE SAVAGES
TRACKS: ''Til the Following Night' b/w 'Good Golly Miss Molly'
CAT #: HMV POP953
RELEASED: 12/1961

ARTIST: JOHN LEYTON
TRACKS: 'Son This Is She' b/w 'Six White Horses'
CAT #: HMV POP956
RELEASED: 12/1961

ARTIST: JOY & DAVE AND THE HOT SHOTS
TRACKS: 'Joe's Been a'Gittin There' b/w 'They Tell Us Not to Love'
CAT #: Parlophone R4855
RELEASED: 12/1961

ARTIST: JOHN LEYTON
TRACKS: 'Wann Bist Du Bei Mir' b/w 'Six White Horses'
CAT #: Electrola 22089
RELEASED: 12/1961
NOTE: German only release. B-side is the same version as The English 45.

ARTIST: CARTER-LEWIS AND THE SOUTHERNERS
TRACKS:'Two Timing Baby' b/w 'Will It Happen to Me'
CAT #: Ember 145
RELEASED: c.12/1961
NOTE: Recorded at Meek's studio but produced by Terry Kennedy. Meek involved in an engineering capacity.

ARTIST: MICHAEL COX
TRACKS: 'Young Only Once' b/w 'Honey 'Cause I Love You'
CAT #: HMV POP972
RELEASED: 1/1962

ARTIST: THE CHARLES BLACKWELL ORCHESTRA
TRACKS: 'Taboo' b/w 'Midnight in Luxembourg'
CAT #: HMV POP977
RELEASED: 1/1962

ARTIST: MIKE BERRY AND THE OUTLAWS
TRACKS: 'It's Just a Matter of Time' b/w 'Little Boy Blue'
CAT #: HMV POP979
RELEASED: 1/1962

ARTIST: DON CHARLES
TRACKS: 'Walk with Me My Angel' b/w 'Crazy Man Crazy'
CAT #: Decca F11424
RELEASED: 1/1962

ARTIST: THE STONEHENGE MEN
TRACKS: 'Big Feet' b/w 'Pinto'
CAT #: HMV POP981
RELEASED: 2/1962

ARTIST: THE OUTLAWS
TRACKS: 'Last Stage West' b/w 'Ku-Pow'
CAT #: HMV P0P990
RELEASED: 2/1962

ARTIST: JOHN LEYTON
TRACKS: 'Lone Rider' b/w 'Heart of Stone'
CAT #: HMV POP992
RELEASED: 3/1962

ARTIST: THE MOONTREKKERS
TRACKS: 'There's Something at the Bottom of the Well' b/w 'Hatashai (Japanese Sword Fight)'
CAT #: Parlophone R4888
RELEASED: 3/1962

ARTIST: DANNY RIVERS AND THE RIVERMEN
TRACKS: 'We're Gonna Dance' b/w 'Movin' In'
CAT #: HMV POP1000
RELEASED: 3/1962

ARTIST: CLIFF BENNETT AND THE REBEL ROUSERS WITH THE PEPPERMINTIES
TRACKS: 'Poor Joe' b/w 'Hurtin' Inside (Slow Twist)'
CAT #: Parlophone R4895
RELEASED: 3/1962

ARTIST: THE TORNADOS
TRACKS: 'Love and Fury' b/w 'Popeye Twist'
CAT #: Decca F11449
RELEASED: 4/1962

ARTIST: TONY VICTOR
TRACKS: 'There Was a Time' b/w 'Dear One'
CAT #: Decca F11459
RELEASED: 4/1962

ARTIST: IAIN GREGORY
TRACKS: 'Mr. Lovebug' b/w 'Pocketful of Dreams (And Eyes Full of Tears')
CAT #: Pye 7N15435
RELEASED: 4/1962

ARTIST: JOHN LEYTON
TRACKS: 'Lonely City' b/w 'It Would Be Easy'
CAT #: HMV POP1014
RELEASED: 4/1962

ARTIST: THE FLEE REKKERS
TRACKS: 'Stage to Cimmaron' b/w 'Twistin' the Chestnuts'
CAT #: Pye-Piccadilly 7N35048
RELEASED: 4/1962
NOTE: Recorded at Pye studios. Meek may only have been involved in an engineering capacity.

ARTIST: BRIAN WHITE AND THE MAGNA CITY JAZZ BAND
TITLE: "MAGNA CITY JAZZ BAND" (ALBUM)
TRACKS: 'Babette'/'I'm Confessing'/'Calamity'/'Ida'/'Baby Won't You Please Come Home'/'Goody Goody'/'You're Just in Love'/'Ukulele Lady'/'Misty Morning'/'Softly As in a Morning Sunrise'/'Marchita'/'Don't Dilly Dally'
CAT #: HMV CLP1534
RELEASED: 5/1962

ARTIST: DON CHARLES
TRACKS: 'The Hermit of Misty Mountain' b/w 'Moonlight Rendezvous'
CAT #: Decca F11464
RELEASED: 5/1962

ARTIST: ALAN KLEIN
TRACKS: 'Striped Purple Shirt' b/w 'You Gave Me the Blues'
CAT #: Oriole CB1719
RELEASED: 5/1962

ARTIST: ANDY CAVELL
TRACKS: 'Hey There Cruel Heart' b/w 'Lonely Soldier Boy'
CAT #: HMV POP1024
RELEASED: 5/1962

ARTIST: ALAN KLEIN
TRACKS: 'Three Coins in the Sewer' b/w 'Danger Ahead!'
CAT #: Oriole CB1737
RELEASED: 7/1962

ARTIST: MIKE BERRY
TRACKS: 'Every Little Kiss' b/w 'How Many Times'
CAT #: HMV POP1042
RELEASED: 7/1962

ARTIST: JOHN LEYTON
TRACKS: 'Down the River Nile' b/w 'I Think I'm Falling in Love'
CAT #: HMV POP1054
RELEASED: 7/1962

ARTIST: THE DOWLANDS AND THE SOUNDTRACKS
TRACKS: 'Little Sue' b/w 'Julie'
CAT #: Oriole CB1748
RELEASED: 8/1962

ARTIST: THE TORNADOS
TRACKS: 'Telstar' b/w 'Jungle Fever'
CAT #: Decca F11494
RELEASED: 8/1962

ARTIST: MICHAEL COX
TRACKS: 'Stand Up' b/w 'In April'
CAT #: HMV POP1065
RELEASED: 9/1962

ARTIST: JOHN LEYTON
TITLE: "THE JOHN LEYTON HIT PARADE" (E.P.)
TRACKS: 'Lone Rider'/'Son, This Is She'/'Lonely City'/'It Would Be Easy'
CAT #: HMV 7EG8747
RELEASED: 9/1962

ARTIST: PAT READER
TITLE: 'Cha-Cha on the Moon' b/w 'May Your Heart Stay Young Forever'
CAT #: Pye Piccadilly 7N35077
RELEASED: 9/1962

ARTIST: GEOFF GODDARD
TRACKS: 'My Little Girl's Come Home' b/w 'Try Once More'
CAT #: HMV POP1068
RELEASED: 9/1962

ARTIST: THE OUTLAWS
TRACKS: 'Sioux Serenade' b/w 'Fort Knox'
CAT #: HMV POP1074
RELEASED: 10/1962

ARTIST: JOHN LEYTON
TRACKS: 'Lonely Johnny' b/w 'Keep on Loving You'
CAT #: HMV POP1076
RELEASED: 10/1962
NOTE: Credited to RGM Sound, but probably produced by Robert Stigwood.

ARTIST: MARK DOUGLAS
TRACKS: 'It Matters Not' b/w 'Upside Down'
CAT #: Ember EMB-S166
RELEASED: 10/1962

ARTIST: ANDY CAVELL
TRACKS: 'Always on Saturday' b/w 'Hey There Senorita'
CAT #: HMV POP1080
RELEASED: 10/1962

ARTIST: HOUSTON WELLS AND THE MARKSMEN
TRACKS: 'This Song Is Just for You' b/w 'Paradise'
CAT #: Parlophone R4955
RELEASED: 10/1962

ARTIST: THE FLEE REKKERS
TRACKS: 'Sunburst' b/w 'Black Buffalo'
CAT #: Pye-Piccadilly 7N35081
RELEASED: 10/1962
NOTE: Recorded at Pye studios. Meek may only have been involved in an engineering capacity.

ARTIST: THE TORNADOS
TITLE: "THE SOUND OF THE TORNADOS" (E.P.)
TRACKS: 'Ridin' the Wind'/'Dreamin' on a Cloud'/'Red Roses and a Sky of Blue'/'Earthy'
CAT #: Decca DFE8510
RELEASED: 10/1962

ARTIST: THE TORNADOS
TITLE: "TELSTAR" (E.P.)
TRACKS: 'Telstar'/'Popeye Twist'/'Love and Fury'/'Jungle Fever'
CAT #: Decca DFE8511
RELEASED: 11/1962

ARTIST: DON CHARLES
TRACKS: 'It's My Way of Loving You' b/w 'Guess That's the Way It Goes'
CAT #: Decca F11528
RELEASED: 11/1962

CAT #: Oriole CB1781
RELEASED: 12/1962

ARTIST: KENNY HOLLYWOOD
TRACKS: 'Magic Star' b/w 'The Wonderful Story of Love'
CAT #: Decca F11546
RELEASED: 12/1962

ARTIST: THE CHAPS
TRACKS: 'Poppin' Medley (part 1)' b/w 'Poppin' Medley (part 2)'
CAT #: Parlophone R4679
RELEASED: 12/1962

ARTIST: HOUSTON WELLS AND THE OUTLAWS
TRACKS: 'Shutters and Boards' b/w 'North Wind'
CAT #: Parlophone R4980
RELEASED: 12/1962

ARTIST: MIKE BERRY AND THE OUTLAWS
TRACKS: 'Don't You Think It's Time' b/w 'Loneliness'
CAT #: HMV POP1105
RELEASED: 12/1962

ARTIST: CARTER-LEWIS AND THE SOUTHERNERS
TRACKS: 'Tell Me' b/w 'My Broken Heart'
CAT #: Ember ??M
RELEASED: ?/1962
NOTE: Recorded at Meek's studio, but produced by Terry Kennedy. Meek involved only in an engineering capacity.

DISCOGRAPHY/JOE MEEK PRODUCTIONS (1963)

ARTIST: THE TORNADOS
TRACKS: 'Globetrotter' b/w 'Locomotion with Me'
CAT #: Decca F11562
RELEASED: 1/1963

ARTIST: GERRY TEMPLE
TRACKS: 'Angel Face' b/w 'Since You Went Away'
CAT #: HMV POP1114
RELEASED: 1/1963

ARTIST: JAMIE LEE AND THE ATLANTICS
TRACKS: 'In the Night' b/w 'Little Girl in Blue'
CAT #: Decca F11571
RELEASED: 1/1963

ARTIST: TOBY VENTURA
TRACKS: 'If My Heart Were a Storybook' b/w 'Vagabond'
CAT #: Decca F11581
RELEASED: 2/1963

ARTIST: JOHN LEYTON
TRACKS: 'Cupboard Love' b/w 'Land of Love'
CAT #: HMV POP1122
RELEASED: 2/1963
NOTE: Credited to R.G.M. Sound, but probably produced by Robert Stigwood.

ARTIST: THE OUTLAWS
TRACKS: 'Return of the Outlaws' b/w 'Texan Spiritual'
CAT #: HMV POP 1124
RELEASED: 2/1963

ARTIST: THE FLEE REKKERS
TRACKS: 'Fireball' b/w 'Fandango'
CAT #: Pye 7N35109
RELEASED: 2/1963
NOTE: Recorded at Pye studios. Meek may have only been involved in an engineering capacity.

ARTIST: PETER JAY AND THE JAYWALKERS
TRACKS: 'Totem Pole' b/w 'Jaywalker'
CAT #: Decca F11593
RELEASED: 2/1963

ARTIST: MIKE BERRY AND THE OUTLAWS
TITLE: "IT'S TIME FOR MIKE BERRY" (E.P.)
TRACKS: 'Don't You Think It's Time'/'Loneliness'/'Every Little Kiss'/'How Many Times'
CAT #: HMV 7EG8793
RELEASED: 3/1963

ARTIST: SCREAMING LORD SUTCH
TRACKS: 'Jack the Ripper' b/w 'Don't You Just Know It'
CAT #: Decca F11598
RELEASED: 3/1963

ARTIST: DON CHARLES
TRACKS: 'Angel of Love' b/w 'Lucky Star'
CAT #: Decca F11602
RELEASED: 3/1963

ARTIST: THE CHECKMATES
TRACKS: 'You've Got to Have a Gimmick Today' b/w 'Westpoint'
CAT #: Decca F11603
RELEASED: 3/1963

ARTIST: THE TORNADOS
TRACKS: 'Robot' b/w 'Life on Venus'
CAT #: Decca F11606
RELEASED: 3/1963

ARTIST: THE TORNADOS
TITLE: 'Life on Venus' b/w?
CAT #: ?????
RELEASED: c.3/1963
NOTE: German only release. Spoken introduction re-recorded in German.

ARTIST: THE TORNADOS
TITLE: "MORE SOUNDS FROM THE TORNADOS" (E.P.)
TRACKS: 'Chasing Moonbeams'/'Theme from 'a Summer's Place'/'Swinging Beefeater'/'The Breeze and I'
CAT #: Decca DFE8521
RELEASED: 3/1963

ARTIST: THE TORNADOS
TRACKS: 'Ridin' the Wind' b/w 'The Breeze and I'
CAT #: London 9581
RELEASED: c.3/1963 NOTE: U.S. only release. A-side is an alternate take with added sound effects.

ARTIST: WES SANDS
TRACKS: 'There's Lots More Where This Came From' b/w '3 Cups'
CAT #: Columbia DB4996
RELEASED: 3/1963

ARTIST: TONY HOLLAND
TRACKS: 'Sidewalk' b/w 'Time Goes By'
CAT #: HMV POP1135
RELEASED: 3/1963

ARTIST: MICHAEL COX
TRACKS: 'Don't You Break My Heart' b/w 'Hark Is That a Cannon I Hear?'
CAT #: HMV POP1137
RELEASED: 3/1963

ARTIST: MIKE BERRY AND THE OUTLAWS
TRACKS: 'My Little Baby' b/w 'You'll Do It, You'll Fall in Love'
CAT #: HMV POP1142
RELEASED: 3/1963

ARTIST: THE DOWLANDS AND THE SOUNDTRACKS
TRACKS: 'Breakups' b/w 'A Love Like Ours'
CAT #: Oriole CB1815
RELEASED: 4/1963

ARTIST: DON CHARLES
TRACKS: 'Heart's Ice Cold' b/w 'Daybreak'
CAT #: Decca F11645
RELEASED: 4/1963

ARTIST: THE TORNADOS
TITLE: "JUST FOR FUN" (SOUNDTRACK ALBUM)
TRACK: 'All the Stars in the Sky'
CAT #: Decca LK4524
RELEASED: 4/1963 NOTE: This in the only Meek production on the album.

ARTIST: CHAD CARSON
TRACKS: 'They Were Wrong' b/w 'Don't Pick on Me'
CAT #: HMV POP1156
RELEASED: 4/1963

ARTIST: GEOFF GODDARD
TRACKS: 'Saturday Dance' b/w 'Come Back to Me'
CAT #: HMV POP1160
RELEASED: 5/1963

ARTIST: HEINZ
TRACKS: 'Dreams Do Come True' b/w 'Been Invited to a Party'
CAT #: Decca F11652
RELEASED: 5/1963

ARTIST: GLENDA COLLINS
TRACKS: 'I Lost My Heart at the Fairground' b/w 'Feels So Good'
CAT #: HMV POP1163
RELEASED: 5/1963

ARTIST: PETER JAY AND THE JAYWALKERS
TRACKS: 'Poet and Peasant' b/w 'Oo La La'
CAT #: Decca F11659
RELEASED: 5/1963

ARTIST: THE TORNADOS
TRACKS: 'The Ice Cream Man' b/w 'Theme from 'The Scales of Justice''
CAT #: Decca F11662
RELEASED: 5/1963

ARTIST: FREDDIE STARR AND THE MIDNIGHTERS
TRACKS: 'Who Told You?' b/w 'Peter Gunn Locomotion'
CAT #: Decca F11663
RELEASED: 5/1963

ARTIST: HOUSTON WELLS AND THE MARKSMEN
TRACKS: 'Only the Heartaches' b/w 'Can't Stop Pretending'
CAT #: Parlophone R5031
RELEASED: 5/1963

ARTIST: MIKE BERRY
TITLE: "A TRIBUTE TO BUDDY HOLLY" (E.P.)
TRACKS: 'Tribute to Buddy Holly'/'It's Just a Matter of Time'/'My Little Baby'/'You'll Do It, You'll Fall in Love'
CAT #: HMV 7EG8808
RELEASED: 6/1963

ARTIST: JENNY MOSS
TRACKS: 'Hobbies' b/w 'Big Boy'
CAT #: Columbia DB7061
RELEASED: 6/1963

ARTIST: JOHN LEYTON
TRACKS: 'I'll Cut Your Tail Off' b/w 'The Great Escape'
CAT #: HMV POP1175
RELEASED: 6/1963
NOTE: Credited to R.G.M. Sound, but probably produced by Robert Stigwood.

ARTIST: BURR BAILEY AND THE SIX-SHOOTERS
TRACKS: 'San Francisco Bay' b/w 'Like a Bird Without Feathers'
CAT #: Decca F11686
RELEASED: 6/1963

ARTIST: THE ORIGINAL CHECKMATES
TRACKS: 'Union Pacific' b/w 'The Spy'
CAT #: Decca F11688
RELEASED: 6/1963

ARTIST: DON CHARLES
TITLE: "DON CHARLES" (E.P.)
TRACKS: 'Walk with Me My Angel'/'The Hermit of Misty Mountain'/'It's My Way of Loving You'/'Heart's Ice Cold'
CAT #: Decca DFE8530
RELEASED: 6/1963

ARTIST: CLIFF BENNETT AND THE REBEL ROUSERS
TRACKS: 'Everybody Loves a Lover' b/w 'My Old Standby'
CAT #: Parlophone R5046
RELEASED: 7/1963

ARTIST: ANDY CAVELL
TRACKS: 'Andy' b/w 'There Was a Boy'
CAT #: Pye 7N15539
RELEASED: 7/1963

ARTIST: THE SAINTS
TRACKS: 'Wipeout' b/w 'Midgets'
CAT #: Pye 7N15548
RELEASED: 7/1963

ARTIST: HEINZ
TRACKS: 'Just Like Eddie' b/w 'Don't You Knock at My Door'
CAT #: Decca F11693
RELEASED: 7/1963

ARTIST: THE PACKABEATS
TRACKS: 'Dream Lover' b/w 'Packabeat'
CAT #: Pye 7N15549
RELEASED: 7/1963

ARTIST: THE TORNADOS
TITLE: "TORNADO ROCK" (E.P.)
TRACKS: 'Ready Teddy'/'My Babe'/'Blue Moon of Kentucky'/'Long Tall Sally'
CAT #: Decca DFE8533
RELEASED: 7/1963

ARTIST: JOHN LEYTON
TITLE: "ALWAYS YOURS" (ALBUM)
TRACKS: 'I'm Gonna Let My Hair Down'/'On Lover's Hill'/'Sweet and Tender Romance'/'Johnny My Johnny'/'That's the Way It Is'/'Too Many Late Nights'/'Lover's Lane'/'Funny Man'/'Another Man'/'Buona Sera'/'A Man Is Not Supposed to Cry'/'How Will It End?'
CAT #: HMV CLP1664
RELEASED: 7/1963
NOTE: Credited to R.G.M. sound, but probably produced by Robert Stigwood.

ARTIST: THE THUNDERBOLTS
TRACKS: 'March of the Spacemen' b/w 'Lost Planet'
CAT #: Dot DOA16496
RELEASED: 7/1963
NOTE: U.S. only release.

ARTIST: THE CAMEOS
TRACKS: 'Powercut' b/w 'High, Low and Lonesomely'
CAT #: Columbia DB7092
RELEASED: 8/1963

ARTIST: MIKE BERRY
TRACKS: 'It Really Doesn't Matter' b/w 'Try a Little Bit Harder'
CAT #: HMV POP1194
RELEASED: 8/1963

ARTIST: THE OUTLAWS
TRACKS: 'That Set the Wild West Free' b/w 'Hobo'
CAT #: HMV POP1195
RELEASED: 8/1963

ARTIST: SOUNDS INCORPORATED
TRACKS: 'Keep Moving' b/w 'Order of the Keys'
CAT #: Decca F11723
RELEASED: 8/1963

ARTIST: THE TORNADOS
TITLE: "AWAY FROM IT ALL" (ALBUM)
TRACKS: 'Indian Brave'/'Flycatcher'/'Dreams Do Come True'/'Lullaby for Giulia'/'Costa Monger'/'Lonely Paradise'/'Chattanooga Choo Choo'/'Rip It Up'/'Alan's Tune'/'Cootenanny'/'Night Rider'/'Hymn for Teenagers'
CAT #: Decca LK4552
RELEASED: 8/1963

ARTIST: THE PUPPETS
TRACKS: 'Everybody's Talking' b/w 'Poison Ivy'
CAT #: Pye 7N15556
RELEASED: 8/1963

ARTIST: THE BEAT BOYS
TRACKS: 'That's My Plan' b/w 'Third Time Lucky'
CAT #: Pye 7N15556
RELEASED: 9/1963

ARTIST: HOUSTON WELLS AND THE MARKSMEN
TITLE: "JUST FOR YOU" (E.P.)
TRACKS: 'This Song Is Just for You'/'Paradise'/'Shutters and Boards'/'North Wind'
CAT #: Parlophone GEP8878
RELEASED: 9/1963

ARTIST: JOHN LEYTON
TRACKS: 'On Lover's Hill' b/w 'Lover's Lane'
CAT #: HMV POP1204
RELEASED: 9/1963
NOTE: Credited to R.G.M. sound, but probably produced by Robert Stigwood.

ARTIST: THE TORNADOS
TRACKS: 'Dragonfly' b/w 'Hymn for Teenagers'
CAT #: Decca F11745
RELEASED: 9/1963

ARTIST: SCREAMING LORD SUTCH
TRACKS: 'I'm a Hog for You' b/w 'Monster in Black Tights'
CAT #: Decca F11747
RELEASED: 9/1963

ARTIST: THE AMBASSADORS
TRACKS: 'Surfin' John Brown' b/w 'Big Breaker'
CAT #: Dot DOA 16528
RELEASED: 9/1963
NOTE: U.S. only release.

ARTIST: GEOFF GODDARD
TRACKS: 'Sky Men' b/w 'Walk with Me My Angel'
CAT #: HMV POP1213
RELEASED: 10/1963

ARTIST: HEINZ
TITLE: "HEINZ" (E.P.)
TRACKS: 'I Get up in the Morning'/'Talkin' Like a Man'/'That Lucky Old Sun'/'Lonely River'
CAT #: Decca DFE8545
RELEASED: 10/1963

ARTIST: MICHAEL COX
TRACKS: 'Gee What a Party!' b/w 'Say That Again'
CAT #: HMV POP1220
RELEASED: 10/1963

ARTIST: HOUSTON WELLS AND THE MARKSMEN
TRACKS: 'Blowing Wild' b/w 'Crazy Dreams'
CAT #: Parlophone R5069
RELEASED: 10/1963

ARTIST: PETER JAY AND THE JAYWALKERS
TRACKS: 'Kansas City' b/w 'Parade of the Tin Soldiers'
CAT #: Decca F11757
RELEASED: 10/1963
NOTE: The A-side is believed to have had no Meek involvement.

ARTIST: PAMELA BLUE
TRACKS: 'My Friend Bobby' b/w 'Hey There Stranger'
CAT #: Decca F11761
RELEASED: 10/1963

ARTIST: MICHAEL COX
TITLE: "MICHAEL COX IN SWEDEN" (E.P.)
TRACKS: 'Gee What a Party!'/'I've Been Thinking'/'In This Old House'/'Say That Again'
CAT #: HMV 7EGS296
RELEASED: c.10/1963 NOTE: Swedish only release.

ARTIST: JOHN LEYTON
TRACKS: 'Beautiful Dreamer' b/w 'I Guess You Are Always on My Mind'
CAT #: HMV POP1230
RELEASED: 11/1963
NOTE: Credited to R.G.M. sound, but probably produced by Robert Stigwood.

ARTIST: HEINZ
TRACKS: 'Country Boy' b/w 'Long Tall Jack'
CAT #: Decca F11768
RELEASED: 11/1963

ARTIST: THE RAMBLERS
TRACKS: 'Dodge City' b/w 'Just for Chicks'
CAT #: Decca F11775
RELEASED: 11/1963

ARTIST: THE SAINTS
TRACKS: 'Husky Team' b/w 'Pigtails'
CAT #: Pye 7N15582
RELEASED: 11/1963

ARTIST: GLENDA COLLINS
TRACKS: 'If You've Got to Pick a Baby' b/w 'In the First Place'
CAT #: HMV POP1233
RELEASED: 11/1963

ARTIST: HEINZ
TITLE: "LIVE IT UP" (E.P.)
TRACKS: 'Live It Up'/'Don't You Understand'/'Dreams Do Come True'/'When Your Loving Goes Wrong'
CAT #: Decca DFE8559
RELEASED: 11/1963

ARTIST: FREDDIE STARR AND THE MIDNIGHTERS
TRACKS: 'It's Shaking Time' b/w 'Baby Blue'
CAT #: Decca F11786
RELEASED: 11/1963

ARTIST: GUNILLA THORNE
TRACKS: 'Merry Go Round' b/w 'Go on Then'
CAT #: HMV POP1239
RELEASED: 11/1963

ARTIST: THE OUTLAWS
TRACKS: 'Law and Order' b/w 'Do Da Day'
CAT #: HMV POP1241
RELEASED: 12/1963

ARTIST: ROGER LAVERN AND THE MICRONS
TRACKS: 'Christmas Stocking' b/w 'Reindeer Ride'
CAT #: Decca F11791
RELEASED: 12/1963

ARTIST: JOE MEEK ORCHESTRA
TRACKS: 'The Kennedy March' b/w 'The Theme of Freedom'
CAT #: Decca F11796
RELEASED: 12/1963

ARTIST: THE DOWLANDS AND THE SOUNDTRACKS
TRACKS: 'Lucky Johnny' b/w 'Do You Have to Make Me Blue'
CAT #: Oriole CB1892
RELEASED: 12/1963
NOTE: Withdrawn shortly after release.

ARTIST: THE DOWLANDS
TRACKS: 'All My Loving' b/w 'Hey Sally'
CAT #: Oriole CB1897
RELEASED: 12/1963

DISCOGRAPHY/JOE MEEK PRODUCTIONS (1964-1967)

ARTIST: THE RALEIGH ROUNDERS
TRACKS: 'The Bike Beat (part 1)' b/w 'The Bike Beat (part 2)'
CAT #: Lyntone LYN574
RELEASED: ?/1964
NOTE: Double sided flexi disc produced for the Raleigh Bicycle Company.

ARTIST: MICHAEL COX
TRACKS: 'Love My Life Away' b/w 'Just a Gentle Word'
CAT #: HMV X 8654
RELEASED: ?/1964
NOTE: Swedish only release.

ARTIST: THE SHARADES
TRACKS: 'Dumb Head' b/w 'Boy Trouble'
CAT #: Decca F11811
RELEASED: 1/1964

ARTIST: DEKE ARLON AND THE OFFBEATS
TRACKS: 'I'm Just a Boy' b/w 'Can't Make Up My Mind'
CAT #: Columbia DB7194
RELEASED: 1/1964

ARTIST: HOUSTON WELLS AND THE MARKSMEN
TITLE: "WESTERN STYLE" (ALBUM)
TRACKS: 'I Won't Go Hunting with You, Jake'/'You Left Me with a Broken Heart'/'Call Me Another Time'/'Squaws Along the Yukon'/'Little Black Book'/'Kissing Tree'/'I'll Be Your Sweetheart for a Day'/'Blowing Wild'/'Best Job Yet'/'We're Gonna Go Fishin''/'All for the Love of a Girl'/'I'm Gonna Change Everything'/'Behind the Footlights'
CAT #: Parlophone PMC1245
RELEASED: 1/1964

ARTIST: KIM ROBERTS
TRACKS: 'I'll Prove It' b/w 'For Loving Me This Way'
CAT #: Decca F11813
RELEASED: 1/1964

ARTIST: HOUSTON WELLS AND THE MARKSMEN
TRACKS: 'Anna Marie' b/w 'Moon Watch over My Baby'
CAT #: Parlophone R5009
RELEASED: 1/1964

ARTIST: THE CAMEOS
TRACKS: 'My Baby's Comin Home' b/w 'Where 'Ere You Walk'
CAT #: Columbia DB7201
RELEASED: 1/1964

ARTIST: JIMMY LENNON AND THE ATLANTICS
TRACKS: 'I Learned to Yodel' b/w 'Louisiana Mama'
CAT #: Decca F11825
RELEASED: 1/1964

ARTIST: HEINZ
TRACKS: 'You Were There' b/w 'No Matter What They Say'
CAT #: Decca F11831
RELEASED: 2/1964

ARTIST: ANDY CAVELL
TRACKS: 'Tell the Truth' b/w 'Shut Up'
CAT #: Pye 7N15610
RELEASED: 2/1964

ARTIST: THE TORNADOS
TRACKS: 'Joystick' b/w 'Hot Pot'
CAT #: Decca F11838
RELEASED: 2/1964

ARTIST: THE CHECKMATES
TRACKS: 'Sticks and Stones' b/w 'Please Listen to Me'
CAT #: Decca F11844
RELEASED: 2/1964

ARTIST: BURR BAILEY
TRACKS: 'Chahawki' b/w 'You Made Me Cry'
CAT #: Decca F11846
RELEASED: 2/1964

ARTIST: CLIFF BENNETT AND THE REBEL ROUSERS
TRACKS: 'Got My Mojo Working' b/w 'Beautiful Dreamer'
CAT #: Parlophone R5119
RELEASED: 3/1964
NOTE: 'Beautiful Dreamer' was recorded in 1963 with Meek. The A-side is a post-Meek production.

ARTIST: JOHN LEYTON
TITLE: "BEAUTIFUL DREAMER" (E.P.)
TRACKS: 'Beautiful Dreamer'/'On Lover's Hill'/'I'll Cut Your Tail Off'/'Lover's Lanc'
CAT #: HMV 7EG8843
RELEASED: 3/1964
NOTE: Credited to R.G.M. Sound, but probably produced by Robert Stigwood.

ARTIST: THE SYNDICATS
TRACKS: 'Maybelline' b/w 'True to Me'
CAT #: Columbia DB7238
RELEASED: 3/1964

ARTIST: DAVY KAYE
TRACKS: 'A Fool Such As I' b/w 'It's Nice Isn't It?'
CAT #: Decca F11866
RELEASED: 3/1964

ARTIST: HEINZ
TITLE: "A TRIBUTE TO EDDIE" (ALBUM)
TRACKS: 'Tribute to Eddie'/'Hush-A-Bye'/'I Ran All the Way'/'Summertime Blues'/'Don't Keep Picking on Me'/'Cut across Shorty'/'Three Steps to Heaven'/'Come on and Dance'/'Twenty Flight Rock'/'Look for a Star'/'My Dreams'/'I Remember'/'Rumble in the Night'/'Just Like Eddie'
CAT #: Decca LK4599
RELEASED: 3/1964

ARTIST: THE OUTLAWS
TRACKS: 'Keep A-Knockin' b/w 'Shake with Me'
CAT #: HMV POP1277
RELEASED: 4/1964

ARTIST: GLENDA COLLINS
TRACKS: 'Baby It Hurts' b/w 'Nice Wasn't It'
CAT #: HMV POP1283
RELEASED: 4/1964

ARTIST: THE TORNADOS
TRACKS: 'Monte Carlo' b/w 'Blue Blue Blue Beat'
CAT #: Decca F11889
RELEASED: 4/1964

ARTIST: THE PUPPETS
TRACKS: 'Baby Don't Cry' b/w 'Shake with Me'
CAT #: Pye 7N15634
RELEASED: 4/1964

ARTIST: JOHN LEYTON
TITLE: " TELL LAURA I LOVE HER" (E.P.)
TRACKS: 'Tell Laura I Love Her'/'The Girl on the Floor Above'/'Johnny Remember Me'/'Wild Wind'
CAT #: HMV 7EG8854
RELEASED: 5/1964

ARTIST: THE DOWLANDS
TITLE: 'I Walk the Line' b/w 'Happy Endings'
CAT #: Oriole CB1926
RELEASED: 5/1964

ARTIST: MICHAEL COX
TRACKS: 'Rave On' b/w 'Just Say Hello'
CAT #: HMV POP1293
RELEASED: 5/1964

ARTIST: BOBBY CRISTO AND THE REBELS
TRACKS: 'The Other Side of the Tracks' b/w 'I've Got You out of My Mind'
CAT #: Decca F11915
RELEASED: 5/1964

ARTIST: HOUSTON WELLS AND THE OUTLAWS
TRACKS: 'Galway Bay' b/w 'Livin' Alone'
CAT #: Parlophone R5141
RELEASED: 5/1964

ARTIST: HEINZ
TRACKS: 'Please Little Girl' b/w 'For Loving Me This Way'
CAT #: Decca F11920
RELEASED: 6/1964

ARTIST: THE HONEYCOMBS
TRACKS: 'Have I the Right?' b/w 'Please Don't Pretend Again'
CAT #: Pye 7N15664
RELEASED: 6/1964

ARTIST: SCREAMING LORD SUTCH AND THE SAVAGES
TRACKS: 'She's Fallen in Love with the Monster Man' b/w 'Bye Bye Baby'
CAT #: Oriole CB1944
RELEASED: 6/1964

ARTIST: THE DOWLANDS
TRACKS: 'Wishing and Hoping' b/w 'You Will Regret It'
CAT #: Oriole CB1947
RELEASED: 6/1964

ARTIST: GLENDA COLLINS
TRACKS: 'Lollipop' b/w 'Everybody's Gotta Fall in Love'
CAT #: HMV POP1323
RELEASED: 7/1964

ARTIST: BENNY PARKER AND THE DYNAMICS
TRACKS: 'Boys and Girls' b/w 'You'll Be on Your Way'
CAT #: Decca F11944
RELEASED: 7/1964

ARTIST: THE TORNADOS
TRACKS: 'Exodus' b/w 'Blackpool Rock'
CAT #: Decca F11946
RELEASED: 8/1964

ARTIST: HOUSTON WELLS
TITLE: "RAMONA" (E.P.)
TRACKS: 'Ramona'/'Girl down the Street'/'I Wonder Who's Kissing Her Now'/'Nobody's Child'
CAT #: Parlophone GEP8914
RELEASED: 8/1964

ARTIST: TONY DANGERFIELD AND THRILLS
TRACKS: 'I've Seen Such Things' b/w 'She's Too Way Out'
CAT #: Pye 7N15695
RELEASED: 9/1964

ARTIST: THE HONEYCOMBS
TITLE: "THE HONEYCOMBS" (ALBUM)
TRACKS: 'Colour Slide'/'Once You Know'/'Without You It Is Night'/'That's the Way'/'I Want to Be Free'/'How the Mighty Have Fallen'/'Have I the Right'/'Just a Face in the Crowd'/'Nice While It Lasted'/'Me from You'/'Leslie Ann'/'She's Too Way Out'/'It Ain't Necessarily So'/'This Too Shall Pass Away'
CAT #: Pye NPL18097
RELEASED: 9/1964

ARTIST: SHADE JOEY AND THE NIGHT OWLS
TRACKS: 'Bluebirds over the Mountain' b/w 'That's When I Need You Baby'
CAT #: Parlophone R5180
RELEASED: 9/1964

ARTIST: THE HONEYCOMBS
TRACKS: 'Hab Ich Das Recht' b/w 'Du Sollst Nicht Traurig Sein'
CAT #: Vogue DV14210
RELEASED: c.9/1964
NOTE: German only release.

ARTIST: HEINZ
TRACKS: 'Questions I Can Answer' b/w 'The Beating of My Heart'
CAT #: Columbia DB7374
RELEASED: 10/1964

ARTIST: THE HONEYCOMBS
TRACKS: 'Is It Because' b/w 'I'll Cry Tomorrow'
CAT #: Pye 7N15705
RELEASED: 10/1964

ARTIST: FREDDIE STARR
TRACKS: 'Never Cry on Someone's Shoulder' b/w 'Just Keep on Dreaming'
CAT #: Decca F12009
RELEASED: 10/1964

ARTIST: SCREAMING LORD SUTCH
TRACKS: 'Dracula's Daughter' b/w 'Come Back Baby'
CAT #: Oriole CB1962
RELEASED: 11/1964

ARTIST: FLIP AND THE DATELINERS
TRACKS: 'My Johnny Doesn't Come around Anymore' b/w 'Please Listen to Me'
CAT #: HMV POP1359
RELEASED: 11/1964

ARTIST: THE HONEYCOMBS
TRACKS: 'Eyes' b/w 'If You Gotta Pick a Baby'
CAT #: Pye 7N15736
RELEASED: 11/1964

ARTIST: THE BLUE RONDOS
TRACKS: 'Little Baby' b/w 'Baby I Go for You'
CAT #: Pye 7N15734
RELEASED: 11/1964

ARTIST: VALERIE MASTERS
TRACKS: 'Christmas Calling' b/w 'He Didn't Fool Me'
CAT #: Columbia DB7426
RELEASED: 11/1964

ARTIST: THE HONEYCOMBS
TITLE: 'I Can't Stop' b/w 'I'll Cry Tomorrow'
CAT #: Interphon IN-7713
RELEASED: c. 12/1964
NOTE: U.S. only release. The A-side is a totally different version to the track on "It's The Honeycombs."

ARTIST: THE SYNDICATS
TRACKS: 'Howlin' for My Baby' b/w 'What to Do'
CAT #: Columbia DB7441
RELEASED: 1/1965

ARTIST: THE TORNADOS
TRACKS: 'Granada' b/w 'Ragunboneman'
CAT #: Columbia DB7455
RELEASED: 1/1965

ARTIST: JOHNNY GARFIELD
TRACKS: 'Stranger in Paradise' b/w 'Anyone Can Lose a Heart'
CAT #: Pye 7N15758
RELEASED: 1/1965

ARTIST: DAVY KAYE
TRACKS: 'In My Way' b/w 'All the Stars in Heaven'
CAT #: Decca F12703
RELEASED: 2/1965

ARTIST: ALAN DEAN AND HIS PROBLEMS
TRACKS: 'Thunder and Rain' b/w 'As Time Goes By'
CAT #: Pye 7N15749
RELEASED: 2/1965

ARTIST: HEINZ AND THE WILD BOYS
TRACKS: 'Diggin' My Potatoes' b/w 'She Ain't Coming Back'
CAT #: Columbia DB7482
RELEASED: 2/1965

ARTIST: DAVID JOHN AND THE MOOD
TRACKS: 'Bring It to Jerome' b/w 'I Love to See You Strut'
CAT #: Parlophone R5255
RELEASED: 3/1965

ARTIST: BOBBY RIO AND THE REVELLES
TRACKS: 'Boy Meets Girl' b/w 'Don't Break My Heart and Run Away'
CAT #: Pye 7N15790
RELEASED: 3/1965

ARTIST: THE HONEYCOMBS
TRACKS: 'Something Better Beginning' b/w 'I'll See You Tomorrow'
CAT #: Pye 7N15827
RELEASED: 3/1965

ARTIST: THE BLUE RONDOS
TRACKS: 'Don't Want Your Lovin' No More' b/w 'What Can I Do'
CAT #: Pye 7N15833
RELEASED: 4/1965

ARTIST: TOM JONES
TRACKS: 'Chills and Fever' b/w 'Baby I'm in Love'
CAT #: Tower 190
RELEASED: c.4/1965
NOTE: U.S. only release.

ARTIST: THE DOWLANDS
TRACKS: 'Don't Make Me Over' b/w 'Someone Must Be Feeling Sad'
CAT #: Columbia DB7547
RELEASED: 4/1965

ARTIST: MICHAEL COX
TRACKS: 'Gypsy' b/w 'It Ain't Right'
CAT #: HMV POP1417
RELEASED: 4/1965

ARTIST: PETER COOK
TRACKS: 'Georgia' b/w 'There and Bach Again'
CAT #: Pye 7N15847
RELEASED: 4/1965

ARTIST: HEINZ AND THE WILD BOYS
TRACKS: 'Don't Think Twice, It's Alright' b/w 'Big Fat Spider'
CAT #: Columbia DB7559
RELEASED: 4/1965

ARTIST: TOM JONES
TRACKS: 'Little Lonely One' b/w 'That's What We'll Do'
CAT #: Columbia DB7566
RELEASED: 5/1965

ARTIST: JESS CONRAD
TRACKS: 'Hurt Me' b/w 'It Can Happen to You'
CAT #: Pye 7N15849
RELEASED: 5/1965

ARTIST: THE TORNADOS
TRACKS: 'Early Bird' b/w 'Stompin' Through the Rye'
CAT #: Columbia DB7589
RELEASED: 4/1965

ARTIST: SCREAMING LORD SUTCH
TRACKS: 'The Train Kept A'Rollin'' b/w 'Honey Hush'
CAT #: CBS 201767
RELEASED: 6/1965

ARTIST: THE SAXONS
TRACKS: 'Saxon War Cry' b/w 'Click-Ete-Clack'
CAT #: Decca F12179
RELEASED: 6/1965

ARTIST: THE SHAKEOUTS
TRACKS: 'Every Little Once in a While' b/w 'Well Who's That'
CAT #: Columbia DB7615
RELEASED: 6/1965

ARTIST: REG AUSTIN
TRACKS: 'My Saddest Day' b/w 'I'll Find Her'
CAT #: Pye 7N15885
RELEASED: 6/1965

ARTIST: GLENDA COLLINS
TRACKS: 'Johnny Loves Me' b/w 'Paradise for Two'
CAT #: HMV POP1439
RELEASED: 7/1965

ARTIST: DAVY MORGAN
TRACKS: 'Tomorrow I'll Be Gone' b/w 'Ain't Got Much More to See'
CAT #: Columbia DB7624
RELEASED: 7/1965

ARTIST: DAVID JOHN AND THE MOOD
TRACKS: 'Diggin' for Gold' b/w 'She's Fine'
CAT #: Parlophone R5301
RELEASED: 7/1965

ARTIST: JUDY CANNON
TRACKS: 'The Very First Day I Met You' b/w 'Hello Heartache'
CAT #: Pye 7N15890
RELEASED: 7/1965

ARTIST: THE HONEYCOMBS
TRACKS: 'That's the Way' b/w 'Can't Get Through to You'
CAT #: Pye 7N15890
RELEASED: 7/1965

ARTIST: BOBBY RIO AND THE REVELLES
TRACKS: 'Everything in the Garden' b/w 'When Love Was Young'
CAT #: Pye 7N15897
RELEASED: 7/1965

ARTIST: HEINZ
TRACKS: 'End of the World' b/w 'You Make Me Feel So Good'
CAT #: Columbia DB7656
RELEASED: 7/1965

ARTIST: THE HOTRODS
TRACKS: 'I Don't Love You No More' b/w 'Ain't Coming Back No More'
CAT #: Columbia DB7693
RELEASED: 9/1965

ARTIST: THE SYNDICATS
TRACKS: 'On the Horizon' b/w 'Crawdaddy Simone'
CAT #: Columbia DB7686
RELEASED: 9/1965

ARTIST: THE TORNADOS
TRACKS: 'Stingray' b/w 'Aqua Marina'
CAT #: Columbia DB7687
RELEASED: 9/1965

ARTIST: GLENDA COLLINS
TRACKS: 'Thou Shalt Not Steal' b/w 'Been Invited to a Party'
CAT #: HMV POP1475
RELEASED: 9/1965

ARTIST: PETER LONDON
TRACKS: 'Bless You' b/w 'Baby I Like the Look of You'
CAT #: Pye 7N15957
RELEASED: 10/1965

ARTIST: BOBBY RIO AND THE REVELLES
TRACKS: 'Value for Love' b/w 'I'm Not Made of Clay'
CAT #: Pye 7N15958
RELEASED: 10/1965

ARTIST: THE HONEYCOMBS
TITLE: "THAT'S THE WAY" (E.P.)
TRACKS: 'That's the Way'/'She's Too Far Out'/'Colour Slide'/'This Too Shall Pass Away'
CAT #: Pye NEP24230
RELEASED: 10/1965

ARTIST: TOM JONES
TRACKS: 'Lonely Joe' b/w 'I Was a Fool'
CAT #: Columbia DB7733
RELEASED: 10/1965

ARTIST: CHARLES KINGSLEY CREATION
TRACKS: 'Summer Without Sun' b/w 'Still in Love with You'
CAT #: Columbia DB7758
RELEASED: 11/1965

ARTIST: THE HONEYCOMBS
TRACKS: 'This Year Next Year' b/w 'Not Sleeping Too Well Lately'
CAT #: Pye 7N15979
RELEASED: 11/1965

ARTIST: HEINZ
TRACKS: 'Heart Full of Sorrow' b/w 'Don't Worry Baby'
CAT #: Columbia DB7759
RELEASED: 11/1965

ARTIST: THE HONEYCOMBS
TITLE: "ALL SYSTEMS GO" (ALBUM)
TRACKS: 'I Can't Stop'/'I Don't Love Her No More'/'All Systems Go'/'Totem Pole'/'Emptiness'/'Ooee Train'/'She Ain't Coming Back'/'Something I Got to Tell You'/'Our Day Will Come'/'Nobody But Me'/'There's Always Me'/'Love in Tokyo'/'If You Should'/'My Prayer'
CAT #: Pye NPL18132
RELEASED: 11/1967

ARTIST: TOM JONES
TITLE: "TOM JONES" (E.P.)
TRACKS: 'Little Lonely One'/'I Was a Fool'/'Lonely Joe'/'That's What We'll Do'
CAT #: Columbia SEG8464
RELEASED: 12/1965

ARTIST: JASON EDDY AND THE CENTREMEN
TRACKS: 'Whatcha Gonna Do Baby' b/w 'Come on Baby'
CAT #: Parlophone R5388
RELEASED: 12/1965

ARTIST: THE FOUR MATADORS
TRACKS: 'A Man's Gotta Stand Tall' b/w 'Fast Cars and Money'
CAT #: Columbia DB7806
RELEASED: 1/1966

ARTIST: DIANE AND THE JAVELINS
TRACKS: 'Heart and Soul' b/w 'Who's the Girl?'
CAT #: Columbia DB7819
RELEASED: 1/1966

ARTIST: THE RIOT SQUAD
TRACKS: 'Cry Cry Cry' b/w 'How It Is Done'
CAT #: Pye 7N17041
RELEASED: 1/1966

ARTIST: GLENDA COLLINS
TRACKS: 'Something I've Got to Tell You' b/w 'My Heart Didn't Lie'
CAT #: Pye 7N17044
RELEASED: 2/1966

ARTIST: THE CRYIN' SHAMES
TRACKS: 'Please Stay' b/w 'What's News Pussycat?'
CAT #: Decca F12340
RELEASED: 2/1966

ARTIST: THE HONEYCOMBS
TRACKS: 'Who Is Sylvia' b/w 'How Will I Know'
CAT #: Pye 7N17059
RELEASED: 2/1966

ARTIST: THE TORNADOS
TRACKS: 'Pop Art Goes Mozart' b/w 'Too Much in Love to Hear'
CAT #: Columbia DB7856
RELEASED: 3/1966

ARTIST: THE BUZZ
TRACKS: 'You're Holding Me Down' b/w 'I've Gotta Buzz'
CAT #: Columbia DB7887
RELEASED: 4/1966

ARTIST: THE RIOT SQUAD
TRACKS: 'I Take It That We're Through' b/w 'Working Man'
CAT #: Pye 7N17092
RELEASED: 4/1966

ARTIST: PETER CHRIS AND THE OUTCASTS
TRACKS: 'Over the Hill' b/w 'The Right Girl for Me'
CAT #: Colmubia DB7923
RELEASED: 5/1966

ARTIST: HEINZ
TRACKS: 'Movin' In' b/w 'I'm Not a Bad Guy'
CAT #: Columbia DB7942
RELEASED: 6/1966

ARTIST: THE CRYIN' SHAMES
TRACKS: 'Nobody Waved Goodbye' b/w 'You'
CAT #: Decca F12425
RELEASED: 6/1966

ARTIST: JASON EDDY AND THE CENTREMEN
TRACKS: 'Singing the Blues' b/w 'True to Me'
CAT #: Parlophone R5473
RELEASED: 6/1966

ARTIST: THE RIOT SQUAD
TRACKS: 'It's Never Too Late to Forgive' b/w 'Try to Realise'
CAT #: Pye 7N17130
RELEASED: 7/1966

ARTIST: THE HONEYCOMBS
TRACKS: 'It's So Hard' b/w 'I Fell in Love'
CAT #: Pye 7N17138
RELEASED: 7/1966

ARTIST: GLENDA COLLINS
TRACKS: 'It's Hard to Believe It' b/w 'Don't Let It Rain on Sunday'
CAT #: Pye 7N17150
RELEASED: 7/1966

ARTIST: THE MILLIONAIRES
TRACKS: 'Wishing Well' b/w 'Chatterbox'
CAT #: Decca F12468
RELEASED: 8/1966

ARTIST: THE TORNADOS
TRACKS: 'Is That a Ship I Hear?' b/w 'Do You Come Here Often?'
CAT #: Columbia DB7984
RELEASED: 8/1966

ARTIST: PAUL RITCHIE AND THE CRYIN' SHAMES
TRACKS: 'September in the Rain' b/w 'Come on Back'
CAT #: Decca F12483
RELEASED: 8/1966

ARTIST: THE HONEYCOMBS
TRACKS: 'That Lovin' Feeling' b/w 'Should a Man Cry?'
CAT #: Pye 7N17173
RELEASED: 9/1966

ARTIST: THE IMPAC
TRACKS: 'Too Far Out' b/w 'Rat Tat Ta Tat'
CAT #: CBS 202402
RELEASED: 11/1966

ARTIST: THE RIOT SQUAD
TRACKS: 'Gotta Be a First Time' b/w 'Bitter Sweet Love'
CAT #: Pye 7N17237 RELEASED: 1/1967

Appendix B

KIM LOWDEN'S DISCOGRAPHY OF U.S.-RELEASED JOE MEEK PRODUCTIONS

ARTIST: ANNE SHELTON
TRACKS: 'Lay Down Your Arms' b/w 'Madonna in Blue'
CAT #: Columbia 40759
RELEASED: 1956

ARTIST: LONNIE DONEGAN
TRACKS: 'Rock Island Line' b/w 'John Henry'
CAT #: London 1650
RELEASED: 1956

ARTIST: LONNIE DONEGAN
TRACKS: 'Lost John' b/w 'Stewball'
CAT #: Mercury 70872
RELEASED: 1956

ARTIST: LONNIE DONEGAN
TRACKS: 'Bring a Little Water Sylvie' b/w 'Dead or Alive'
CAT #: Mercury 70949
RELEASED: 1956

ARTIST: LONNIE DONEGAN
TRACKS: 'Don't You Rock Me Daddy-O' b/w 'How Long, How Long Blues'
CAT #: Mercury 71026
RELEASED: 1957

ARTIST: LONNIE DONEGAN
TRACKS: 'Cumberland Gap' b/w 'Wabash Cannonball'
CAT #: Mercury 71094
RELEASED: 1957

ARTIST: LONNIE DONEGAN
TRACKS: 'Puttin' on the Style' b/w 'Gamblin' Man'
CAT #: Mercury 71181
RELEASED: 1957

ARTIST: LONNIE DONEGAN
TRACKS: 'My Dixie Darling' b/w 'I'm Just a Rolling Stone'
CAT #: Mercury 71248
RELEASED: 1957

ARTIST: CHRIS BARBER
TRACKS: 'Petite Fleur' b/w 'Wild Cat Blues'
CAT #: Laurie 3022
RELEASED: 1958

ARTIST: LONNIE DONEGAN
TRACKS: 'Grand Coulee Dam' b/w 'Nobody Loves Like an Irishman'
CAT #: Dot 15792
RELEASED: 1958

ARTIST: MIKE PRESTON
TRACKS: 'A House a Car And a Wedding Ring' b/w 'My Lucky Love'
CAT #: London 1834
RELEASED: 1958

ARTIST: JOY & DAVID
TRACKS: 'Whoopee' b/w 'My Oh My'
CAT #: Capitol 4106
RELEASED: 1958?

ARTIST: MIKE PRESTON
TRACKS: 'Girl Without a Heart' b/w 'In Surubaya'
CAT #: London 1865
RELEASED: 1959

ARTIST: ACKER BILK
TRACKS: 'Summer Set' b/w 'Acker's Away'
CAT #: Atco 6160
RELEASED: 1960

ARTIST: EMILE FORD & THE CHECKMATES
TRACKS: 'What Do You Want to Make Those Eyes at Me For' b/w 'Don't Tell Me Your Troubles'
CAT #: Andie 5018
RELEASED: 1960

ARTIST: LANCE FORTUNE
TRACKS: 'Be Mine' b/w 'Action'
CAT #: Signature 12030
RELEASED: 1960?

ARTIST: CLIFF BENNETT & THE REBEL ROUSERS
TRACKS: 'I'm in Love with You' b/w 'You Got What I Like'
CAT #: Capitol 4621
RELEASED: 1961

ARTIST: JOHN LEYTON
TRACKS: 'Johnny Remember Me' b/w 'There Must Be'
CAT #: ABC Paramount 10257
RELEASED: 1961?

ARTIST: MIKE BERRY
TRACKS: 'Tribute to Buddy Holly' b/w 'Every Little Kiss'
CAT #: Coral 62341
RELEASED: 1962

ARTIST: JOHN LEYTON
TRACKS: 'Son This Is She' b/w 'Six White Horses'
CAT #: ABC Paramount 10292
RELEASED: 1962

ARTIST: THE CHARLES BLACKWELL ORCHESTRA
TRACKS: 'Taboo' b/w 'Midnight in Luxembourg'
CAT #: Bethlehem 3058
RELEASED: 1962?

ARTIST: THE TORNADOES
TRACKS: 'Telstar' b/w 'Jungle Fever'
CAT #: London 9561
RELEASED: 1962

ARTIST: MIKE BERRY
TRACKS: 'Don't You Think It's Time' b/w 'Loneliness'
CAT #: Coral 62357
RELEASED: 1963

ARTIST: THE TORNADOES
TITLE: "THE ORIGINAL TELSTAR (THE SOUNDS OF THE TORNADOES)" (ALBUM)
TRACKS: 'Telstar'/'Red Roses and a Sky of Blue'/'Chasing Moonbeams'/'Earthy'/'Swinging Beefeater'/'Theme from a Summer Place'/'Love And Fury'/'Dreamin' on a Cloud'/'Ridin' the Wind'/'The Breeze and I'/'Jungle Fever'/'Popeye Twist'
CAT #: London LL3279
RELEASED: 1963
NOTE: Appears in some listings as "Telstar" or confused with London LL3293 (see below)

ARTIST: KENNY HOLLYWOOD
TRACKS: 'Magic Star' b/w 'The Wonderful Story of Love'
CAT #: London 9574
RELEASED: 1963

ARTIST: THE TORNADOES
TRACKS: 'Globetrottin' b/w 'Like Locomotion'
CAT #: London 9579
RELEASED: 1963

ARTIST: THE TORNADOES
TRACKS: 'Ridin' the Wind' b/w 'The Breeze and I'
CAT #: London 9581
RELEASED: 1963

ARTIST: THE TORNADOES
TITLE: "THE SOUNDS OF THE TORNADOES" (ALBUM)
TRACKS: 'Telstar'/'Ridin' the Wind'/'Red Roses And a Sky of Blue'/'Chasing Moonbeams'/'Earthy'/'Swinging Beefeater'/'Globetrottin'/'Theme From a Summer Place'/'Love And Fury'/'Dreamin' on a Cloud'/'The Breeze And I'/'Popeye Twist'
CAT #: London LL3293
RELEASED: 1963
NOTE: Very similar to London LL3279—different color cover, track order shuffled and 'Globe-trottin' replaces 'Jungle Fever,' band photo on reverse sleeve different

ARTIST: SCREAMING LORD SUTCH
TRACKS: 'Jack the Ripper' b/w 'Don't You Just Know It'
CAT #: London 9591
RELEASED: 1963

ARTIST: THE TORNADOES
TRACKS: 'Robot' b/w 'Life on Venus (Telstar II)'
CAT #: London 9599
RELEASED: 1963

ARTIST: THE TORNADOES
TRACKS: 'The Ice Cream Man' b/w 'Theme from 'The Scales of Justice''
CAT #: London 9614
RELEASED: 1963

ARTIST: HEINZ
TRACKS: 'Just Like Eddie' b/w 'Don't You Knock on My Door'
CAT #: London 9619
RELEASED: 1963

ARTIST: THE AMBASSADORS (aka The Saints)
TRACKS: 'Surfin' John Brown' b/w 'Big Breaker'
CAT #: Dot 16528
RELEASED: 1963
NOTE: US only issue

ARTIST: CLIFF BENNETT & THE REBEL ROUSERS
TRACKS: 'Everybody Loves a Lover' b/w 'My Old Stand-By'
CAT #: Ascot 2146
RELEASED: 1964

ARTIST: CLIFF BENNETT & THE REBEL ROUSERS
TRACKS: 'One Way Love' b/w 'I'm in Love with You'
CAT #: Capitol 5309
RELEASED: 1964
NOTE: B-side only is Joe Meek production

ARTIST: JOHN LEYTON
TRACKS: 'Beautiful Dreamer' b/w 'I Guess You Are Always on My Mind'
CAT #: Liverpool Sound 901-V
RELEASED: 1964?

ARTIST: THE DOWLANDS
TRACKS: 'All My Loving' b/w 'Hey Sally'
CAT #: Tollie 9002
RELEASED: 1964

ARTIST: THE HONEYCOMBS
TRACKS: 'Have I the Right?' b/w 'Please Don't Pretend Again'
CAT #: Interphon IN-7707
RELEASED: 1964

ARTIST: THE HONEYCOMBS
TRACKS: 'I Can't Stop' b/w 'I'll Cry Tomorrow'
CAT #: Interphon IN-7713
RELEASED: 1964
NOTE: Originally issued with picture sleeve

ARTIST: THE HONEYCOMBS
TITLE: "HERE ARE THE HONEYCOMBS (SINGING HAVE I THE RIGHT AND OTHER
HITS)" (ALBUM)
TRACKS: 'Colour Slide'/'Once You Know'/'Without You It Is Night'/'That's the Way'/'I Want
to Be Free'/'How the Mighty Have Fallen'/'Have I the Right?'/'Just a Face in the Crowd'/'Nice
While It Lasted'/'Me From You'/'Leslie Anne'/'She's Too Way Out'/'Ain't Necessarily So'/'This
Too Shall Pass Away'
CAT #: Interphon 88001
RELEASED: 1964
NOTE: Four slightly different issues: Interphon label with Interphon sleeve, mono or electronically
reprocessed stereo; reissued shortly after with Vee-Jay label with Interphon sleeve & catalogue
number, tracks identical, mono or electronically reprocessed stereo

ARTIST: JOHN LEYTON
TRACKS: 'Make Love to Me' b/w 'I'll Cut Your Tail Off'
CAT #: Atco 6319
RELEASED: 1964

ARTIST: THE THUNDERBOLTS (aka Charles Kingsley Creation)
TRACKS: 'Lost Planet' b/w 'March of the Spacemen'
CAT #: Dot 16496
RELEASED: 1964
NOTE: US only issue

ARTIST: THE JOE MEEK ORCHESTRA
TRACKS: 'The Kennedy March' b/w 'The Theme of Freedom'
CAT #: London 9634
RELEASED: 1964

ARTIST: THE BLUE RONDOS
TRACKS: 'Little Baby' b/w 'Baby I Go for You'
CAT #: Parkway 937
RELEASED: 1964

ARTIST: THE TORNADOES
TRACKS: 'Telestar' b/w 'Jungle Fever'
CAT #: London (Gold Demand Performance) 11003
RELEASED: 1964
NOTE: Misspelled on A-side label

ARTIST: GEOFF GODDARD
TRACKS: 'Sky Men' b/w 'Walk with Me My Angel'
CAT #: Lawn L235
RELEASED: 1964

ARTIST: HEINZ
TRACKS: 'Questions I Can't Answer' b/w 'The Beating of My Heart'
CAT #: Tower 110
RELEASED: 1964

ARTIST: THE HONEYCOMBS
TRACKS: 'That's the Way' b/w 'Color Slide'
CAT #: Interphon 7717
RELEASED: 1965
NOTE: Originally issued with picture sleeve

ARTIST: GLENDA COLLINS
TRACKS: 'Lollipop' b/w 'Everybody's Got to Fall in Love'
CAT #: Lawn L250
RELEASED: 1965

ARTIST: VARIOUS (credited to FREDDIE & THE DREAMERS)
TITLE: "I'M TELLING YOU NOW" (ALBUM)
TRACKS: Includes 'Questions I Can't Answer' and 'The Beating of My Heart' by Heinz
CAT #: Tower T5003 (mono), DT5003 (electronically reprocessed stereo)
RELEASED: 1965
NOTE: Marketed as a Freddie & The Dreamers LP, actually contains only two tracks by them. Basically a commercial sampler of British artists signed to the Tower label.

ARTIST: THE HONEYCOMBS
TRACKS: 'Something Better Beginning' b/w 'I'll See You Tomorrow'
CAT #: Warner Brothers 5634
RELEASED: 1965

ARTIST: THE HONEYCOMBS
TRACKS: 'That's the Way' b/w 'Can't Get Through to You'
CAT #: Warner Brothers 5655
RELEASED: 1965

ARTIST: TOM JONES
TRACKS: 'Little Lonely One' b/w 'That's What We'll Do'
CAT #: Tower 126
RELEASED: 1965
NOTE: Originally issued with picture sleeve

ARTIST: THE TORNADOES
TRACKS: 'Early Bird' b/w 'Stompin' through the Rye'
CAT #: Tower 152
RELEASED: 1965

ARTIST: THE TORNADOES
TRACKS: 'Stingray' b/w 'Aqua Marina'
CAT #: Tower 171
RELEASED: 1965?

ARTIST: HEINZ
TRACKS: 'Diggin' My Potatoes' b/w 'Don't Think Twice It's All Right'
CAT #: Tower 172
RELEASED: 1965

ARTIST: BOBBY RIO & THE REVELLES
TRACKS: 'Boy Meets Girl' b/w 'Don't Break My Heart & Run Away'
CAT #: ABC Paramount 10656
RELEASED: 1965

ARTIST: TOM JONES
TRACKS: 'Lonely Joe' b/w 'I Was a Fool'
CAT #: Tower 176
RELEASED: 1965
NOTE: Originally issued with picture sleeve

ARTIST: SCREAMING LORD SUTCH
TRACKS: 'She's Fallen in Love with the Monster Man' b/w 'Bye Bye Baby'
CAT #: Cameo 341
RELEASED: 1965

ARTIST: THE HONEYCOMBS
TRACKS: 'Who Is Sylvia' b/w 'How Will I Know'
CAT #: Warner Brothers 5803
RELEASED: 1966

ARTIST: THE CRYIN' SHAMES
TRACKS: '(Don't Go) Please Stay' b/w 'What's News Pussycat'
CAT #: London 10001 (?)
RELEASED: 1966

ARTIST: TOM JONES
TRACKS: 'Baby I'm in Love' b/w 'Chills and Fever'
CAT #: Tower 190
RELEASED: 1966
NOTE: B-side only is Joe Meek production

ARTIST: HEINZ
TRACKS: 'Heart Full of Sorrow' b/w 'Don't Worry Baby'
CAT #: Tower 195
RELEASED: 1966

ARTIST: HEINZ
TRACKS: 'Movin' In' b/w 'I'm Not a Bad Guy'
CAT #: Tower 253
RELEASED: 1966

ARTIST: THE RIOT SQUAD
TRACKS: 'Cry Cry Cry' b/w 'How Is It Done'
CAT #: Reprise 457
RELEASED: 1966

ARTIST: THE BUZZ
TRACKS: 'You're Holding Me Down' b/w 'I Gotta Buzz'
CAT #: Coral 62492
RELEASED: 1966?

ARTIST: JASON EDDIE & THE CENTREMEN
TRACKS: 'Singing the Blues' b/w 'True to You'
CAT #: Capitol 5727
RELEASED: 1966?

ARTIST: RIOT SQUAD
TRACKS: 'I Take It That We're Through' b/w 'Working Man'
CAT #: Hanna-Barbara HBR485
RELEASED: 1966

Index

About the CD

I Hear A New World
The Blue Men with Rod Freeman

I Hear a New World (2:46)
Glob Waterfall (3:13)
Entry of the Globbots (3:19)
Valley of the Saroos (2:55)
Magnetic Field (3:11)
Orbit around the Moon (2:50)
The Bublight (2:44)
March of the Dribcots (2:19)
Love Dance of the Saroos (2:33)
Dribcot's Space Boat (2:22)
Disc Dance of the Globbots (2:17)
Valley of No Return (2:56)
I Hear a New World (Alternate Mix) (2:23)

Originally recorded by Joe Meek at Arundel Gardens, London, England in 1959.
This version is a direct copy from a "white label" demo LP on Triumph Records, 1960.
Minimal sound restoration by Alex Artaud, Estudio Tribu, Oakland, CA.
Digital preparation and editing by Barry Cleveland, Eleveneleven Recorders, Oakland, CA.
Copyright RPM Records. Licensed to artistpro.com 2001.

ABOUT THIS VERSION

RPM Records in England released a remastered CD version of *I Hear a New World* in 1991. It was assembled from various sources, some of them not particularly good, and enhanced to make it more presentable to modern listeners. The masterfully executed restoration process eliminated a great deal of the surface noise, brought out previously obscured sounds, and added overall clarity. However, it changed the stereo balance as well. Also, in some places (digital?) delay was added to conceal some serious problems. In addition to the sonic changes, the original sequencing of the songs was altered.

The CD of *I Hear a New World* included with this book was created using a different source than the RPM version, and presents it more or less "warts and all." Very minimal restoration was done, and the clicks, pops, and other surface noises are there to prove it. However, the natural deterioration caused by aging and the distortion in some sections notwithstanding, this is the original version of the recording, as Joe Meek intended it to be heard, presented for the first time since its original limited release. Also presented for the first time is an alternate mix of the title track, which appears at the end of the disc.

See Chapter 4 for more detailed information on *I Hear a New World*.